The Life of a
BURMA SURGEON

This book is a compendium of material from
Dr. Gordon S. Seagrave's best-selling
Burma Surgeon, and *Burma Surgeon Returns*,
including excerpts from his combat diary.

The Life of a Burma Surgeon was edited by
Charles B. Pintchman and Ben Wechsler.

THE LIFE OF A
Burma Surgeon

By Gordon S. Seagrave, M.D.

Foreword by CHESTER BOWLES

W · W · NORTON & COMPANY · INC · *New York*

This book is a compendium of material from Dr. Gordon S. Seagrave's best selling *Burma Surgeon* and *Burma Surgeon Returns,* including excerpts from his combat diary.

The Life of a Burma Surgeon was edited by Charles B. Pintchman and Ben Wechsler.

Library of Congress Catalog Card No. 61-17684

CONTENTS

FOREWORD *by Chester Bowles*　　　　　　　　viii

PART ONE: BURMA MISSION

1　WASTEBASKET SURGERY　　　　　　　13
2　BURMA ROAD　　　　　　　　　　　33
3　THE PLAGUE　　　　　　　　　　　39
4　MALARIA AND AIRPLANES　　　　　　45

PART TWO: BATTLE OF BURMA

5　THE BEGINNING　　　　　　　　　　55
6　UNDER GENERAL STILWELL　　　　　61
7　NOTES FROM A DIARY　　　　　　　66
8　RETREAT!　　　　　　　　　　　　79
9　OVER THE MOUNTAINS　　　　　　　89
10　ASSIGNMENT IN ASSAM　　　　　　　98

PART THREE: THE LONG ROAD BACK

11　RAMGARH TRAINING CENTER　　　　107
12　THE TRAIL OF THE REFUGEES　　　116
13　THE FIRST OFFENSIVES　　　　　　137
14　MYITKYINA! MYITKYINA!　　　　　　153
15　SURGERY AT THE AIRSTRIP　　　　　162

PART FOUR: RETURN TO NAMKHAM

16　THE TASTE OF PEACE　　　　　　　171
17　HOME　　　　　　　　　　　　　193
Epilogue　　　　　　　　　　　　　218

MAPS

General Map of Burma　　　　　　　　vi-vii
Naga Hills and Hukawng Valley　　　　121
Ledo Road from Tingkawk Sakan to Myitkyina　152
Myitkyina to Namkham　　　　　　　183
Namkham Area　　　　　　　　　　　203

List of Illustrations

Oldest hospital building
Dr. Seagrave, his wife and their two young boys
Nurses' home
In the bazaar at Namkham
Scene on the Burma Road
Chit Sein "Miss Burma 1942"
Committee on Buddhist affairs
Grandma Naomi
Nurses resting
Dr. Silgardo and Dr. Ba Saw
Pansy Po, center, and two Buddhist friends
Dr. Seagrave attending wounded Chinese soldiers
Making raft shelters on the retreat
General Stilwell leads off
Burmese nurses on the Irrawaddi Ferry
Little Bawk prepares a meal
Operating at Myitkyina Airstrip
Intravenous department
A casualty is brought in
Burma Surgeon is joyously welcomed back to Namkham
Dr. Seagrave watches the celebration of his return to Namkham
Dr. Seagrave giving informal lecture
Nurse Esther Po administering anesthesia
Dr. Seagrave operating
Two operations at once

FOREWORD

In 1897, when Gordon S. Seagrave was born in Rangoon, Burma, the American people stood poised on the verge of a curious and unprecedented Pacific adventure. With our seizure of the Philippines a year later, we awakened—with surprise and some misgivings—to find ourselves an Asian colonial power.

Of course, our indirect involvement with Asia, of which Gordon Seagrave is a product, had begun long before Dewey's victory at Manila Bay. During the late 18th century, New England shipowners and merchants played a major role in the China trade. As early as 1834 Peter Parker, a graduate of Yale, set up a mission hospital in Canton. In the next decades, American traders and missionaries were among the leaders in pressing for the "opening" of China. At mid-century it was Americans who took the initiative in forcing Japan out of isolation.

From such facts it is clear that our relations with Asia have been an outgrowth of mixed motivations. Yet running throughout this record is a remarkably constant current of vigorous humanitarianism.

To be sure, Americans were active in the notorious opium and coolie trade. Yet such traders were displaced ultimately by missionaries of every sort—by teachers, doctors and nurses as well as evangelists. Propelled by a rugged faith, these newcomers were, inevitably, revolutionaries as well. For they brought with them most of the elements—the good and the less good—of a radically different civilization. Their impact was explosive.

Today we are reaping the harvest of this long relationship with Asia and Asians. Gone are the days of colonialism. In their place is a new age of explosive nationalism, when millions of men and women are awakening to a new sense of opportunities for a better life. The revolution first triggered by merchant and missionary alike is now at flood tide.

The new Asia confronts us with radically new challenges. To live with it in peace, we Americans need to understand its people and their cultures. We need sensitivity to their aims and respect for their way of life.

In this revolutionary world, the record of individual Americans of vision, courage and long experience among Asian peoples can serve to guide the rest of us in our quest for understanding. Gordon Seagrave is one such American. To be sure his story is similar in many ways to that of other men and women who gave their lives to serving the people of Asia. And yet there is uniqueness in his perseverence and in the long family tradition of service to one nation to which he is the heir.

Gordon Seagrave's forebears went to Burma in 1835 as a part of that early trickle of Americans who left friends, family, home and country to pioneer in the cause of the Christian Gospel. To their neighbors, their decision often seemed foolhardy, dangerous and ill-conceived.

Yet theirs was not a choice motivated by the traditional causes of migration—escape from oppression and economic hardship, or a craving for greater material opportunity. The early Seagraves had no personal fortunes to make, no political axe to grind; nor were they carrying the flag on a colonial adventure.

Theirs was a mission of faith.

In the years since the coming of the first Seagraves, Asia and change have become almost synonymous. As a young man who knew only Burma as his home, Gordon Seagrave was already able to perceive the needs of an awakening people.

When he traveled from Rangoon to the U.S. in 1909, he was determined to acquire the medical skills necessary to heal his fellow man. He doubtless felt misgivings about missionary work which sought exclusively to substitute one religion for another in a country already deeply spiritual. He understood, too, what has in recent years become a truism—that worthwhile souls require healthy bodies and free minds.

In any event, Gordon Seagrave acquired his medical training at Johns Hopkins and in 1922 returned to Burma as a young doctor in search of a practice.

It is characteristic of Gordon Seagrave that the practice he sought and found could never be remunerative in any but spiritual terms. He chose a most remote part of Burma—the town of Namkham on the Chinese border, some 700 miles from Rangoon where his family had lived before him for generations.

He chose this place on the basis of need, not comfort or

acceptance. He chose a community which had never before experienced the service of a modern trained doctor. His greatest challenge was consequently that of proving he was needed to thousands of chronically ill but curable people who did not as yet believe they could be cured.

During the twenty years prior to the war with Japan, young Dr. Seagrave set out to teach the basically illiterate tribesmen and diverse nationality groups in the Northern Shan States that life was not inevitably an endless torment of ill-health.

Through skillful surgery and constant teaching, he slowly spread the wonders of modern medicine in ever-widening circles throughout Northern Burma and Southwest China. His clinic became the center of a quiet up-country revolution which gave new meaning to lives which would have otherwise been lost or wasted.

The challenge of disease was everywhere. Malaria was as common in Burma as colds in New York or Seattle. Also present in abundance were cholera, typhoid, tuberculosis, goiter—indeed almost every variety of tropical and temperate disease known to the medical profession.

It is difficult to say which was Gordon Seagrave's greater contribution—the lives he healed and saved or the influence of his person and character on the Northern Shan peoples. Living in a place so remote from modern technological America, he has preserved qualities which sometimes seem rare among contemporary Americans.

Like the men who wrested our country from the wilderness, he is a pioneer oblivious to danger whether physical or intellectual. He is almost flint-like in his indestructibility.

For decades, disease has wracked his body. War and insurrection have plagued his life and destroyed his hospital. Supplies, equipment and money have been the exception rather than the rule. The inevitably suspicious Burmese minorities he had chosen to serve learned but slowly that he was their friend. Strength of character against these adversities was as necessary as strength of body.

In looking back, I have often wondered which other quality was most important to Dr. Seagrave's work—his Yankee stubbornness or his irrepressible sense of humor. Perhaps he needed both to weather the forty years at Namkham.

From my own experiences in Asia, I can guess that nothing endeared him more to the local populace than an appropriate sense of humility, for Gordon Seagrave never deluded himself into believing in his own superiority. He never assumed that he carried with him all the answers. He remained as ready to learn as to teach. From his books the reader clearly senses Dr. Seagrave's appreciation of the values of another culture and his respect for the dignity of the people he has served.

Yet when his country faced its greatest crisis—the Second World War—a patriotism which in lesser men might have been extinguished by distance and time was keenly awakened. The story recounted in his book is remarkable. With the advance of the Axis armies, Gordon Seagrave reacted instinctively and volunteered at age 47 without hesitation. In 1942 this extraordinary man marched out of Burma on foot with Stilwell, and many months later marched back again under combat conditions, healing Allied soldiers and holding together large hospital units.

Here, in the life of one man, is a rare combination of brotherhood and patriotism, of service and courage, that seems to me distinctly American. I could no more picture Gordon Seagrave as of another nationality than I could imagine Gandhi a Frenchman or Churchill an Indian.

The story of Dr. Seagrave is the story of the best of America overseas. What he has tried to do in Burma is something of which we can be justly proud, for his actions are a natural extension of our traditional national purpose— the widening of opportunities for all men everywhere.

Since World War II, we have begun slowly to do as a people what Gordon Seagrave and others have done as individuals. We have begun to understand our critical stake in the peaceful economic and political development of free nations. We have begun to build on the foundation of good will provided by our private agents of humanitarianism down through the years.

In many respects, our present effort is as much a promise as it is a record of achievement. For all the good works accomplished by individual Americans in isolated places with the private and public support of their countrymen, the size of the undertaking is still inadequate to the challenge. Indeed, we are only just beginning to achieve the indispensable coordination and planning which the necessarily limited earlier activities of private citizens lacked.

Today Asia, Africa and Latin America are in the throes of a revolution of rising expectations whose end none can foretell. Where earlier dozens, even hundreds of Seagraves seemed to suffice, today we need thousands, tomorrow tens of thousands.

We need dedicated medical, educational, and technological experts in every field—men and women who are willing to pool their efforts in the service of villagers and workers everywhere. We need people who are willing to live and work in the tradition of Gordon Seagrave.

Ahead of us is a vast frontier which only our young people of today can cross. Are we as a nation prepared to inspire and encourage these young people to undertake this historic effort? Are we willing to instill in them the sense of mission, and to equip them with the necessary skills to help the people of Asia, Africa and Latin America to create prosperous free societies within the framework of their own cultures?

The answers to these questions may well determine mankind's future course.

We have in our national heritage the ideals and examples for such action. Although there is only one Gordon Seagrave, let us hope that his brilliant example may inspire countless other Americans to similar deeds in the future.

This may well be his greatest and most enduring contribution.

CHESTER BOWLES

PART ONE: BURMA MISSION

1 WASTEBASKET SURGERY

RANGOON, 1902—I was about five years old. A great hulking Irishman stamped up the steps to the huge verandah of the house my great-grandfather had built to live in when, after the second Burmese War, the British took over all of Lower Burma as far north as Toungoo. The Irishman sat me on his lap and told me stories of wild jungles and great deeds: about service in the Royal Irish Constabulary as a young man; about his later adventures in Canada in the Royal Northwest Mounted Police; about stray rifle bullets that whizzed past him as he sat in his bungalow in the Shan States and that bored through the side of his bookcase. Then he grasped the top of a heavy dining-room chair in his teeth and swung it up over his head. I was fascinated! I tried it out on my tiny nursery chair, but it didn't work; my teeth couldn't have been much better then than they are now. Then he asked me for a glass of water to quench his thirst, and drank it down—standing on his head. I was completely overwhelmed!

After he had gone I asked my mother who the big chap was.

"He is Doctor Robert Harper, a medical missionary at Namkham on the border between the Northern Shan States and China."

That made it still more romantic.

"When I grow up I'm going to be a medical missionary in the Shan States," I declared.

Mother didn't say anything. The vaporizings of a five-year-old didn't worry her. After a few years her only son would undoubtedly become an evangelistic missionary to the Karens of Lower Burma like his father, grandfather and great-grandfather, and a smattering of uncles and aunts, great-aunts, and what not had been before him. Blood would tell.

Perhaps blood would have told if the Karens hadn't taken

13

their new national religion so seriously. To them religion meant going to church on Sunday in a big way. Their chapel next door boasted the largest bell purchasable in America and they rang it twice for each service. Half-past five every Sunday morning it woke them up. Fifteen minutes later it told them to hurry along for the morning prayer service. At six o'clock it warned stragglers that the service was beginning. At seven the women had a special meeting to pray for the souls of their errant males. Then breakfast, then Sunday school, then the main service, followed by assorted Christian Endeavor meetings till nine o'clock at night.

My parents were very lenient. The only service I had to go to was at ten o'clock. Now a good Karen preacher almost always begins his sermons with the lapse from grace of Adam—it being Eve's fault, of course. An outline of the more dramatic sins of the poor Israelites follows, and then, after people have subsided into coma, he ends up with a little intricate exegesis of some of St. Paul's more difficult remarks.

My father preached some of the most convincing, simply worded sermons I ever heard in English or Karen, and his prayers were poetry. But one day after a long-winded Karen sermon he stood up and prayed. I had been hoping for the best when the preacher sat down. This was too much, even if it was my father who was praying. I rolled the paper boat, which I had been making, into a wad and threw it at him in disgust. I hadn't meant to, but I hit him squarely on the cheek. The means I took to bring the meeting to a close were effective—very! So effective it still hurts me to sit down when I think of it.

I had three sisters, all older than I. Now that isn't right. If parents are going to divide their children eccentrically with regard to sex, the oddly-sexed one should be the eldest so that he should have some chance to lick the others when they gang up on him. That's what I did. I had three sons and one daughter, so I fathered the daughter first, and she can still hold her own though the eldest boy is about a foot taller than she is. But I had good training, taking on those three older sisters. I eventually stood up to my mother and dad and told them I was going to be a *medical* missionary— and made them like it.

Some time that same year a little girl was learning to toddle around in the not-very-famous city of Carlinville, Illinois, where her civil-engineer father was taking on more jobs than

14

he could handle. She must have been "Tiny" then, and I bet she was cute. When I first saw her, some seventeen years later, she was, at least in my eyes, the glamor girl to end all glamor girls.

1909—The Atlantic was in a turmoil. I ate a ham sandwich as we pulled out of Southampton and my next meal—to stay down—was a banana as we passed the Statue of Liberty.

We settled down in the university town of Granville, Ohio.

Granville knew about missionary children, and since we had come there for an education, education was what we should have. I still bear on my bruised carcass the marks of that education. As soon as I got into long pants I began to work for my board in the college girls' commons, waiting on tables, since my father, being a missionary, never had any spare cash. I got quite adept at the art. I could carry five full coffee cups in my bare hands without very much of the coffee slopping into the saucers. I could carry out all the dishes for eighteen girls on one tray without having a crash more often than once in two weeks. That was good training for my shoulders, so I decided to go out for pole vaulting. I became an expert. Once in Johns Hopkins, at the end of the first World War, I actually got a gold medal for pole vaulting. That night the Baltimore *Sun* gave me a good write-up: POLE VAULT—SEAGRAVE, JOHNS HOPKINS, FIRST. NO OTHERS RAN.

I earned my room rent by working in the college library, and my tuition by correcting papers for the English and/or Mathematics departments.

1918—I was sick of the smells of the dissecting room at Johns Hopkins, smells that would empty the balcony around you if you went to a movie without a bath. I wanted some fresh air. I applied for and got a job at a summer camp in Lake Geneva, Wisconsin. I am glad I didn't know, in advance, what the job was going to be. At dawn we got up, fetched the tank car, went into all the cottage rooms and emptied the slop pails into the tank. But I used to come across a damsel there who was making up beds. Since 1902 she had been creating havoc on the farm her father bought for a hobby. When she wasn't hoeing the corn and the potatoes, she and her ten brothers and sisters had been generally raising Cain riding the horses bareback, falling out of trees, stealing apples and otherwise producing a crop of scars for identification purposes.

15

I had kept my fingers crossed whenever I cast my eye on these neurotic little creatures. I had seen many a first-flight missionary who had had to give up a grand job and come back to the States because his wife couldn't take it. But Tiny looked as if she could take it, with a little education!

It took me two summers to convince Tiny she couldn't do better than marry me and go to Burma, but it was worth it.

1921—Tiny was going to have a baby. I decided to find out something about babies with a summer internship in the Pediatrics Hospital at Mt. Airy, Maryland.

Then came my real internship at the Union Memorial Hospital in Baltimore. During our first emergency appendix a telephone call came telling me Tiny's pains had set in.

One day in the operating room there was comparative quiet, and the operating-room superintendent decided to clear out all the useless broken-down surgical instruments that could no longer be repaired. I happened in as she was having the orderly take away a basketful of these instruments. Since I knew my Burman mission and the extent of surgical instruments I would find there, I asked for, and was given, that wastebasketful. With them all my surgical work was done for five years, in spite of the fact that they were broken and not mates. Many of the hemostats would not remain clamped but would spring apart and permit large hemorrhages in the most embarrassing parts of the operations.

So in August, 1922, Tiny, Leslie Mae and I set sail for Burma, well equipped with shaving soap and toothpaste (which some fool told us couldn't be bought in Burma), with our wastebasket of surgical instruments, but, most of all, with dreams of the marvelous surgery we were going to do for the aborigines of the Shan States of Burma.

Before we left Baltimore, we had been told that we would be stationed in Loikaw, in the Karenni States. We had accordingly studied up all the known facts about the Red Karens, the Padaungs who stretch the necks of their women with brass rings till they are about a foot long, about that special variety of Karens that does not permit its men to marry outside of their own village and is thereby rapidly dying out, and about the other people of the Karenni. When we reached New York we were told that the mission could no longer afford to put a medical missionary at Loikaw, and we would

16

have to go to Kengtung, the largest * and easternmost Shan
State that borders on China, Indo-China and Siam.

I didn't care. All I wanted was plenty of jungle and thousands of sick people to treat, preferably with surgery. We
disembarked in Rangoon, where Leslie and Tiny both promptly came down with dengue fever after the minimum incuba-
tion period of three days.

Dr. Harper was in Rangoon when we arrived. The mission
committee had a session and Dr. Harper, for Namkham,
and Dr. Henderson, for Kengtung, went into a tussle to see
who could get us. Dr. Harper won by promising me his practice, all his good will, and a free hand, since he was going
to retire permanently in the spring. The committee agreed
and ordered me to Namkham. The committee was anxious
that Tiny remain in Rangoon till our son was born, two
months later. But Tiny, in spite of dengue fever, was so anxious to get to the place where we would at last have our own
home that she voted to start at once.

We went by train to Mandalay and then by river steamer
three days up the Irrawaddy to Bhamo. From Bhamo on we
rode native ponies. We did twelve miles a day, spending
the nights in government bungalows. On the fourth day we
crossed the great seven-mile-wide Shweli River plain and
passed through Namkham Town up the hundred-foot-climb
to the Shan compound on the right and the Kachin compound on the left. Our hearts were pounding. What sort of
setup were we going to find in this place where we were to
spend twenty years? The hospital was a rotten wooden building with twenty wooden beds bare of all furnishings. The
floor was stained with blood and pus and medicine, and was
so rotten you had to step carefully not to break through.
Nurses have, since then, scrubbed that floor so thoroughly
and so often that the boards are about half as thick as when
they were nailed down; yet the stains are still there, for the
jungle wood is as porous as a sponge. The walls were covered with large red splashes of the saliva of betel-nut chewers.

There was one patient, with a leg ulcer.

That night Tiny and I broke down and sobbed in each
other's arms.

The next morning we set our teeth and decided that if
Namkham wasn't what we wanted it to be, we would
get off to an early start and do something about it. I found
a Karen preacher chap who spoke English and Shan well, and
made him sit with me all day long and help me teach myself
Shan. At the end of three months I preached my first Shan

17

sermon. That was the worst sermon I ever heard preached in any language. You have to sing Shan, not speak it, and preferably your mouth should be full of betel nut as you sing. I persisted in singing my sermon in the wrong key!

Take the one word *hsu*. If you say it with an even sound it means "a tiger." If you say it gruffly, down in your belly, it means "straight." When you cut the word off sharp with an axe it means "coat." Sung on high C for a couple of measures it means "happy," and high C staccato means "buy."

Still, I thought I was pretty good. It was time now to kill two birds with one stone: give the accepted evangelistic type of missionary work a fair trial, and, incidentally, advertise Johns Hopkins. I gathered together a gospel team, loaded a mule with medicines, and started off on tour. At each village we called on the headman. When we announced free medicine for all sick, the villagers crowded in. It was too good to miss. We gave each patient just enough of the right medicine to make him want more. One patient didn't want more. He had pylorospasm and I had no belladonna, so I gave him three tablets of pure atropine and told him to take one after every meal and report to me how he felt the next day. He reported in great disgust. He had decided to hurry the cure by taking all three of those tiny tablets at once. His pylorospasm had been cured, but he hadn't been able to spit all day, no matter how much betel nut he chewed. He would, he said, like to have his spit and his pylorospasm back again!

After medicines were distributed, one of the preachers got up and started preaching; everyone immediately got up and went out.

Luck was with me, though, on that trip. A man came to me with tuberculosis. I went over him carefully and told him I was sorry, I couldn't do a thing for him. With those lungs he couldn't live more than a year. One year later, to a day, he died, and my reputation among the Shans was made!

Soon after that tour the Kachins threw a huge convention in their mission compound across the street. They had heard of the new doctor, so as soon as they had registered they came over to put me to the test. One man had a huge adenomatous goiter. "You'll have to have the thing cut out," I said, and nearly fainted when he replied, "All right, go ahead."

I ran up to the house.

"Tiny," I called, "I've got an operation to do. A goiter as big as a grapefruit. Will you give the anesthetic for me? I'll tell you what to do."

Tiny agreed. I got out my pressure cooker and sterilized

some towels. The instruments were put on to boil. Tiny got the chloroform bottle and started to pour. Then I began to cut. I cut darn near everything that man had in his neck before I got the goiter out. When he was fully conscious I said, "Listen, fellow, I want you to promise me to lie flat on your back for several days. If you try to sit up your neck's going to fall apart. Understand?"

Yes, he understood. He would be a good boy.

Much relieved that he had not died on the table, I went up to breakfast. When I came down, half an hour later, he was already sitting up in bed.

Next day the Kachin convention was having a feast out on the grass. A Kachin man was standing near, dressed in a most extraordinary manner. As Kipling says, "Nothin' much before, an' rather less than 'arf o' that be'ind." He had a bandage around his neck. I looked again. Yes, there was my goiter patient! He had smelled the pork curry and had come across the street to get it. And yet he couldn't die!

This was the first time in northern Burma and the Shan States that a goiter had been successfully removed. People came in willing to take a chance at other operations. A few key cases opened up whole districts to a confidence in us. There was a cancer of the breast that had already reached the cauliflower stage but was not yet fastened irremovably to the chest wall. For years she spread the news of how her breast had been removed and skin from her leg grafted onto her bare chest in sheets! There was a woman with a sarcoma of the orbit pushing her eyeball way out of her head. We removed the eyeball and the tumor, and, until last year, she was still sending patients to us. A rich Chinese had been inexpertly operated on for amebic abscess of the liver, and the fistula had never closed. He wanted another operation, but we cured him with injections of emetine and irrigations of quinine and salvarsan. A high-class woman of wide influence had had one girl baby followed by several abortions, and wanted a boy badly. We removed a dermoid cyst of the ovary and a year later she did have a boy.

In lots of these cases we had the breaks. I had not had more than a minimum variety of operations on which to acquire experience under guidance in America. When a new operation needed to be done, I got out my books and studied every detail. Then I was profusely sick, went to bed on it, and the next morning, still nauseated, started operating. Somehow or other, the first three operations of each variety were more or less uncomplicated and the patients got along well.

In medicine, also, we had the breaks. I was called once to see the sawbwa of Chefang State in China who was "dying" of malaria. When I got there the prince had just about got control of his fever; but I gave him an intravenous injection of quinine and then, when all his lords and ladies gave me the credit for a marvelous cure, I just kept my mouth shut and smiled my gratitude.

These Shan sawbwas are what in England would be dukes, earls, or baronets, according to the size of their respective states. In the Shan States of Burma, the sawbwas are chiefs.

Having one or two on our side didn't hurt our reputation at all.

With surgery in the offing it was immediately apparent that we must have nurses. The hospital staff consisted of Tiny and myself, a Karen doctor, and a girl who had had a year of training in Rangoon. Our milkman came down with malaria one day. I put him to bed and gave him fifteen grains of quinine, for I believed in large doses in those days. Then I went home for dinner. When I came back an hour later I discovered to my horror that not only had my "nurse" come in and, seeing a fever case, given him ten grains of quinine, but my assistant doctor had turned up and given him fifteen grains more. The patient almost died of quinine poisoning, but it cured his fever!

We decided then and there that we would train our own nurses. We began with a Shan and a Kachin girl. The language made things difficult. I taught the Shan girl in Shan and she taught the Kachin girl in Burmese! In our operations we had four languages, English, Burmese, Shan, and Kachin, going at once.

Shan girls were hard to obtain, so, after two years, we had one Shan and five Kachin nurses, and my Shan was practically useless. I started to study Kachin but gave it up at once. Kachin is a child's language compared to Shan. It is easy to learn because there isn't anything to it. It has no term for anything important. All the girls, however, had had to study Burmese in school, and Burmese is more expressive even than Shan. So I set myself to learning Burmese by the simple expedient of having the nurses teach me Burmese while I taught them nursing. It worked pretty well except in anatomy where the only names for the genitourinary organs with which the nurses were acquainted were the filthy terms that they had heard used in the bazaars when Burmese women cursed each other. Without realizing it, they were teaching me to be very proficient in profane Burmese.

By this time our training school had reached government standards and obtained government recognition and our first class of English-speaking nurses had passed their state examinations with credit. The top girl in the class was a charming Shan girl named E Hla, with a first-class brain. We put her in as head nurse and she was still head nurse at the time of the evacuation of Burma.

Unless you have seen the jungle races of the Shan States you cannot possibly grasp the problem of training nurses, or appreciate the girls we trained. We have girls of ten or twelve races continually represented in the school, each with their own language entirely unintelligible to the other race groups. Their only common language is Burmese which they learn in the school—and also in the bazaars—and in the whole history of the school we have had only four pupil nurses who were actually Burmese. The largest race group was Kachin, the next Shan, the next Karen, and then a smattering of other tribes, Hkamti, Padaung, Taungthu, Lahu, Red Karen, Black Karen, Maru, Atsi, Lashi, Pwo, Bghai, and Paku. There were two Indian girls and one Intha. There was one Hkun. The only race we wanted represented, but without success, was the Chinese.

Of them all, the Kachins were the most hopeless-looking when they came for training. The Kachins have a stocky, lowslung chassis, and are, by nature and preference, brigands. They migrated down, the last to come to Burma, from the Chinese-Tibetan divide. With their skill in the use of dahs they were fast chopping themselves southward through the Shans and Burmese, and if the British had not taken over Burma, they would by this time have been unquestioned masters of the country. Living in the mountaintops where it is cold and water very difficult to obtain, the Kachin villager never bathes unless someone puts it over on him. That happens three times in his life: once when he is born, once when he is married, and once when he dies. That means that only once in a lifetime does a normal jungle Kachin voluntarily take a bath. A missionary asked a villager once if he ever bathed and he replied, "Yes, teacher, twenty years ago I had a bath and a month later my uncle died. Five years later I had another bath and my cousin died. I haven't dared bathe since!"

The people known as Shans were the original inhabitants of southern China. Driven out by the Chinese, they migrated

21

west and south. One branch filtered into Siam and became the Siamese. Those that came into East Burma became the Shans, into West Burma, the Hkamti, and into Assam, the Assamese. They have been civilized for a thousand years. They had kings of their own and contributed at least one dynasty to the throne of Burma. They built walled cities. Subjugated by the Burmese kings, they had Buddhism forced on them, though they retain some of their original spirit worship. Six hundred years ago a great Burmese monk adapted the Burmese script to Shan needs and they developed a literature of their own. The Kachins have only the English script given them fifty years ago by Baptist missionaries.

Shan women are the most beautiful in Burma. With charming figures, they have lovely light skins and, when healthy, bright rosy cheeks. Chit Sein, one of our nurses, is so gorgeous that the Americans called her "Miss Burma, 1942."

The Karens were in Burma before the Burmese. They are mountain people. Burmese kings subjugated all but those in the Karenni States, and have treated them like scum ever since. They were very religious, with a mythology very close to that of the Jews.

With all these varieties in training, the proper way to maintain discipline was a very serious problem requiring real thought. The ordinary Kachin enjoys being bossed by a man with a loud voice, reinforced by an occasional slap and a couple of kicks. Shans resent even the loud voice, and if you get angry with a Karen girl she becomes positively ill. The only way we could influence them at all was to treat them with respect and affection; affection even when an occasional nurse did not deserve affection, and respect even when it was pretty difficult to respect many, especially in those first days when they were so dirty. Astonished at being treated with respect they tried all the harder to deserve respect. Receiving affection, they became worthy of affection.

And the nurses did try. Bathed and bathed and bathed— until they were as clean and sweet a group of girls as you could find in any country.

Then they tried a bit of powder to take the shine off their faces. One of the girls got up her courage and bought some rouge. They decided that was fine. Then someone appeared with a lipstick and overdid the business badly. Some of the others bought one and showed her how ladies of taste did those things.

Teaching them nursing is not very simple. Only a few of them have very quick minds. The rest are taught and taught

22

until they finally understand. Those later years we began to understand their difficulties. Unlike Americans they do not grow up in an atmosphere where modern medical facts and ideas are overheard daily and seen in articles in the press. Medical terms are never heard. But with three and four years under you, living in hospital, seeing thousands of cases, they pick up so much new vocabulary as to amount almost to a new language.

One thing I learned from sore experience. You could not hope to handle these nurses, no matter of what race, in groups. No argument, no matter how sound, is ever effective with them as long as they are permitted to gang up on you. Singly, and handled with affection and respect, they see the point of your argument at once, and respond. Handled as individuals and with respect and affection, we can get twelve and fourteen hours of very efficient work per day out of these girls, and they sing and smile and joke as they work. But let them gang up, even with only one other person, and you can't argue with them at all. This has been proved numberless times. In a gang they give each other courage to resist the "old man," as they used to call me.

In a hospital it is as important as in any army that orders be obeyed. But there is much more co-operation if the reason for the order is explained, when it is not in itself apparent. Also, it is much easier to lead than to drive. That is where human beings differ from horses. In no Indian or Burmese hospital do the nurses do any dirty work. There are special castes to do individual jobs. It makes the hospital bulky with lazy personnel. It is costly. It makes it hard for the patient to get real service, unless he has plenty of money for "backsheesh." We were determined that any nurses we trained should be willing to do anything needed, no matter how foul. All I had to do was do the dirty job myself. Lose face? A big man cannot lose face. It is the petty person who has to fret about losing face. I can open up the manhole in our sewer system and clean it out with my bare hands in front of a crowd and not lose face thereby. In fact, the crowd will turn in and help me clean it out so they won't lose face by doing nothing when the old man is busy.

The first order any nurse received when she entered training was that she must be gentle. Any lack of gentleness in doing dressings or giving nursing treatment of any sort is punished drastically. If nurses don't care what happens to their patients when they first enter training they soon throw it off. Once a patient with cerebral malaria walked out of

23

the ward, while the nurse's back was turned, and disappeared. We searched all over the neighborhood without success. Twenty-four hours later a party of soldiers discovered him lying in a marsh, half under water. They brought him back to the ward, and his temperature went steadily up till, at dawn, it reached 107° and he died. When the night-duty nurses came off, two of them were sobbing.

"What are you crying about now?" I asked.

"We tried so hard to keep that patient of yours alive, and all the time he was dying the other patients stood around and made fun of him. Nobody cared about his dying except us!"

Nursing Chinese patients is about as difficult a job as a nurse can possibly be asked to handle. They simply won't take their medicine. Hla Sein solved the problem. I was walking by her ward when I heard her singing at the top of her voice. I thought she must be mad so I peeped in the door. She had her bottle of quinine solution in one hand and her dram glass in the other. All the malaria patients were lying at attention. She stepped up to one after another, sang him a verse until he started to laugh, and when he had his mouth wide open poured in the bitter stuff.

The girls are tiny. About five feet tall, they weigh from eighty to a hundred and ten pounds. But you should see them heave their patients around, move them from stretcher to operating table and back again. They stood the long, hard tramp out of Burma better than the Americans, and got through into India in much better physical condition.

The United States Army speaks of these girls of ours as Seagrave's Burmese nurses. The nurses are not Burmese. Only Than Shwe is Burmese. But I don't mind. The other girls were born Karen, Shan, Kachin, Taungthu, and so forth, but we wouldn't tolerate their remaining Taungthu, Kachin, Shan, and Karen. We wouldn't tolerate any race differentiation. They had to be bigger than their race or we had no further use for them. Now race has nothing to do with any of them. Little Bawk and Chit Sein, Kachin and Shan. When Bawk goes off on sick leave Chit Sein mopes around and gets sick herself. The Shan girl can't live without the Kachin. Koi and Saw Yin, Shan and Karen. Roi Tsai and Lu Lu, Kachin and Karen.

They are bigger than race, bigger than nationalists. What price a solution of this horrible world's difficulties. If Germans were bigger than Germans. If English and Americans and Russians were bigger than Russians, Americans, and

English. If there were something bigger than patriotism, bigger than love of country!

With nurses to help, we began to take on all sorts of cases. It was to Kachins that we owed our ability to develop surgery. Having lived by the dah they were not afraid of the knife and came to have a most unbalanced admiration for my prowess with that instrument. One day in Bhamo, a Kachin with a gastric ulcer came to me to be examined. When I told him he needed an operation, he took off his shirt, pulled out his gigantic sword, put it into my hand, lay down on the floor and said, "O.K., Doctor, go ahead."

I opened my first pus abdomen and put in a rubber-tube drain. When I did the first dressing, the drain had disappeared. I probed around in the man's belly but couldn't find it.

"What are you looking for, Doctor?" asked the patient.

"I'm looking for that rubber tube I stuck in you. It's lost."

"Oh, that thing. Well it was hurting me so I pulled it out and threw it away."

In those days we were so poor I couldn't afford to lose that tube. I couldn't find it in the ward, but on the verandah I was delighted to come across a baby using it for a pacifier.

No appendix case came to me those first years unless the appendix had been ruptured at least a month, and one patient had ruptured his three months before I saw him. Sulfanilamide had not appeared.

I always wished I could specialize in gynecology. But how can you limit yourself to specializing in any one thing in a country like that? Still we had plenty of gynecological cases to keep life interesting. The medical colleges in Burma and India were alike in that very little gynecology could be studied by male medical students, and the status of gynecological operative work was poor. Women came to a medical missionary much sooner than to government men.

Next to gynecology, I would like to be an obstetrician. And what a chance I had to be an obstetrician! No woman, much less her husband, would call me for a normal delivery, in those first days. But when everything went wrong, even the husband would call me.

The only obstetrical instrument the natives have is the sharp hook. They tear the baby apart with it, rupture the uterus and even rip out half the vagina. But they get the baby out, which to them is the essential point, even if the

25

mother and baby both die. The mother would lose face if she died with the baby still in her.

They carried in a woman with pain down below the appendix region. "She has an extrauterine pregnancy and will have to be operated on at once," I told her employer.

"Nonsense," said he, "who ever heard of a baby growing anywhere else than in the uterus?"

"Well, this one is, and I am going to operate right away."

"Not if I can help it. You have to send for her husband and operate after he gives his permission."

"He lives so far away it will take him two days to get here, and by that time there won't be any woman left to operate on," I said, and started to scrub up.

The employer, with a grim face, insisted on remaining in the operating room so as to have the goods on me if I had missed my diagnosis—remained until, on incising the peritoneum, a couple of pints of clotted blood burst forth, and then he had himself carried out by the nurses quite content, and convinced that babies were sometimes indiscreet in their choice of residence.

My first mastoid case was a charming little Kachin schoolgirl. I had never done a mastoid, but I had an old dry skull in the hospital. I pulled it out and did a mastoid operation on it, and when nothing happened to that patient I operated on the little girl, and she did well.

My first gastrectomy for cancer of the stomach did well until the patient went home, and then he sent back word that I was a rotten doctor; he couldn't stow away the gigantic amounts of rice that Shans eat twice a day without getting terrible pains. It took two months to persuade him he would have no pains if he would eat smaller amounts several times a day.

There was a lot of plastic surgery forced on us. There was a Chinese who had literally "lost face." A bear disposed of most of it including one eye, the nose, and the upper lip. A bit of skin was left on the forehead which I used as a pedicle flap to line his new nose. Then I took cartilage from one of his ribs, grafted it in for a support, and finished off his new nose with a caterpillar graft from his chest. It was rather a flat nose, but what better for a Chinese?

A woman came in one day with the worst infection of lice I had ever seen. Her hair had millions of them in permanent occupation. They had bitten her on the forehead and nose until she itched so badly she had scratched the front of her head full of sores. Flies had laid their eggs and now

26

her sores were full of maggots. They had eaten into her nose until the cartilaginous part was separating itself from the bone. After we had excised the worst areas and rid her of the maggots, the front of her head had no scalp left. We left pedicles in both temporal regions, moved the scalp from the top of her head forward, grafted skin from her leg on the newly denuded area, so that when she got well she could comb her hair up over the bald spot and hide it very effectively. She came back to me last year with an attack of malaria. This time she had no lice.

I even tried my hand at dentistry, and once I filled one of my own teeth. I had a wisdom tooth that was giving me a lot of trouble and there was no chance to go to Rangoon. So I got out my dental machine and began to grind. I was rather clever at that part of it. I did just like the dentists in the States. I ground around until I found a place that hurt, and then I ground there a little extra! Then I mixed up the amalgam and pressed the filling home. But somehow, down in the bottom of that cavity I had left a bit of cotton so that when I did finally get down to civilization the whole tooth had to come out. But I filled the tooth anyway.

And always there were goiters. One was so large it looked like a ham. I had the reputation of being the goiter specialist of Burma. And how I hate goiter surgery. Those huge adenomata would seem to be fed by twenty-five jugular veins, and the walls of so many were so very fragile. I used to be nauseated for every operation. But they would keep referring those confounded cases to me from Rangoon and Monywa, Bassein and Yenangyaung. I have never even read of abscessed goiters as large as many we saw.

In a country like that, you cannot do what you want to do and you cannot avoid doing things that you don't want to do. Still I did specialize, and on something new! Surgery with wastebasket instruments. Orthopedic surgery without an X-ray. Urological surgery without a cystoscope. Surgery without any actual cautery except a stray soldering iron. Surgery without electricity. Medicine without a laboratory, and without medicines, often. Hospitalization without a real hospital or any adequate equipment.

I used to be bitter about it, but now I am rather glad that I had to use wastebasket instruments for so many years, for I have seen what would have happened to me if I had had real tools. I had a Chinese carpenter working for me who had wonderful tools. He had the best saw that money could buy. The result was that when I asked him for a two-foot

27

board he never handed me one from a pile of two-foot boards. He pulled out his saw and sawed off two feet from a fourteen-foot board every time. That is what happens to you when you have good tools. I, on the other hand, have become a very conservative surgeon!

As a missionary I was a most unorthodox pain in the neck. As a doctor also I was decidedly unorthodox. A good doctor frequently is the one who gets his diagnosis, no matter what has happened to the patient in the meantime. In a country where 97 per cent of the fevers are malaria, and malignant malaria at that, and where 99 per cent of the dysenteries are amebic, a good doctor will give no quinine or atabrine to the fever case or emetine to the dysentery unless and until the laboratory turns in a positive report for plasmodium and/or amebae. The fact that only one out of ten laboratory men in the country is capable of seeing malaria parasites and amebae makes no difference. If the parasites are not seen, the malaria patient is treated with aspirin and the amebic dysentery with saline cathartics. If the patient dies he is being most unco-operative. Even when the report from the laboratory is positive, treatment has been delayed for anything from twenty-four to seventy-two hours. I would personally rather treat the patient according to his smell and get him well.

The medical examiner of the Mission Board in New York once said, "If Seagrave were a good doctor, he would not allow himself to get infected with malaria and dysentery." That is quite correct. If I had been a good doctor, missionary doctor, I would have climbed under the mosquito net at 6:00 P.M. every night and stayed there and I would have boiled all my drinking water myself. I certainly would not have let my cook "boil" it for me, nor would I ever have answered those numberless emergency calls at night to villages near and far. I would have let the crazy fools go ahead and die unassisted.

With these two diseases the most common everywhere, the nurses became very proficient with the hypodermic and intravenous syringes, much to the distress of the medical profession in Burma, who wanted these money-making procedures in their own hands. When nurses needed practice, they practiced on me. I had a government official visiting me one day. As we left the offices and started down the stairs, the nurse came up with my emetine. I rolled up my sleeves and she stuck it in.

"Good Lord! You don't let a nurse give you a hypodermic,

28

do you?" I certainly do. I would rather any one of our nurses gave me an intravenous quinine than any doctor. Tiny and our son, John, went to Rangoon alone once, and John developed dysentery; so she took him to a doctor there. The doctor put the syringe together, broke off the neck of the emetine ampoule, sucked up the solution and wiped the needle on his thumb.

On Tiny's insistence he condescended to put the needle into alcohol a second. Then Tiny wiped John's arm with alcohol to make sure it would be done, but the doctor wiped off the alcohol with his bare hand and plunged the needle in before Tiny could object. Our first-year girls can do better than that.

There is not much tuberculosis among Shans. They live in comparatively bright and open houses under better circumstances than the other tribes. Kachins have less-open houses, full of smoke, and they sleep with their heads buried in blankets. Still, as long as they remain where they belong, in the mountaintops, tuberculosis is not too common. It is when they come down into the plains that they get tuberculosis readily. The Chinese have the largest proportion of tuberculosis. Yunnanese live in mud-brick houses with practically no air and they are very unsanitary. For their tuberculosis their only treatment is opium. Opium will stop the cough temporarily, and sometimes permanently!

The most expensive department of our hospital was the pediatrics department. Milk costs much more for one baby per day than rice and vegetables would cost for three adults. But there were a lot of babies whose mothers had died soon after birth, and the babies would die too if we did not take them in. There were a few abandoned babies also, usually twins. Orientals detest twins, and I know of several instances where newborn twins were left to die unfed.

The year we reached Burma, the road that later became the Burma portion of the famous Burma Road had just been completed from Lashio to Namkham. It was just a mud road and was only usable six months of the year, and not always then. During the first year we had no car. The second year we got a second-hand Harley-Davidson motorcycle with a sidecar. It simply could not manage those awful hills even without the sidecar. Just then the government announced compulsory physical exams for all schoolchildren in Burma, the examiner to be paid fifteen cents for every pupil. I examined so many thousands during my vacations that we managed to buy a Model T. Still most of our traveling had to be done on foot or on tiny native ponies. On a good many trips I could cover double distance; I would ride fifteen miles, leave the horse, and walk another fifteen before dark. The first time I did this I arrived in Wurraboom, halfway to Bhamo, at night, without food or bedding. The local teacher's wife, one of the most attractive Kachin women I have ever met, saw me and brought over some lovely clean blankets and sheets, killed the fatted chicken, and served me up a nice dinner with her one-year-old daughter strapped on her back. That daughter was Myi Tung Bawk, later known as M. T. Bawk, or "Big Bawk." Sixteen years later, her mother having in the meanwhile died of tuberculosis, Big Bawk came to us for training.

That same year, the wife of the most attractive Kachin man I have ever met had a daughter born by the breech. They called her Bawk, too: Maru Bawk, alias "Little Bawk." When she was seventeen, she also entered the nursing school. Bawk is the given name, or rather number. Big Bawk was number-two girl of the Myi Tung family, and Little Bawk was number-two girl of the Maru family. I used to see Big Bawk occasionally on my trips to Bhamo. I saw Little Bawk all the time. She went to school across the street and used to play around with Ruth Sword. They had been playing with my eldest son on the morning of the day he was drowned.

A couple of years later a Shan family moved down from China and settled in our Christian village. They had a skinny little daughter named Koi: "the last one." I can always get a rise out of Koi by asking her how her father and mother knew she was going to be the last one! She did all her school work in our school. She has an astonishing brain. I asked her to let me look at her notes on one of my lectures once. No one knows better than myself how difficult it is to lecture in a foreign language without messing up idioms and failing to connote correctly one's real meaning. In her notes Koi had not only taken down every word I had said, but, at full speed, had changed to correct Burmese idioms and had changed a word here and there so as to get the proper connotation that I had desired.

The American Baptist Foreign Mission did not believe in any more large hospitals than they could possibly avoid. The nearest hospitals that ever did any surgery were at Bhamo, sixty miles west, Mandalay and Maymyo, three hundred miles

30

southwest with jungle paths in between, Lashio, a hundred and twenty miles south, and Kunming, about six hundred miles northeast. I could understand no mission work that cared not to alleviate in a really practical way the ghastly physical misery of the people. The Student Volunteer Group for Foreign Missions had the motto, "The Evangelization of the World in This Generation." Even if you have hundreds of thousands of missionaries you can't really evangelize except by consistent work for at least three generations. All in all, with my eccentric ideas of mission work, I was a thorn in the side of the Burma mission for years.

For twenty years our hospital had to fight to keep out of the wastebasket. The only way we could make financial ends meet was with our fees. These would have been enormous if the hospital had been located in a city, but Namkham is just a country town with only a few wealthy people, and they are both miserly and very, very nationalistic. That is, they would pay a hundred rupees to a Shan quack, call me only when that quack had given them up for lost, and pay me five rupees—or at the outside ten. But with those tiny fees, tens of thousands of them, we kept out of debt. Chinese coolies paid us nothing. Rich Chinese paid us almost enough for themselves and for the Chinese coolies. Kachins made us tiny token payments, and the Shans averaged just about what it cost to treat them.

During our first five and a half years in Burma, Dr. Harper died. His church at Detroit, desiring to build a lasting memorial to him, gave us twenty thousand dollars to build a hundred-bed hospital. Tiny and I had the plans all ready. The plans called for an expenditure of forty thousand dollars. The Mission Property Committee in Rangoon, however, was in those days quite imaginative, and they felt I could get all but one wing of the hospital with the funds at my disposal, providing I built it myself. To a man of my temperament, that was like a red rag to a bull.

We decided to make the hospital out of cobblestone, unlimited amounts being available in the river beds within two miles of the hospital site. I telegraphed to my father to buy us a ton-and-a-half truck in Rangoon, ship it loaded to Mandalay by steamer, where Tiny and I would pick it up.

Then we began to haul stone. We hired a few coolies to gather the stone, and then after the hospital work was done the nurses would pile on board and we would go out, throw the stones on, and haul back several loads. I asked my Chinese carpenter if he could estimate how much stone we would need. He could. He took the plans and a pencil and in a few minutes said we would need so many tons of stone. Later I discovered that if we had hauled as much stone as that Chinese carpenter told me to haul, the hospital would have been solid throughout like the pyramids!

In my medical course in Johns Hopkins they had not taught me how to mix dental cement, even, let alone lime and sand mortar. But there was a missionary named Weeks in Moulmein who had put up a lot of fine buildings. I telegraphed him inviting him to spend his summer vacation in Namkham. He accepted, but could spare only one week. On the afternoon of the day he arrived for his "vacation" we started putting in the foundations, and by the time he left, a week later, we had one corner of the hospital built up to the tops of the windows of the lower story. Now I understood how to fasten those rocks together. His vacation had been such a success that I invited other knowledgeful missionaries to spend their vacations in Namkham. What a summer that was! At our meals together we ate and laughed so loudly they could hear us at the hospital a couple of blocks away.

Hundreds of tons of building material had to be brought in from Lashio, a hundred and thirty miles away. Tiny and I used to do this job together.

We started from Namkham at dawn and covered a hundred and thirty miles into Lashio by three in the afternoon, threw on a load of stuff, and started right back.

Aside from three good Chinese carpenters for the woodwork and, later, a fine Indian chap to do the plastering, most of our work was done by Shan and Kachin coolies, and a great deal of it by voluntary free labor. We chose half a dozen of the most intelligent and taught them to be expert masons for cobblestone work. The roof was completed just as the rains were breaking. Then we put in the electricity and plumbing. I was determined to have modern plumbing even if I had no hospital.

Not having to pay out half our funds to contractors, we not only completed the entire building according to the plans, but had a much more firmly constructed building, since we had used tons more cement than the specifications called for.

But we had no money left for beds. All I could do was saw up the lumber from the scaffolding and use it for beds.

Termite ridden, it furnished the most wonderful hide-outs. Passing through a ward one day I saw a nurse down on her knees with a crochet hook in her hand jabbing at one of the beds. I stood by and counted. She got fifteen out of each crack!

When we moved into the new hospital the nurses used the old wooden building for a home.

The new building filled up rapidly, until it was running to capacity. But we were not satisfied. We were not reaching the countless sick in the jungles who were too ill to travel. We felt we ought to have branch hospitals and dispensaries out in the wilds where we could place graduate nurses. The girls had had an overwhelming experience in the wards with the common diseases of the country so that they knew almost as much about them as I did myself, and, after all, it was those diseases they would be sent to treat. Anything unusual that they did not understand, they could send in to me. We opened three hospitals in our second period of service, one thirty miles west, one forty miles east, and one a hundred miles, as the crow flies, to the east of the Salween River. The girls were all graduate midwives as well as nurses, and the good they did was immeasurable.

In the last year of our second term of service, an insignificant-appearing road was built for automobiles, running north from our Lashio-Namkham road to Chefang, in China, a total distance of about thirty miles. The Lashio-Namkham road was also continued over an enormous suspension bridge to Bhamo, the head of shipping on the Irrawaddy. These roads ran right through our hospital's sphere of influence. We hoped the road would continue north to Chefang and Mangshi, but didn't suppose it ever would.

2 BURMA ROAD

1937—We came back from a trip to America with an X-ray and a lot of brand new surgical instruments. I hoped I was done with my specialization in wastebasket surgery.

Namkham was growing by leaps and bounds. Japan and China were having an "incident." China was pushing a road through from Kunming to our border, working feverishly at both ends and in the middle as well. Already our road had reached Mangshi. I was hoping for an excuse to travel up by car as far as the road was completed, when a telegram came in from Tengyueh saying that a China Inland Mission lady at Longling, twenty miles north of Mangshi, was ill with pneumonia. Two nurses and I started off in our second-hand Buick.

In many places the road was only six inches wider than the car, with tremendous precipices dropping away from the side of the road. Beyond Mangshi no bridges had been built. So we had to leave the car. We drove into the grounds around the Mangshi palace, and my friend, the sawbwa, was luckily at home. It was late so he put us up for the night and, the next morning, started us off on three of the smallest native ponies it has ever been my ill luck to ride.

Our mule path was along the route followed by the new motor road. Even on that short stretch there must have been ten thousand coolies at work. The hillsides were black with them: Chinese, Shans, Kachins, chipping off an inch or two at a time. Ants on a hillside! But ants work together, and what they can't accomplish!

As we climbed up out of Mangshi we left behind the Shan States of China. Now we are entering Chinese China. Graves, graves everywhere! Nothing had ever been permitted to disturb those cemeteries during the centuries; but the road must go through! The Japs were pressing in. The generalissimo was looking ahead. This road must go through! Cemeteries got in the way. They cut right through them, disinterring the bones of the sacred ancestors. China was looking backward over her shoulder no longer.

Deeply impressed with the new road, we pulled into Longling Town and discovered the home of the sick missionary. She had right lobar pneumonia and was very ill. But, as usual, I had the breaks. One of the nurses, tired as she was, went on duty while the other got a few hours of sleep. For no apparent reason, the patient within four hours had a favorable crisis. In twenty-four hours she was so far along the road to recovery that there was no point in our staying further.

We returned to Namkham the second morning. Two months later the Burma Road was completed into Longling.

That year the hospital was filled to overflowing. The nursing school had grown till there was not sufficient room for all the nurses in the old hospital building. With great days in the offing it would be the worst thing for the government if we had to shut down part of our hospital and decrease the number of nurses on account of lack of funds. Days were coming when every hospital bed and every trained nurse would be needed. I wrote to the commissioner of the Federated Shan States, Mr. P. C. Fogarty, requested a grant of five thousand dollars for a clinic for women and children, and asked that our annual grant of one thousand dollars for hospital expenses be doubled.

Ten days later Mr. Fogarty appeared unexpectedly at Namkham. I asked if he would like to look over the hospital. He was astounded at the amount of surgery, the extent of pediatric work, the large number of cases of venereal disease of all sorts being treated in the same wards as the other patients. But nothing can describe his amazement as he went through the women's ward and saw women, with all manner of diseases, being treated on the floor as well as on the beds.

"Why don't you have more iron beds?" he asked.

"No money, sir," I replied.

"How much do they cost?"

"About twelve rupees for the welded iron in Rangoon. We rivet the pieces together ourselves in Namkham."

"Would three hundred rupees help you out?"

"Yes, sir."

He walked on to the row of smaller rooms intended for one patient. There were four to six women patients on the floor of each.

"I'll send you five hundred rupees."

A week later we got a check for seven hundred and fifty! Mr. Fogarty took up the question of building grants with the Defense Department. Things like that take time.

But two months later, approval was given for a grant toward the nurses' home, payable at once, and one for the women's clinic building the following year. Close on the arrival of this notification came a personal letter from Mr. Arthur K. Potter, of the Defense Dept. A ten thousand rupee personal check dropped out. The money, said Mr. Potter, was a much-too-small effort on his part to help us in the development of our program of medical work in the Northern Shan States. We deposited it in the bank as a buffer fund to save the hospital from any debt liable to occur if we pursued our policies of medical development forcefully. Tremendously encouraged and emboldened by the availability of this fund we went ahead, drawing on it when in trouble, and repaying funds into it as we received occasional windfalls from grateful patients. But word leaked out among the Kachins that Mr. Potter's gift had amounted to a hundred thousand rupees, and thereafter they paid even less price in hospital fees than before.

So in the rainy season of 1938, Tiny and I sat down and drew up plans for a two-story nurses' home. She made suggestions from a woman's, and I from a structural, point of view. As we were drawing the plans, we had in the hospital a patient from the royal family of Mangshi State. Representatives of both Mangshi and Chefang were continually visiting this patient, so Tiny and I used every opportunity, in and out of season, to describe our program to them, emphasizing our difficulties in putting up the nurses' building. We even gave them practical demonstrations. With a great deal of effort I repaired our old ton-and-a-half truck until it could run—sometimes—and converted our Chev touring car into an ugly half-ton truck. Day by day they saw nurses jump on board after the day's work and help haul stone. They were so astonished that they even volunteered to help load and unload. Luckily for us the two cars broke down several times when these people were helping us and, members of royal families though they were, they had to walk home. Soon after they left the hospital, a rumor filtered down that the sawbwa of Mangshi would like to lend us two new three-ton trucks to haul stone as his contribution to the hospital work. Rumor though it was, I promptly hired the Shan who had helped drive my truck when we were building the main hospital, and we started north over the Burma Road that night. The rainy season was just over, and there was plenty of mud to plough through.

The sawbwa was very gracious. Dinner was just being served and he wanted us to join him. As we were disposing of a fifteen-course Chinese meal I told him of the rumor and of our very great need for the assistance he was ready to give.

"But you have no drivers," he objected.

"Yes, I have, and they are both here, ready to start in the morning."

That was so typically American that it floored him completely.

"All right," he said. "The two trucks will be ready in the morning." He seemed to like Americans, for in the morning it was three trucks instead of two, and the sawbwa furnished his own driver for the third truck. He went the Americans one better!

Nine tons at a time instead of a ton and a half! We had to haul rapidly, for when the country really dried out after the rains, the sawbwa would need the trucks to fulfill his

36

responsibilities in the construction of the Burma Road. When the Shan driver finished a day's work, Tiny took his truck and we continued to haul.

Knowing that with the completion of the nurses' home we would begin the construction of the women's building, we took time by the forelock and began leveling the site of the latter. Tons of earth had to be removed. Trained in wastebasket surgery, we felt that that waste earth should be put where it would do some good. Where could we put it? Our only remaining dream was a decent little stone bungalow for us to live in, where we could be properly screened from the mosquitoes that constantly made havoc of our work. We had the site already picked out on the little hill beyond the hospital. We could use the waste earth as a fill for a future road connecting the hospital with the doctor's residence.

The first wall of the nurses' home was about four feet above the ground in November, 1938. I was setting a window in place with a plumb bob, when from nowhere appeared the handsomest man I ever met. His name was Dan Gourley and he was, he said, advance agent for an American airplane manufacturing company that had been bombed out of Hangchow and Hankow and had decided to set up their factory in Kunming. While they were settling in Kunming, Japan had begun to bomb that city also, so they had determined to find that spot in China, farthest from Japan, which still had possibilities for easy transportation. On the map, the Namkham valley seemed the most promising. He had been referred to me as the man best acquainted with the valley. Would I be willing to help him locate some spot where nature facilitated the building of runways above the level of the paddy fields?

Great Scott! an airplane factory in the Namkham valley!

I spread out the map and showed him my choice, as well as two other plateaus, much smaller, but closer to the Burma border. Then I took him to the hospital verandah and pointed out the actual spots in the distance.

The next morning, armed with the map and an English-speaking Shan guide whom I furnished, Mr. Gourley set out to explore. He returned delighted.

"Your first suggestion is a perfect spot," said he, "but it is too far from that little spur of the Burma Road. I have selected the two other sites. They are within a quarter mile of the border and we will have no trouble transporting our supplies."

Mr. Gourley returned to Rangoon. We went on building

37

the nurses' home, not quite sure why Gourley had tried to excite us.

Then, one day, a station wagon, the first I had ever seen, drew up under the banian tree. A thick-set, muscular man stepped out. It was Mr. "Chuck" Hunter, manager of the Central Aircraft Manufacturing Company. He had come down the Burma Road from Kunming as far as the Salween River and then, one day's journey by car from his goal, had had to turn back to Kunming and come to Burma by air. There were Chinese engineers with him. After paying his compliments, he went across the river to Pang Kham, the English bungalow nearest the chosen site at Loiwing, and set up headquarters in a grass shack.

Though their headquarters were so close to us, they were busy and we were busy and we did not see much of each other.

A letter appeared in the post one morning—an application from a young Karen doctor named Ba Saw. After graduating from the medical school of Rangoon University he had developed tuberculosis and had been refused a government position. Months at Taunggyi, in the Southern Shan States, had improved his condition very greatly. If I could arrange to take him on as an interne he would, he said, be glad to work without pay. He was the son of Karen missionaries to the Chins of the wild mountains of West Burma. I was fed up with all my previous assistant doctors, whether Kachin, Indian, or Karen. Since they had each passed the Rangoon University examinations, sometimes on the third or fourth try, they knew it all and were not willing to learn more. Give them a chance to operate and they were too proud to study up on the operation the night before, no matter what happened to the patient! Not knowing much myself, after passing my examinations the first time at Johns Hopkins and zealously studying every book I could find for sixteen years, I was apt to be a bit impatient at their "complete" knowledge. But I couldn't do all the routine work myself.

Ba Saw came. His right lung was collapsed with a pleural effusion. I ordered him to work no longer than a maximum of four hours a day. It was the only order I gave him that he ever disobeyed. With only one lung he was forever on the job. No matter what nurses you put on his side in a baseball game he would lead them to victory over my side three games out of every four. Whether he was to do the operation himself or not, he would get out his and my books

38

on operative surgery and study up the next day's operation. A man of completely charming personality. A man whom both men and women love. A perfect Christian, he didn't have a trace of hypocrisy anywhere in his make-up. No fancy phrases and slogans. No prudery. Incapable of exhibiting anger, though capable of deep indignation at the mean things of this world.

I have taught Ba Saw a lot. He has taught me a lot also and continues to teach me.

I gave him ten dollars a month spending money from the start. Six months later I had to argue with him for a long time before he would let me raise him to twenty dollars. A few days before Christmas he came to the office and shamefacedly asked for a loan of a hundred rupees. Every cent went into Christmas presents for nurses and schoolteachers. A year with us, and inevitably romance sprang up between Ba Saw, the most charming Karen male I had ever met, and head nurse Bella, about the sweetest Karen girl you could hope to find! Tiny and I were delighted. In 1941 they had a lovely wedding.

3 THE PLAGUE

CONSTRUCTION had begun at the airplane factory across the plain. Trucks began hauling supplies up.

Food trucks passing from Bhamo to Namkham in five hours when heretofore such articles had taken five days on mules . . . A tremendous fire breaks out in the Bhamo bazaar and destroys half the native town . . . Rats leave the burning houses and have a difficult time finding sufficient food . . . Trucks loaded with food are standing ready to start for Namkham in the morning and the rats leap aboard . . . A month later rats are dying in Namkham by the hundreds . . . Householders pick them up by the tails where they drop on the floor and throw them out into the garden, and the bubonic plague comes to Namkham for the first time in eighty years. Virgin country! I telegraphed for enough plague vaccines for our entire staff and wondered when the first case would appear.

Almost immediately I was called. The patient had been ill since the night before. By the time I reached the house he was dead. He had died so rapidly after the onset that there was no sign of disease on his face. Two rather large ecchymoses on his body were all the signs of plague I could find.

The next day another patient was dead in the adjacent house, and in two days three in this second house had died. All of them were cases of septicemic plague. I telegraphed the civil surgeon in Lashio and the assistant superintendent in Kutkai. I sent our staff through the town urging people to be vaccinated and personally urged vaccination on the lord mayor. Aside from the Chinese community, led by a very intelligent Chinese friend of mine, everyone refused vaccine. We telegraphed for vaccine for the Chinese. Plague cases appeared all over. Rats began to drop dead from the ceiling. Down the street rats would run and fall over dead in front of you. Rats dropped on a group of nurses delivering a labor case in the town. Lashio had done nothing. I telegraphed the superintendent in Lashio himself, asking for a free supply of vaccine from the government, as I could not afford giving free injections by the thousands when each one cost me ten cents. The civil surgeon complained to the superintendent that Seagrave was just having hysterics. Plague was endemic everywhere and not epidemic, and there was nothing to get excited about. Under compulsion from the superintendent, permission was granted for me to order all the vaccine I wanted, bills to be sent to the government. Shans refused to be injected, though by now cases were taking forty-eight hours to die, and they died with terminal plague pneumonia. I wired Lashio again and under pressure from the superintendent, the sawbwa issued an order ordering everyone in the plains to be vaccinated. Then true bubonic plague appeared.

We set a time favorable to the lord mayor and, with a corps of nurses to assist, we started inoculations in a big way. The lord mayor submitted first, but the germs were already in him and in two days he developed bubonic plague and died. We injected more than half of the people in town. Many of those ordered for vaccination refused to appear. The plague began to search out their homes and many of those who had refused vaccination died. Where all but one in a house had been vaccinated, the one unvaccinated person acquired the disease and died.

But occasionally a person who had been vaccinated acquired the disease, and a small per cent even of those died. The nurses and I were constantly exposed to the disease, using every treatment in the books—and out of them, for that matter—to try to save lives.

Plague began to appear in near-by villages. With the local police to help, we went out to give injections in those villages.

The first day was completely wasted. Villagers had heard that we were coming and had evacuated. Not one person was at home. The second time this happened, I telegraphed the assistant superintendent for Kachin troops to help us. The Shans are scared to death of the Kachins. The acting mayor sent for me and begged me not to put this indignity upon him. He would guarantee that his own police would enforce our orders. We tried again with little success. Then the assistant superintendent himself arrived. He was disgusted that I had been put to so much inconvenience. The villagers must come to me. He sent out Kachin troops and arrested the headman and elders of each village where I had had trouble and threw them into jail. Our troubles were over.

That year we gave some ten thousand inoculations of plague vaccine, and as soon as the number of people injected reached 60 per cent of the population, the epidemic stopped.

But we were having real trouble ourselves now. Nurse Nang Leng and I had been trying out various injections on a pregnant plague patient. Our legs were being bitten as we injected. Three days later Nang Leng had a bubo in her groin. I made a smear from the gland which proved positive. The airplane factory had a small stock of plague antitoxin and on our urgent plea for help, sent us over a few c.c. I gave Nang Leng 10 c.c. and then started off on an obstetrics case twenty miles away. On my way there I had a peculiar pain in my right armpit. On the return trip I kept feeling that aching spot, and discovered that I had a bubo myself! I told Tiny about it and she insisted on giving me an injection of the serum. Then I came down with a huge chill and the most gorgeous headache I ever enjoyed in my life. Rats had been dying in our house, and one had died in the bookshelf behind the chair in my office. Every child under ten that had contracted plague in the town had died, even though the child had previously been vaccinated. Tiny and I fought over the matter tooth and nail. She didn't want to leave me and I didn't want our two boys to get the disease and die. I won the argument finally; Tiny turned me over to the head nurse and took the boys out to our school in Muse for the period of quarantine, preparatory to taking them down to Maymyo and safety.

Altogether ten of our hospital staff got the disease, but, thanks to double dosage of vaccine, all of us recovered.

The American engineers had now come and settled in Loi-wing in grass shacks. Many had brought their wives. Thousands of workmen and coolies were at work under American supervision putting up one building after another and installing machine tools. A very attractive Chinese surgeon, Dr. Horace Yu, graduate of Northwestern Medical School, had come. With the help of engineers he had drawn up plans for a factory hospital, and the building was going up rapidly. Dr. Yu's very charming and beautiful wife, an American-born Chinese girl trained as a nurse in Peiping Union Medical College, joined him. Mrs. Yu and her little daughter lived in our home for several weeks. Until their hospital was completed, the factory sent all patients needing hospitalization over to us. Our financial situation, for the first time, eased off a little.

After I had recovered from the plague I received a formal invitation from Messrs. Hunter and Walsh, factory manager and general manager, to dinner. I knew something was up, and made up my mind to refuse. But that dinner was far too delicious. Tiny was still away with the boys and it had been a long time since I had had anything fit to eat. By the time the meal was over I had practically no resistance left! Their idea was for me to stop being a missionary and come over to run their hospital on a generous salary. I had helped order their hospital and surgical equipment and knew there were no "wastebaskets" in the list. I would be practicing medicine and surgery in the way every doctor dreams of doing. But—I liked my stupid idea of missionary work, and I had become badly spoiled by the fun of always having more work on hand than I could ever possibly do. Namkham was my brain child. Even if the American Baptist Mission sent out another missionary, or two, or three, to take my place at Namkham, it would be like divorcing an only son.

I had my alternative suggestion ready: Their job—director of the hospital—was nothing like a full-time job, and if I had no work to employ me other than holding down a chair in the grand new club building, I would soon go mad. I would spend three days a week at Loiwing and assume full responsibility for the work of the hospital, make emergency trips at any time if an American needed special work done. In the other two-thirds of my time I would continue my work at Namkham. They should pay me only a part of the salary suggested and, by mission rule, this money would be used for the Namkham hospital work. I would be able to build the little stone doctor's house Tiny and I had always wanted, and other dreams for Namkham could be realized. Both men objected, but it was a case of accept my offer or have no

American doctor for their Americans, so they finally agreed.

And so thrice-weekly trips to Loiwing began, fourteen miles each way by motor road.

Soon after our nurses' home was completed in 1938, Tiny went out on an obstetrics call. It was a normal case in which a long, long wait was inevitable before the baby could be born. Tiny went into session with her pencil and a piece of paper, and came home with a gorgeous floor plan for the women's and children's clinic. It was such a divine inspiration that all we had to do was work out the dimensions and blueprint it. We built it the first eight months of 1939 before the plague put us temporarily out of commission. When the latter was over and my Loiwing work was running smoothly Tiny and I both went into a huddle to put our dream house on paper. Putting dreams on paper is not too easy a job, but in a few weeks we succeeded beyond our wildest expectations and produced such a good plan that the factory engineer could only add one artistic touch to give it perfection—complete drawings for a fireplace, a small-scale model of the grand fireplace in the Loiwing Club's drawing room. Stone hauling was again the insurmountable obstacle. The factory had plenty of trucks but they were in use all the day long. Finally, the Americans found a solution. After work on Saturday, they would drive over three trucks and haul stone for us till dawn Sunday morning, if the nurses, our few coolies, and I would load the stone. Meanwhile, Bill Cummings and his family had moved to Namkham on a mission plus government agricultural project for the Kachins. Bill is just as crazy a missionary as I am and just as continually up to mischief of some sort. You can tell how crazy he is very easily—he named his youngest son Gordon Seagrave Cummings! This scheme of hauling stone all Saturday night was so insane that it appealed to him as much as it did to me. Tiny and Hazel sobbed in each other's arms, and then took turns producing us some marvelous midnight suppers!

The Burma Road and the Loiwing airplane factory shared first honors for importance in Chungking. Nothing rivaled malaria as the possible cause of failure of these two projects. The United States sent out malaria experts to study our peculiar variety and to institute effective methods of prevention. They made their headquarters at Chefang and spent much time at Loiwing. Even our hospital was not beneath the dignity of their help. Our laboratory had become quite worth while, but we were not satisfied. They offered to give a special six weeks' course in malaria to our two best labora-

43

tory nurses. E Hla and Hara came back from Chefang most efficient in their work, and they have given a two months' course to each pupil-nurse since.

Then the rains of 1940 broke. From that time on I have not had a moment's peace, and I hope I never will.

Plague broke out this time in Muse, at the upper end of the valley. One of the Loiwing workmen spent a night in Muse, picked up the disease, and, after a very short illness, died in Loiwing.

Then began the extraordinary Loiwing rat hunts. Chinese workmen surrounded each house that had a floor near the ground with a barricade of galvanized roofing. Coolies pried up the floor boards one by one, and then the fifteen or twenty men in each enclosure, Americans and Chinese, went mad. Clubs in their hands they struck wildly at each rat as it ran out into the open. As they were killed they were thrown into a five-gallon can. Five gallons of dead rats—a hundred and fifty to two hundred of the rodents—was a normal catch from each house.

The Loiwing hospital staff, doctors and nurses, were quite busy enough with malaria, dysentery, and typhoid, so I brought over Namkham nurses, and we injected 40 per cent of the personnel with 3 c.c. of vaccine and the remaining 60 per cent with a total of 5 c.c. When the factory personnel had completed their injections we vaccinated in the surrounding villages. We continued to kill rats, getting positive smears from their spleens and bone marrow till the end of the rains, but not another case of plague appeared at the factory.

When the nurses moved from the old hospital building into the new nurses' home we shifted some patients to the old hospital, giving us space for new cases. The women's clinic had lovely wards, and single rooms for private patients, while many of our other wealthier patients preferred rooms in the little cottages, for there they could keep their friends with them.

With the beginning of our second plague epidemic, rats began to die in our old home. Though our new house still needed a great deal more work, we decided to move in and keep away from the plague. From then on our workmen wasted no time. Tiny was in the house and kept them on the move. After the epidemic Ba Saw moved up to our old house and had decent quarters at last.

That year I began the same compulsory vaccination of the entire Burma side of the valley that had proved so effective in

44

limiting the disease the year before, and sent nurses out in teams. We gave fifteen thousand injections that rainy season. There were few deaths. No plague went up into China along the Burma Road, and by 1941 plague ceased to be epidemic in our valley.

4 MALARIA AND AIRPLANES

TWO HUNDRED CHINESE troops had been sent to do guard duty at the factory. They were quartered in small bamboo barracks. Coming from nonmalarious parts of China they were not protected by a single trace of natural immunity. The wards of the hospital were so crowded with the factory workers that there was seldom room for sick soldiers. The chief physician and one of the internes paid regular visits to the various barracks, distributing medicines; but the cases of malaria that developed could not be cured without actual hospitalization. The mortality for malaria was higher among the soldiers than was that for plague in the valley this second year of the plague epidemic. As I visited the barracks, I was appalled. I appealed to Mr. Hunter for permission to use the bamboo isolation hospital which the factory had built to house plague patients that never appeared, and urged him to rush construction of more buildings. As the Loiwing staff was too busy to deal with the new wards, I brought over a team of nurses from Namkham.

Then I borrowed a truck to gather in the sick soldiers. Mr. Hunter, thinking I had made much ado about nothing, came along in his station wagon to see for himself. At the first barracks I asked the captain to "fall in" the men so that I could select those for hospital care. They most literally fell in, stumbling, heaving about like drunken men, dragging out companion soldiers slightly sicker than themselves. Mr. Hunter picked up in his arms one erratic patient whose legs could not quite get him into line and deposited him in the truck. Then he leaned himself against the side of the truck a minute, wiped his eyes and blew his nose loudly.

"Doc," he said, "I never saw anything so pitiful in my life. How can a man be as sick as that and live?"

Loaded with malaria cases, we drove to the foot of the hill leading up to the "plague" hospital. Some interested Americans turned in and each carried a sick soldier up the hill. It was late, so we treated them wholesale, while the truck went on to the other barracks for more malaria casual-

45

ties. The nurses were given a little twelve by ten grass shack to live in. It had been built for use as a morgue for plague cases!

I have never seen blood so full of malaria parasites. For several days we lost patients daily; then the value of the treatment began to become apparent. The high proportion of blackwater fever, cerebral malaria, and the algid type decreased and the uncomplicated variety became the rule. To celebrate the improvement in health of the Chinese soldiers, the club threw a party, and three of the nurses put on a series of Burmese dances that brought down the house. It is not surprising that Namkham nurses have developed an extraordinary idea of what constitutes an American. All the Americans they met were hard workers, whether their immediate task was the sort usually done by coolies or an office job requiring brain work of a high type. Every American treated them with great gentleness and amazing respect.

With Loiwing and war news continually filling my mind, it was only natural that I should dream of planes bombing the factory. One day in October, 1940, I had to go to Loiwing, but I had some major operations that morning in our own hospital and was so tired that I lay down for a short nap before going over. This time the dream was so realistic that I could even hear the drone of the engines. Suddenly I heard Tiny screaming for me from the bathroom where she was in the midst of her bath.

"Gordon, Gordon, wake up! Those are Japanese bombers!" I took one look at the flock of "swans" and yelled to our two boys to run to the valley where we had arranged for them to hide. Leaving Tiny to dress frantically, I ran over to the hospital. Nurses were already evacuating the patients according to a prearranged plan, and I passed several who were carrying male patients on their shoulders out into the woods. E Hla and the operating-room nurses were loading the Dodge with all our surgical instruments and baskets of sterile goods.

I started on with a team of nurses, Tiny coming along a few minutes later with another team. Four carloads, in all, went. I reached Loiwing about half an hour after the bombing. Dr. Yu and the first-aid men he had trained had already carried most of the casualties in. With one Chinese nurse and Low Wang, the Chinese orderly who is still with me, to help, our nurses lit primus stoves and boiled instruments. The power mains had been destroyed and we had no electricity.

46

Dr. Yu took the amputation and other orthopedic cases on one table, with Tiny to give his anesthesias, and I took the abdominal cases on the other while E Hla put them to sleep. We both worked fast. As I finished one major abdominal case and the nurses lifted him onto the stretcher, I moved over to the patient nearest the entrance. He moaned to me in Chinese, "Take me next, please take me next." He was covered with a blanket so I could not see just how badly he was hurt. I wheeled him toward my table, but the head factory nurse jerked him back and insisted I take another patient who, she said, needed operation more urgently. Thinking she knew her job, I took her patient, finding it to be a simple flesh wound. Then I went again to the other man, drew back the blanket and found one leg almost completely severed at the thigh with no tourniquet in evidence. Disgusted that favoritisim should come into play during a time like this, I hurried to control hemorrhage; but the patient died. If I had operated on him first, as I intended, I could very probably have saved his life.

It is extraordinary what a ghastly wound can be caused by an insignificant bit of shell.

A woman, eight months pregnant, had a tiny puncture in the left flank, from which oozed a little blood. Sure the shell fragment must have passed into the uterus, I opened the abdomen which contained a lot of blood and amniotic fluid. Tying off the ovarian artery that had been injured, I delivered the baby by Caesarian section. Across the dorsum of the baby's right foot the shell had made a wound, the scar of which that child will carry till the day he dies. Both mother and child did well.

And so on, case after case: splenectomies, removal of several feet of lacerated intestine, amputations of the leg and arm.

Night was coming on and we were not half done. No electricity. Americans were trying to buy Storm King gasoline lamps across the valley and to borrow those the mission owned; but they had not returned. I remembered two packages of candles in the drawer of the desk in my office and sent a nurse for them.

Candles kept us going, with the aid of an occasional flashlight, till the Storm King lamps appeared. Americans had driven thirty-eight miles to Muse to buy them.

At eight the next morning, I started to help operate on the "less seriously injured."

And so, for days, we were operating on bomb casualties, removing arms and legs and using the "Spanish treatment"

47

where we could. Tiny was fascinated by a woman who had lost her arm near the shoulder, but whose baby was untouched. Impervious to pain, she lay with the baby in the crook of her remaining arm, smiling and smiling! Times without number I caught Tiny standing in the doorway gazing in awe at that woman and her child!

After that single bombing, instead of working by day, the factory—such personnel as could be found—worked at night hauling off machine tools to the Burma side and hiding the generalissimo's private amphibian plane which had been flown in for repairs, and other machinery, over miles and miles of the Chinese side of the border. For our part we were paralyzed for fear we would not be in Namkham, near enough to help them, if another raid occurred. We did not dare push our outside work.

Our hospital had never been full, judging by present standards! Now there wasn't one spare inch available. The shock of the bomb raid made many of the pregnant Chinese women go into labor early. Our maternity building was jammed with women outdoing each other.

For months the factory hospital remained closed and patients were sent to us. Our plant had again to be adapted to take care of them. With funds furnished by them, the old hospital and the small cottages were fitted with running-water toilets. Septic tanks were built. Fearful that their precious hospital equipment would be destroyed if the bombers returned, they sent most of it over to us either for our temporary use or to be stored. Our attic was floored, and supplies not susceptible to heat were stored there.

After months had passed, the factory personnel decided that the Japanese were never coming again and consented to go back to work. The hospital reopened. Tiny and I took a deep breath and decided that since we were no longer tied down to the Loiwing job, we would go ahead with some more dreams for Namkham. Taking John to school in Taunggyi and leaving Sterling for a few weeks with his grandmother, Tiny went with me on our first protracted jungle trip together, visiting our most distant hospitals at Kokang and Momeik. It was grand. We were surprised ourselves at how good the work done by these hospitals had turned out to be.

Mr. Fogarty came to us in perplexity one day. He was not satisfied with the medical facilities on the Burma Road. Diseases not known before in Burma were being brought in from China, and there was always the chance that plague would be carried up into China. So many of the truck drivers were unskilled that trucks were being smashed up daily. The morbidity caused by malaria among the road coolies was so great that the Lashio branch could not be kept in condition, nor could the surfacing of the Bhamo branch proceed rapidly. I had plenty of suggestions ready.

"We want to have two more hospitals on the Burma Road besides that one at Nampaka; one at Muse and one at Mong Yu. We want them to have mat walls, thatch roofs, and dirt floors, till we prove them valuable; ten beds in each; salary for the necessary nurse in charge to be paid by the government; and a grant made to cover costs of medicine if you desire us to give free treatment."

"But you can't supervise them satisfactorily," he said, "and they are so far apart they will be of no assistance in preventing malaria among the road coolies."

"That brings us to our next suggestion," I replied. "If the government will buy us a half-ton ambulance and make a grant to cover the cost of necessary petrol, we will make trips twice weekly to Mong Yu and back, dispense to the sick of the villages en route, give preventive doses of cinchona to the coolies, supervise the work of the nurses in each of the hospitals, and bring back to Namkham all those patients whom the nurses are unable to treat satisfactorily."

"It all sounds good, but I do not believe you will ever have much success in roadside dispensing! However, the ambulance will pay for itself even if it only makes possible your supervision of those Burma Road hospitals. You may buy the ambulance, provided you will do one more thing: build a twenty-bed stone hospital where the road crosses the border at Kyuhkok."

"All right, I'll build the hospital and staff it with three nurses." He had gone me one better, as usual, but I had to have that ambulance.

I made the first trip with the ambulance. Two nurses went along each time to make my work easier, give them a change from their monotonous routine, and act as interpreters. We had to travel the first thirty miles on the unpaved Bhamo branch, through Muse, till we reached the main paved road a few miles from the border. Between Namkham and Muse the coolies were almost all Shan. From Muse to the paved road at the "105th mile" were two hundred Indian coolies whom the Burma Oil Company had lent to the government, desiring to haul their oil to China from Bhamo. Beyond 105 the work was done by gangs of Chinese and Kachins. We never had much success in giving preventive doses of quinine to the first group of Shan coolies, probably because I didn't want to waste time arguing with them. They had natural immunity, anyway. From Muse to 105 we never had trouble. The nurses and I walked up to each Indian, opened our jaws wide—at which their mouths opened wide also, in sympathy—and popped in two tablets of cinchona before the cooly could recover from his surprise.

Beyond 105 the Chinese and Kachins were already acquainted with me, and instead of having difficulty in persuading them to take their medicine, we had difficulty in preventing them from running off with our entire supply! At "91" there was a bazaar village—one of the favorite night stops of the Lend-Lease truck drivers.

Stopping again and again, as we came to gangs of coolies at work, we pushed on to Nampaka, instilled pep into the Kachin nurse there who needed that article more than any other we ever had, treated her patients and finished the trip in the evening at the Mong Yu hospital, sixty miles from Namkham.

After dinner we returned to Namkham, picking up stretcher cases at the different hospitals or at the villages along the road. If the day's work had gone well we could reach Namkham at 10:30 P.M. If there had been unusual numbers of patients—well, we had the night before us!

Tiny made the second trip each week. We used to vie with each other to see who would have the most interesting tales to tell after we got back. On my trips I had to see many special cases which she had picked out to refer to me, and that always made my trip longer. It was Tiny who worked up the village dispensing service. By the time she had finished arguing and smiling, smiling and arguing, the most reluctant village was willing to take any medicine, or undergo any operation. The rest of us were satisfied with whatever patients happened to appear for treatment. Tiny made a great many more want to come for treatment.

Certain that the day would come when one or the other of us would be too ill or too busy to make the ambulance trips on the appointed days, we decided to train nurse drivers. Two of our head nurses, Htulum and Nang Leng, had drivers' licenses. Htulum had learned in Maymyo, where she had spent years as a nurse after completing her training with us. Nang Leng had driven around our valley. Neither had driven on the "Burma Road," and driving on that road is one of the most dangerous things one can hope to do. There were blind

50

corners and steep precipices everywhere; unskilled drivers, and, above all, drivers who were driving trucks which they did not own and which cost their transportation companies nothing: Lend-Lease trucks. They were drivers who could earn a pretty penny by putting the gears in neutral, turning off the electricity, coasting down every hill, and then selling in China, at a fat profit, any gasoline thus saved, seldom getting hurt even when their trucks fell over precipices. Htulum was careful but couldn't see well at night. Nang Leng was scatter-brained. It used to take me forty-five minutes to go from Namkham to Loiwing. Nang Leng made it once in twenty-five, and as a result her future husband, Dr. Tu, bragged about what a wonderful nurse she was!

Those were the girls Tiny and I had to train! But always throughout my foolish life, there has been that inner something or other that compelled me to teach people how to do things, no matter how eccentric or unorthodox—a sense of some great event ahead that would need every talent I could develop in all who came under my influence. That strange urge was behind our every decision of policy in our medical work, in our nurses' training; behind acceptance of duties for which I was myself poorly trained: an urge to learn first, how to do the thing myself, and then to find someone whom I could teach to do it for me.

We taught them. First we let them drive only in the valley. Then we let them drive the straight stretches of the Burma Road. When they finally made up their minds to try to drive, as we drove we let them experiment with the worst sections in the daytime. When they graduated with honors they were permitted to drive at night also.

The rainy season of 1941 arrived soon after the ambulance service started. Burma Oil Company trucks soon had ploughed deep ruts in the road to Muse; the ruts filled with rain, and a part of the road was little better than a morass. The B.O.C. drivers were always kind to us and frequently hauled us out of our troubles. As tough as the drivers of the other transportation companies, they had been in the habit of thumbing their noses at us until the day that one of them, starting out from Bhamo, ruptured a gastric ulcer. How that man drove his truck fifty miles with an acute abdomen, I can never think; but he was determined to come to us for treatment rather than turn back to the Bhamo hospital. While he was recovering from his operation, the other drivers stopped in to see him and soon became acquainted with us. From then on,

51

the sight of our ambulance flag caused them to extend every courtesy to us or the nurse-drivers.

During the first month of the rains of 1941 coolies gathered tons of gravel for the hospital at Kyuhkok. It was to be a stucco building. I tried to haul the gravel in the ambulance, but only small amounts could be carried for fear of breaking the springs. Loiwing permitted us to borrow a truck each Saturday evening, after work, and keep it till dawn the following Monday. At first the trucks were old ones, some without brakes, some with no headlamps, some with very faulty engines. It was not much fun driving. But after midnight we had the Burma Road to ourselves, and this offset the other dangers. Our masons were by this time very skilled. There was little supervising to do, and Tiny did this on her ambulance trips. Later, as part of their program to help the A.V.G. (Flying Tigers) which was training in Burma, they bought a lot of new trucks, and my work became much easier. The hospital was completed the first week of December, 1941.

On every trip the ambulance brought home patients, filled to capacity. More than half the cases were surgical. A fourth were complicated malarias, while the rest were a smattering of pneumonias and other medical complaints. Mr. Fogarty was greatly impressed. He said that if we would build two new hospitals on this road, at Namsarawp and Kunlong, and extend our ambulance work to Kunlong and the border, the government would buy us a new ton-and-a-half ambulance to make it possible. All he had to do was tell us about the way those Chinese coolies were dying and we bit!

While the new ambulance was being built we started the longer weekly trip—a hundred and fifty miles each way—with the first ambulance. This trip took two days instead of one. The Kunlong road was much more difficult than the Burma Road. I did not dare let either of the two nurses drive it alone, expert as they had become. Only Tiny and I could manage it. Most of the Kunlong road was so narrow that cars could not pass each other except at rare intervals. If one met a car or truck in a narrow spot there was nothing to do but back up hundreds of yards and let it by.

The Chinese on the Kunlong road finally became acquainted with us. We had loads of fun with them. The new ambulance, when it came, had medicine shelves above the windshield from which we could reach the drugs without having to go outside. The coolies crowded up to the windows and got their cinchona tablets, and whatever other

52

special medicines they asked for, if we were convinced they really needed them. Nurses dispensed out of one window and I out of the other. Soon we discovered patients were getting too clever. Having received all they were entitled to from me, they slipped around and, pretending to be someone else, tried to draw rations from the nurses as well. We always glanced back at the men as we pulled out. Invariably they were gathered in little groups comparing notes to see who had managed to get the largest number of pills of various sorts.

Then the assistant superintendent of Kutkai wired me to join him at Namsarawp, where we could choose a satisfactory site for the new hospital we were to build of mat and thatch. It was the eve of December 7, 1941. I expected that, as usual, we would push on and spend the night up in the mountains sleeping in the ambulance. Mr. Barton insisted, however, that I stay the night with him in the Namsarawp plain, as he had other business to attend to and wished to travel on to Kunlong in the ambulance next day. Never in my whole life have I been so miserably chewed by mosquitoes! It was hot, but I covered my body and head with my blanket, leaving only a small air hole. The mosquitoes chewed my nose. Sweating from the blanket, it was only natural to kick it off the minute I fell asleep, and swarm after swarm of mosquitoes had their blood meal. A glorious feeling greeted the appearance of dawn, with its resultant freedom from my tormentors.

Near Kunlong, we were met by a Chinese official who told us about the attack on Pearl Harbor—a garbled version, because he located the attack at Singapore! So at this time we did not realize that America had been attacked.

"Let's hurry the selection of the site for the Kunlong hospital as much as we can, Mr. Barton," I urged. "I want to get back to our own radio and listen in on this thing; if Japan has cut loose, Burma is in for it."

Hurrying back much faster than the road warranted, I met the Namkham-Lashio bus. The driver waved me to stop, and Dr. Tu, who had hospital business to do for us in Lashio, stepped out.

"Mrs. Seagrave is critically ill with malaria," he said. "She has been delirious and Dr. Ba Saw is very worried."

We stopped for no more patients! At Namkham, Tiny was conscious again, but very weak. Dr. Ba Saw had done a wonderful job giving her various intravenous and intramuscular injections, using the right drugs, as her condition demanded

53

from time to time, and pulling her out of the cerebral malaria attack with the utmost skill. Tiny's favorite nurses had been on with her continually without thought of rest for themselves. She remained critically ill for many days, but the cerebral symptoms, at least, did not return. About the time she was able to be up again, the malaria parasites injected into me by the mosquitoes at Namsarawp that night had multiplied to sufficient numbers to put me in bed for a day. Since then Tiny and I have had relapse after relapse of malaria, neither one being able to afford time to cure it completely by staying in bed.

PART TWO: BATTLE OF BURMA

5 THE BEGINNING

THE NEWS on the radio was not good. Sooner or later they would be in Burma, and then where would our hospital be? I asked "Chuck" Hunter if he could figure out some way in which the hospital could become mobile so that we could move swiftly to the scene of action when hostilities started.

"Listen, Doc, why don't you go down to Rangoon and persuade them to give you some Lend-Lease trucks. The authorities would rather have them given to Americans who they know will not misuse them. They have given us some to help in our work with the A.V.G."

On our way home, Tiny, Hazel, and Bill Cummings and I talked it over. The idea seemed pretty good to us, but there was the difficulty of getting enough drivers. It was Christmas, and I had to go to Rangoon in any case to take delivery of the new ambulance, and Bill consented to go along with me in the Oldsmobile which the factory had presented to us. Tiny was still too weak to drive long distances.

Cooped up in the car for three days on end were two of the craziest missionaries the A.B.M. ever produced in Burma. We saw no scenery the whole trip. Our tongues were moving so rapidly that we persistently interrupted each other. We had started out from Namkham with only a hazy idea; continuous argument caused the pieces of the puzzle to fall into place and the picture gradually came into focus.

Mr. Fogarty was in Rangoon, now chief liaison officer between the government and the Army. Bill and I went to his house at once to lay the project before him; but before we could say a word, he started laying his plans before us!

"Seagrave! I was just hoping I could get hold of you. I want you to start for Prome tomorrow night and open a four-hundred-bed hospital at once for bomb casualties. I will give you three days to set up, and then your first hospital train of patients will arrive. Can you do it?"

"Yes, if you can get a telegram through to Namkham asking for eight of our key nurses to be brought down to help me; and if you will help us with this project of ours," I told him, as I outlined the plans Bill and I had made.

"I'll take you around to Army headquarters first thing in the morning," he said.

The next morning Mr. Fogarty's face was wreathed in smiles.

"It worked," he said. "The governor approved of my plan for sending you to Prome most wholeheartedly; so the Burma Medical Department immediately discovered that they had underestimated their own ability to handle the situation and are no longer talking of evacuating all casualties to Calcutta by sea. They decided that if you could start a four-hundred-bed hospital on three days' notice, so could they; so they are getting busy at once. Now we can go around to the Army." Fogarty moves in mysterious ways. I felt a little dismay at having been used as a red herring, and yet Fogarty would have been quite capable of tying me up in Prome for a month or six weeks if his herring had not produced results. Approval of General Hutton having been obtained, it took only a few minutes over the telephone to secure the trucks and Lend-Lease supplies from the American officers in charge.

Early the next morning we took delivery of the trucks and other supplies and loaded up with all the gasoline we would need during the first month. The medical stores filled our requisitions in record time. Mr. Baxter, financial secretary to the government in Burma, gave us a thousand rupees of his own personal funds to cover incidental expenses liable to occur during the period essential for organizing our unit. Several missionaries were out of constructive jobs because Judson College, of the University of Rangoon, had closed down. Driving our hospital trucks seemed to them to offer possibility of real service to Burma. It certainly would prove more interesting than sitting on chairs for the duration. Paul Geren and Whittington joined us then, and for one of the trucks we secured Mr. Tun Shein, a Karen who had had years of service with Macgregor's, one of the companies handling the teak of Burma. A college graduate, elephant catcher, a little bit of everything that we needed so badly, he took the job first as a lark, then later became just as vitally a part of our work as Bill and myself. Tun Shein could hear the squawk of a hen laying an egg five miles away, and come back with both the hen and the egg!

56

Speaking Burmese, Hindustani, and English as well as his own Karen, and understanding the psychology of each race, he was a perfect liaison as well as supply officer.

That day in Rangoon great pressure was put on us by the mission and by the American consul general to get all American women and children out of the country. Now what were we to do? Rangoon Port was almost out of commission as the result of only two bomb raids. Bill and I had a major problem on our hands. What sort of advice should we give Tiny and Hazel? Each of us had two small sons in Namkham. Hazel was not very well, and Tiny had been very ill for a long while. If Tiny were well she would be of immense service with our unit either at the front or keeping the Namkham hospital open while we were away. If she regained her strength, she might stand the trip to Myitkyina if we had a chance to fly out from there, but from Myitkyina to India on foot would be beyond her in any case. If the Japs gave our friends in Loiwing time enough, they might fly her and the boys out from Loiwing at the last minute. There were too many ifs. If Tiny remained ill (and I had tried so long to restore her to health without success) I would never be free for continued action at the front.

The day after our return, January 2, we put the matter up to them. May I never have to go through another day like that! Finally the two mothers decided they had better go over to India and take no chance with the children. Twenty-four mad hours were spent packing the most essential things, and then Tiny started off in the Oldsmobile, one of the trucks accompanying her to pick up supplies for the unit that we had been unable to bring on the first trip. She reached Rangoon just in time for a week of continuous night bombing. After what seemed like seven years instead of seven days, the three obtained passage on a steamer for Calcutta. The letter Tiny wrote from there on her arrival was the last to reach me till July. Someone told me later that he thought she had sailed from Bombay, but it was not till I reached India that I knew she had safely reached our home in Ohio.

January was a busy month for Bill and me. We had to arrange our trucks for immediate departure when the Army authorities ordered it, while I still had all my regular hospital work to do and ambulance trips to make, and Bill had to wind up some important phases of his agricultural work.

A division of the Chinese Sixth Army was reported to have arrived in Kengtung State. Two other divisions were due to come through into Burma by way of the Burma Road. Somehow we knew the Army in Burma intended to assign us to the Chinese Army. We were the only hospital in Burma that had Chinese-speaking nurses, and we were the only non-British hospital available for military use. It was known that the Sixth Army had no medical-school graduates to do their surgery. But I had begged headquarters not to tie me up with medical work for an idle army. Namkham, the work we had developed in the Northern Shan States, the Burma Road hospitals—all seemed well worth maintaining until there were actual battle casualties that needed treatment. The British liaison officer assigned to the Chinese Sixth Army came in to see us one day.

The first regiment of Chinese, he said, would start on Wednesday. It would be better for us to start on Thursday so that there would be no difficulty getting mixed up with the Chinese convoy on the road. So, on Thursday, we started off under a barrage of pouts and tears from the nurses, whom we had decided to leave behind to keep up the Namkham hospital work. Promises of rotation between Namkham and the front had no effect. Five other nurses started a Gandhiesque non-co-operation strike because they had been left behind.

We spent the first night in Kutkai getting used to Army life. Arriving in Lashio the next morning we drew out our first stock of rations and cooked breakfast in the jungle, ending our second day's journey in the bazaar sheds at Pangkitu. While we were eating our breakfast next day at Laikha, another liaison officer appeared, who told us we were to report at Mongnai instead of at Takaw, on an entirely different road. We got to Mongnai at sunset, and there Brigadier General Martin, chief of the British Liaison Mission to the Chinese Army, met us. He informed us that our orders were more extensive than we had originally been given to understand. Our unit was to serve not just one division but the entire Chinese Sixth Army over a front extending from Kengtung State, three hundred miles east of Loilem, through Mong Pan State a hundred and fifty miles south, and into Loikaw, capital of Karenni, a hundred and fifty miles southwest. Since the main roads to these three stations met in Loilem, a delightfully situated town, General Martin advised us to set up our base hospital there. We pushed back to Loilem that night. What kind of men did these British think we were anyway, giving us a job of that size? They were ordering us to be a whole confounded medical corps! It was well known that the Chinese Medical Corps consisted only of a few men trained in first aid, and of companies of stretcher bearers. We would somehow or other have to do all the hospitalization for the entire Army. My job was so large that a commission as lieutenant colonel was offered me.

I declined with thanks. They could make me an honorary lieutenant colonel—Kentucky variety—but I was taking no chances of losing my American citizenship!

We selected a lovely pine-covered hill east of Loilem, and the government secured contractors to put up a lot of bamboo and thatch wards under the pines.

I did all I could for the few days during which hospital construction was going on, but I knew that my first week away from Namkham would be very difficult for Ba Saw and E Hla. So the first time it seemed possible to leave for a few days, I went back to Namkham.

At Namkham it was just as I had feared. The nurses we had had to leave behind, albeit temporarily, had been just as mean as dirt because we had not taken them to the front. I pointed out to them the fact that they were very lucky in being assigned their share of the Namkham work at the beginning, before hostilities commenced, as they would not need to return to humdrum work in the middle of the excitement that would come later. They were only half convinced. Bella was now at term. Her pelvis was very narrow and she and Ba Saw were terrified at the thought of her having the baby while I was away. As Bella was not very strong and ought not to have another pregnancy soon, it would be more than they could bear if trial labor resulted in the death of the child. That evening I performed a Caesarian section, stayed with Bella for twelve hours, and then went off on the regular ambulance run for Kunlong. From Kunlong I returned to Loilem. Two more regiments of the Sixth Army had gone through to Mong Pan, and the general, whose headquarters was in that town, wished me to open our hospital there at once.

Htulum was the top nurse of our unit. It seemed logical to put her in charge at Mong Pan with two younger girls and Lieng Sing, our Chinese college boy, to help her, Koi remaining in charge at Loilem. Htulum, being such a good driver, could keep a jeep at Mong Pan for use as an ambulance; while, if he was willing, Dr. Gurney of the English mission at Langkhu would answer emergency calls from Mong Pan when Htulum got into trouble.

The sawbwa of Mong Pan built Htulum a fifty-bed hospital of bamboo and teak-leaf thatch, above a cement floor of some unknown origin. There was a nice little nurses' home beside it. I was quite pleased with the arrangements, feeling no qualms at leaving the nurses there. I was sure they would be able to take care of themselves. One of the younger nurses was the Princess Louise, granddaughter of the sawbwa of Lawksawk—who was a very old friend of mine. Louise is unfortunate. Everyone falls in love with her, from my son John to a certain Chinese major at Mong Pan. Htulum and Lieng Sing were worried, at first, at the persistent attentions of the Chinese major, but Louise told them not to fret—she could handle him! So she took the poor man and made him teach her Mandarin until she was an expert.

At Mong Ton, beyond the Salween and only a few miles from the Siam border, advance units of the division that had its headquarters at Mong Pan had made contact with Siamese troops. I picked three nurses, of whom the chief was Chit Sein, "Miss Burma, 1942," to open a small hospital there. Having no doctor to spare, I asked Paul Geren to go with the nurses and add to their prestige as well as protect their morale. A forty-mile walk was necessary from the end of the dirt road beyond Mong Pan. I felt positively ill as I escorted the little party to the road's end. The other two girls were Kachin and had been toughened by many years of life in the mountains, but this little Shan beauty, brought up in comfort, was in for a very, very hard trip which I was sure she could never stand. I was convinced that I was bidding them a permanent good-by. Later a nice long letter came back by messenger from Paul. Chit Sein had smiled and laughed the whole way there, standing the trip much better than he had. One day's journey from Mong Ton the Chinese had sent out a group of dignitaries to welcome them and bring them to the post in style. A tremendous Chinese banquet had been prepared in their honor. Paul, a doctor of science, was assumed to be a doctor of medicine, and all the sick officers sent for him. Being a canny man, Paul took Chit Sein with him on each visit.

"Chit Sein," said Paul in an undertone, as he made a theatrical examination of the patient. "what the dickens is the matter with this fellow?"

"He has malaria," Chit Sein replied without moving her lips.

"What do you think ought to be done for him?"

"Chinese like injections; I think we had better give him a hypodermic of quinine."

"Chit Sein," said Paul in an authoritative tone, as he put away the spare stethoscope, "this officer has a bad attack of malaria. Please give him an injection of quinine."

Mong Pan hospital now had a hundred beds. Htulum had become very popular not only with the Chinese Army but with the medical officers of the Indian troops that still remained there, and the latter continually sent particularly difficult cases to her for treatment. Under the treatment of such a lovely nurse, it was impossible for the patients not to get well!

6 UNDER GENERAL STILWELL

NEXT MORNING we started for Kengtung with the large ambulance loaded with supplies for Dr. Barr-Johnston. Htulum, Esther, Hla Sein, and Roi Tsai went along to study geography. Htulum and I took turns with the driving. We got a few hours of uneasy sleep, scattered as we were on top of bundles of medicines and gauze. Barr-Johnston was at Mong Hpayak near the Siam border. The ambulance engine was running on only half her cylinders, so we did not reach Mong Hpayak till after dark. Barr-Johnston had so many patients that he had taken over a lot of bazaar buildings and had a flourishing two-hundred-bed hospital. Before the Japs burst through, our unit was handling seven hundred and fifty beds over a three-hundred-mile front for the Chinese Sixth Army alone.

With two drivers, we made the return trip in record time.

Next morning we separated at Loilem. I had just heard that Lieutenant General Stilwell had arrived from America to take over command of the Chinese armies in Burma. Was I going to have a chance to work under an American general after all?

I had not the least idea that General Stilwell would see me. What little reputation I had obtained in Burma would be completely unknown to him.

I was mistaken; General Stilwell would see me! His medical chief, Colonel R.P. Williams, would also like to have my ideas with regard to supplies necessary for the Chinese armies. Very diffidently, I asked that my surgical unit be permitted to serve the Fifth Army, which was in action at Toungoo,

61

while the medical unit maintained the hospitals already at work with the Sixth Army. Still more diffidently I begged that our units be transferred from the control of the British Liaison Mission to the American Army. Nobody was more surprised than I when the general approved my suggestions and promised to issue the necessary orders as soon as things could be arranged with the British. I completed the trip to Namkham, relieved that I had not been thrown out on my neck!

At Namkham everything was serene. The nurses had started to co-operate, beginning to believe that I loved them after all! E Hla, especially, was glad to see me. Ba Saw, relieved from his Namkham duties by the arrival of a Burmese woman doctor who had worked with me previously in Namkham, was fretting for permission to return to the front. Bella was well after her operation. The baby was putting on weight. But at Lashio I found tragic news. Htulum, returning to her post in the jeep, was traveling on a perfectly straight, loosely graveled road, when her left front tire burst, and the car turned over. Htulum's skull was crushed by the windshield and she died instantly. The nurse with her had sustained three fractured ribs but was doing well, while Moses, the orderly, had escaped with a few bruises. They buried Htulum among the beautiful pines by our hospital.

It was a sad group of girls that met us that day. Our first casualty the most competent girl of the unit! Something drastic was needed to set the girls back on their feet again. That "something" was lying on my table: orders from General Stilwell to report to General Sibert at Pyawbwe before setting up for active duty at Pyinmana. I called all the girls together.

"I don't want any heroics this time," I said. "I know there is not one of you girls that would not follow me into hell! We will need twelve nurses at Pyinmana, but our Sixth Army work has to go on. The girls who remain are going to have just as hard a task as those who go, and are going to be in just as much danger without having the thrills of Pyinmana to help them in their daily work. Paul Geren and Tun Shein are going with me, but Mr. Cummings is staying on with the Sixth Army group. Take a slip of paper and write on it where you personally feel your real place in this picture is and hand the slips in to me."

The slips returned; we counted them out. Thirteen girls asked for Pyinmana. The others had indicated one or the other of the Sixth Army hospitals as the spot where they felt their work would prove most valuable.

"Well, girls," I said, as we bade them good-by, "you can count on Bill and me. We won't leave you in any of your hospitals unprotected if the Japs ever break through and a retreat becomes necessary. Some of you already know and love Dr. Ted Gurney, who is top doctor now for the Sixth Army, and Ba Saw is coming back to help. Give them the satisfaction in your work that you have given me and scramble for the trenches when the Japs come over!"

Bill accompanied us as far as Kalaw where he had a summer cottage. Spending our first night draped all over his floor and the few beds, we raided his stores for everything the Japs might like to have and then, amid a burst of sobs at the thought of leaving behind the beloved "son-in-law," as the nurses called him, we hurried on down the mountain, our trucks and jeeps camouflaged with branches of trees in the most approved Chinese Army pattern. At Meiktila the British garrison gazed in unbelieving awe at a group of "Burmese" girls heading for the front instead of running away at top speed! On reporting to General Sibert we were informed that a group of British Friends Ambulance men had volunteered to serve with our unit and would follow us down immediately to Pyinmana.

It was midnight when we reached Mr. Case's agricultural school on the outskirts of Pyinmana, the F.A.U. trucks on our heels. Mr. Case was away looking for food for the Chinese Fifth Army that he was feeding, but we assumed he would approve of our using his buildings; so we set up our operating equipment while the F.A.U. boys went on to the front for their first load of patients. When the operating room was ready for action we snatched a couple of hours' sleep, waking up again at 4:00 A.M. to the sound of the returning ambulances.

We started operating at once. Those operations before dawn that morning are hazy memories. All that stands out in my mind is the trouble we had keeping plaster casts on our patients. There was a high percentage of bone injuries requiring "Spanish treatment" and we were using plaster steadily; but it was very inferior and took so long to set that the patient was awake and tearing at it while it was still soft. Nurses tied arms and legs together, but the patients tried so hard to get free that the casts were cracked and broken. While I was removing a foot of intestine from one badly injured patient, Mr. Case walked in. He was delighted that we were doing something for the Chinese, but he could not permit us to remain in the agricultural-school buildings. He had had

63

a great deal of trouble keeping a sufficient number of boys with him to help secure food for the Army. If we remained the boys would be in terror of our drawing a Japanese attack on the buildings and they would run away. During a short lull we piled our packing cases back onto the trucks and moved over to the "Child Welfare Center" where there was one small, very inferior building. On the bottom floor were two small open porches. We chose one of the porches for the operating room and set up four operating tables. The upstairs floor was soon covered with bedrolls, while the main floor was reserved for patients. The ambulances now returned from their second trip to the front, and with a good deal of trouble, the Friends located us in our new setup. We started operating again and were soon in our stride. This was getting to be old stuff. Four of the nurses were upstairs getting a little sleep preparatory to taking over when the first group downstairs dropped from exhaustion. Two of them, with the help of Low Wang and Lieng Sing, were giving first aid to the casualties as they were brought in and deciding the order in which the patients would be sent for operation. Esther and Big Bawk each had two tables assigned to them and were pouring chloroform in a way that would have delighted Tiny, who taught them. Koi, Kyang Tswi, Ruth and Little Bawk were assisting, one at each table. The sun began to scorch us. Off came my surgeon's gown, then my rubber apron. I would rather catch a Japanese bomb than perish from heat stroke as I moved from table to table debriding devitalized tissues, putting bone fragments together, throwing powdered sulfanilamide tablets into the wounds and applying plaster casts. Sweat was still pouring, and my shirt, undershirt, and stockings came off and were thrown into a corner, leaving me in nothing but a pair of bloody shorts. It was grand to be a man! I could work in a pair of shorts without anyone's getting excited! The poor nurses were not so fortunate. Their thin little Burmese jackets plastered tight to their bodies, they had to sweat and gasp and like it! A squadron of Japanese bombers passed over us on its way to Mandalay, and I forced the girls to jump into the slit trenches in the back yard. An hour or so later the formation returned. Since the girls were convinced that all bombs had been disposed of and that the planes were returning empty, I could not persuade them to leave off operating. Just as the planes were straight above us the bombs began to scream downward.

"Lie down, you darn little fools," I yelled as the bombs burst a scant two hundred yards down the street.

Paul had dragged the spare nurses into one of the trenches and heard them praying as the explosions shook the house, "Oh, God, don't let the doctor get hurt; don't let him get hurt!"

As fire began to sweep the town we returned to our operating tables. Civilian bomb casualties were now being brought in. I simply could not locate the bullet in the thigh of one of our Chinese patients.

"Here, let me have a try," said Koi. She inserted one tiny finger in the wound, using it as a guide for a long forceps, and out came the bullet!

"Listen, woman, what are you helping me for? You take over this table and do your own darned operations! I'm busy. Debride each case, get the bullet or shell fragment out if you can, pack the wound, and if the destruction is extensive, put on a plaster cast."

Kyang Tswi and Ruth were getting along pretty well also. All I needed to do was select uncomplicated cases for them, explore, and leave them to trim, while I kept them in view out of the corner of my eye. Little Bawk and I handled the worst cases: abdominal, chest, and head wounds. Just as we were really going to town I looked up and saw General Stilwell standing in the doorway! The room behind him was littered with the patients we had been operating on, lying on our little cotton mattresses. On the ground outside nurses were receiving patients from the trucks and giving first aid. Three Chinese casualties were standing by the wall of the operating room waiting for nurses and Friends to carry away the one who had been operated on so they could climb up on the vacant operating table and sigh thankfully as Bawk or Esther began to chloroform them. My body was covered with blood. Well, I was in for it! The general certainly wouldn't have any use for me now!

The town was blazing merrily. Two Storm King lamps and the burning town furnished us light. Tomorrow, I thought, we must locate some other place where we will not have to worry about fire.

The next day, as we were treating the truckloads of new casualties, Paul explored the town. There was nothing big enough for us but the lousy jail, and he advised our moving three miles closer to the front where there were some abandoned Government Agricultural Institute buildings. I drove out to have a look and was so pleased that on my return the nurses packed up, nurses and Friends loaded the trucks during the first lull, and we moved—the second time in forty-eight hours.

7 NOTES FROM A DIARY

Pyinmana, March 30th—This is a grand place. The school building has a nice cement floor and plenty of windows. There is a laboratory with all sorts of glassware which we must carry with us if we have to move again. There are two teachers' houses. The Friends have moved into one and our group is in the other. There are a lot of huts scattered around the grounds and we can put patients into them. Today bombers passed over us twice, one formation bombing Pyinmana again. It is nice to have clean well water. Our patients had thrown bloody bandages into the other well at Pyinmana. We all got a nice bath by the well, the nurses bathing in their *longyis* (skirts) and us menfolks in our shorts. We can have water carried to our bathrooms tomorrow.

March 31st—Another big day. The F.A.U. brought in several more truckloads from Yedashe where the Chinese are making a big stand. They lost the Toungoo airfield. Magwe field has been bombed, they say, and about thirty A.V.G. planes were destroyed on the ground. I guess that leaves us without any air support. The only decent landing ground this side of Namkham seems to be Pyawbwe and the Japs are over Pyawbwe every day. While we were getting ready to operate, an American officer drove up and said he was Captain O'Hara of the Dental Corps. General Stilwell had ordered him to come down to help us. After he had watched us for a while he offered to do some of the smaller operations. He made a mess of a couple of simple cases and then the F.A.U. brought in another of those shattered jaws like the one that took me so long to put together in Pyinmana. While I was exploring the possibilities of the case, O'Hara took a look.

"Listen," he said, "I don't know anything about surgery, but I can put that jaw together for you."

I let him go to it with a sigh of relief. By George, that fellow certainly knew his job! By the time he had finished I had something I could really drape that face over.

Friends are the funniest Englishmen I ever met. They pick those blood-covered patients up in their arms as if they were

66

sweet and lovely. Every Chinese seems to them to have been named "George." The Friends themselves don't seem to have any last names; they are teaching the nurses to call them "Bill" and "Eric" and "Martin." The girls get a great kick out of calling white men by their first names.

April 2nd—We have five tables now. The F.A.U. stole one from an abandoned hospital in town. They are going to steal me a sterilizer tomorrow—"salvage" it, I mean. Captain O'Hara doesn't seem to object quite so much to having to work with me as he did. But he doesn't like our food!

April 3rd—Another captain turned up today while I was matching the nurses for blood transfusion: Captain Grindlay trained in the Mayo Clinic after finishing Harvard. Looks just like a Mayo Clinic man, too! I will have to keep a stiff upper lip and do the best surgery I can. At least he hasn't operated on as many different parts of the body as I have! One of my cases today was a man with a bullet through his skull. I asked Grindlay if he didn't want to handle that patient, but he preferred an abdominal case. There was nothing for it but to go ahead as if O'Hara and Grindlay were not there. I used my old wastebasket trephine to remove about three square inches of shattered skull. The brains were beginning to ooze out even before I cut the dura mater. I simply could not locate the bullet, so I put in a vaseline wick and sewed a few stitches in his scalp. Bet he dies tonight!

We stopped for a while and had dinner again on the floor. All the available furniture is being used in the operating room. Grindlay and O'Hara look disgusted when they see us eating the rice and curry with our hands. We have very little silverware, but I am eating with my hands myself as a morale measure. No oriental likes to be bombed, but if I can make these girls realize that their old man is in this thing on an equal footing with them and takes no privileges, they will keep on the way they have done, ignoring the bombings as if they liked them. Later I can start using silverware again. This responsibility for the mess of these officers weighs heavily on me. Ko Nyunt cannot possibly cook two messes. Tun Shein is helping in the kitchen as it is, like any menial. We make a special effort to give O'Hara and Grindlay silverware and a suitcase or box to sit on, but I know they are still horribly shocked.

There has been tremendous traffic on the road past us all day. The trucks are going down empty and coming back full. Liaison men say the Chinese are retreating from Yedashe. What worries me is that bridge across the Sittang at Pyinmana. The bombs today dropped very near it. If they should destroy it we would cease to be of any use to the Chinese Army. We had a consultation of all hands, and decided to move on tonight.

Shwemyo Cliff, April 4th—We packed up late last night. I am afraid I was not of much use. One of the darned boxes lit on my foot and took off some skin, and I was so tired from the operations that I could make only a pretense of bossing the packing. It was a pretense, all right, because Koi and Esther can do a much better job than I can. Those Friends were Herculean in their efforts. Eric can throw a hundred-and-fifty-pound case into a truck without any help. Big Bawk is almost as good as he is when she gets excited. Paul is such a handsome chap it doesn't seem possible that he could do half what he did tonight, and Tun Shein continually astonished me. I am afraid I am getting old. Had some fever yesterday.

The Shwemyo Cliff bungalow is where we are now: first place we could find north of the Sittang bridge. Got here at four o'clock this morning, so tired we just dropped down on our bedrolls and slept till nine. My brain case is still alive and, furthermore, conscious and up to mischief, although he seems a bit crazy. We unpacked and set up for work, but had to run for the nullahs every two hours as squadron after squadron passed over us. We are much too much in the public (Jap) eye here. The bungalow is right on the brow of the hill where they can't miss us, and today the planes swooped down and machine-gunned the village at the foot of the hill. Every time the planes had passed by and we returned from the nullahs, someone had to go after that brain case. Once he had run half a mile away. Why *does* he live? Hasn't even got a fever!

April 5th, Sunday—Didn't have any casualties because the Friends can't locate the front! Bill Brough, top man of our special group of Friends, and I took the opportunity to run around in a jeep and find a more suitable place. Tatkon, a few miles nearer Pyawbwe, was our choice. Every Sunday is moving day!

Tatkon, April 6th—An observation plane circled over us as we got up. There was no place to hide except in a sugar-cane field, and I am scared to death of snakes. Prefer bombs any day! About a quarter of a mile away there was a government "Rural Uplift Center," the compound of which is full of beautiful banian trees under which we could hide the trucks as well as ourselves. All of us felt this was a much nicer place, so we moved again. The American officers and the Friends have taken over a little bungalow, and our unit is in the upstairs floor of the school building, which is quite nice, now that we have torn out the wooden partitions between the rooms to let the air through. Blistering hot! Ko Nyunt burned the oatmeal again this morning, much to the disgust of Grindlay and O'Hara. But what can I do! No use getting angry with Ko Nyunt who has his troubles trying to cook food without any cooking facilities whatever. I keep getting fever, so I don't care what they feed us. The nurses give me so many injections that I manage to keep on working, which is the most important thing. First the English and now General Stilwell have so much faith in us that we must keep going!

In spite of our horrible food Grindlay and O'Hara seem to be getting over their antipathy for our unit. Grindlay can't understand the nurses insisting on making up his bed for him every day although they are as tired as he is. Tonight, not having been worked to death, our morale was at a low ebb, so we had a sing. I think the thing that astonishes our honored guests the most is the wide variety of songs the nurses sing: anything from the grand old hymns to the jazz "gospel songs."

April 7th—Tun Shein has found some Burmese coolies to dig slit trenches for us. They work in the early morning and late afternoon, disappearing during Jap bombing time. Planes have been over again and again today. The nurses pulled a new gag on me so that I wouldn't make them jump into the trenches—the sand keeps getting into their hair! Silly fools stand on the edge of the trenches in full sight waiting for me to jump in first! Unless I jump in there is no possible way to make them take cover.

For some time I have noticed that O'Hara never takes shelter in the same trench that I do, no matter where it is. I figured, as a result of my inferiority complex, that it must be due to some personal objection to me, but it turned out today that he was afraid both he and I might be hit by the same bomb! He was willing to be hit by a bomb in the pursuit of

69

his duty, but wanted me, in such a case, to be still alive and able to operate on him!

The Friends brought in thirty-four patients, of whom all but two were serious casualties. There were three brain cases, and I did them all. Since my first brain case is doing so well, walking all over the place, everyone thinks I am a brain surgeon! Two of these died on the table, but I still feel cocky, for the third was the worst, and he is still alive! The girls put him on the table soon after the ambulances arrived, but in addition to having a shell fragment in his brain, he had shell wounds all over him and looked so ghastly that I told the nurses to carry him out and let him die in peace while I went on operating on the other seriously injured cases that I might possibly save. When all the operations were done I was about to take off my gloves; but Ruth asked me if I wasn't going to operate on the patient they had thrown out behind the kitchen.

"Golly," I said, "is he still alive? Gosh darn it, bring him in." It took me another hour to finish him off. I don't believe he is going to die after all. Grindlay is helping the nurses give him a huge intravenous injection of glucose.

The bugs are awful. The only way I can stand it is to operate naked except for the pair of thin Shan pants that Tun Shein located for me today. The nurses obligingly scratch my back at frequent intervals. Grindlay is apparently getting over his shyness, a bit. He can stand the bugs anywhere but on his bald head. O'Hara will not go to bed as long as there is any work to do. Even if he can't find a patient to operate on he sticks around helping the nurses with their jobs. Grindlay had trouble with a neck wound today, tearing into the jugular vein as he was debriding. He packed the wound and the patient is O.K. I was away at Yamethin at the time trying to "salvage" some hospital equipment.

I have been jealous for some time of the way the girls have a nickname for everyone, or call them by their first names. They have already adopted Grindlay and call him "Uncle" quite shamelessly. O'Hara, as soon as they caught sight of his hairy chest, became "Mr. Bear." Tun Shein is "Little Uncle," Geren "Big Brother," Gurney "First Love." Bill Cummings, being the favorite of all the nurses, is known as my "son-in-law"; but they won't call me anything but "Doctor" to my face, "The Old Man" behind my back, and "Our Father and Mother" when they write me letters. This afternoon at lunch, before the casualties began to arrive, the Friends were having a lot of fun kidding the nurses, and they were certainly up to mischief! One of the Friends decided that Roi Tsai needed to be spanked and chased after her. She naturally ran to me for protection.

"That's right, run to daddy," said the Friend. Koi, ringleader in everything, began to call me "daddy," and now none of the nurses calls me anything else unless I am administering a rebuke. It makes me homesick for John and Sterling.

April 8th—The Friends arrived with twenty-five casualties at dawn. There were two belly cases two days old that I turned over to Grindlay. He had to remove two feet of bowel from one case, doing a beautiful anastomosis. I took time out to watch him. He sure knows his stuff! Both those cases are doing right well. So is my brain case of yesterday! He is still unconscious, but his condition is good. I shall have to send away the first brain case I did south of Pyinmana, since we have no room for him. Most of the cases today had serious shattering wounds of bone. Grindlay had one case with four compound fractures. That guy is a hound for work! The nastier the case the better he likes it. The Friends brought in another eighty cases. The older girls were all in, so I put Little Bawk on as first assistant to Grindlay when he was operating on his abdominal cases. Mean way to make a young kid like her the one and only assistant at the sort of abdominal cases he was operating on; but he seemed to like her. At dinner tonight he said she was a "natural," and the best assistant he had ever had. And he comes from the Mayo Clinic!

April 10th—Time after time the ambulances went back to the front yesterday, until by three this morning we had had to operate on a hundred and twenty patients more.

We used up all our sterile supplies yesterday, so the nurses turned out at dawn to wash out the bloody towels and gauze. They were just as tired as I, so I got up and joined them in washing out the stuff in the near-by stream where we could take cover and still enjoy the sight of the bombers. Those crazy sores I got on my feet at Pyinmana just won't get well. The nurses dress them several times a day, but the foul discharges from the wounds of the several-day-old casualties keep my shoes wet and the sores dirty.

On our return for lunch I found that Grindlay and O'Hara had been scrubbing out the operating room themselves with cresol. Grindlay had found pieces of amputated fingers and toes in the plaster of Paris and wound refuse on the floor!

April 11th—Twenty-five more cases arrived at eight-thirty this morning. No more can be brought till after dark as the shelling is so incessant that the stretcher bearers can't evacuate them from the front lines till then. We all decided to have a good sleep during the day, but it didn't work very well. It's too hot! Today is Bill Brough's twenty-third birthday. Wherever we set up, regiments of Chinese soon move in beside us. They are moving in next door. They won't get out of sight when observation planes come over; but the pollution of our precious wells is distressing. These wells were never supposed to supply water to so many hundreds. Personnel of the Air Force is reported to have reached Karachi, but they have no planes.

Had only thirty-five cases today. We have been burning up the bloody remnants of clothes we have had to cut off our patients and cleaning up the grounds and the little hut next door where we place postoperative cases until the ambulances can cart them off. My, what a stink!

April 13th—We were just dropping asleep at night when Paul drove in with three more nurses from Loilem. Jap raiders were strafing the Taunggyi-Kalaw road as he came along. He made a record trip to Namkham and back—up in a jeep and back in a "pregnant" truck. We had quite a time delivering that jeep from the body of the truck. Wished I had had my obstetrical instruments! Paul had brought along Tiny's cache of Waldorf toilet paper. I was almost as glad to see it as I was to see the nurses! E Hla had written me a nice long letter with all the news of the crowd. Hkawn Tawng, angry at not yet having been brought to the front, had run off with a Chinese shopkeeper. All the wards were comfortably full. Dr. Grey had flown back from India and she and Dr. Ahma were busily at work, leaving E Hla in charge of the hospital finances. Japanese planes had brought the front to Namkham, as they tried to wipe the A.V.G. out of Loiwing. So far the A.V.G. had had the best of it, shooting down Jap planes in dogfights over the valley. The nurses had had a ringside seat for the whole show.

April 14th—Just got to bed last night when twenty more casualties were brought in. We worked on them till two

72

in the morning. Terribly hot and dry today! Tun Shein has located several nice thin Shan pants for Grindlay and me. They are so comfortable to work in.

April 15th—It is 136° in the sun. Villages are burning all around us. I was finishing a bath at sunset when a plane circled over us and then made a forced landing west of town. We started off in jeeps to catch the pilot if he were a Jap or help him if he were an A.V.G. man. We must have made a complete circle around the plane without locating it, while the pilot had made the edge of the town under his own steam when we got back.

"Are you an A.V.G. pilot?" we asked.

"Yes, I had to make a forced landing in a dry river bed, and the plane cracked up. My name is Patech."

"Come on over to our 'Little America,' " I said, and he jumped in.

We gave him a lot of coffee and a little "snake poison." He almost sobbed at finding friends so soon. We sent him on into Pyawbwe with a truckload of patients.

April 16th—Soon after Patech left, the trucks came in with seventy cases which kept us busy till 8:00 A.M. It was too hot to sleep, so we had a discussion as to what to do. The Japanese had been advancing rapidly along the Irrawaddy and their soldiers were said to have been on the main road north of Meiktila. Other Japanese patrols were reported trying to cut the Shan States road at Kalaw, while two drives were being made toward the Sixth Army headquarters at Loikaw, one from Toungoo on the Thandaung-Mawchi road and one westward from Chiengmai in Siam. If these drives succeeded we would be encircled. That would not matter for our personnel, as we could sneak out on the same mountain paths; but we would certainly lose all our precious equipment. Grindlay and I went to Pyawbwe to see General Stilwell.

April 18th—General Sibert dropped in at dawn and ordered us to retreat to the first decent place beyond the junction of the two roads to Mandalay from Myingyan and Meiktila. We began to pack at six-thirty, had breakfast, and after a little fun smashing up all the furniture and windows to let off steam, were off at nine just in time to avoid the retreating Chinese. So far all the Burmese villagers have been very

73

good and kind to our group, recognizing us as the Americans and "Burmese" that we are.

It was ghastly hot! We nearly perished of thirst before we got to Kyaukse, the first place beyond the junction General Sibert mentioned. A few miles south of the road junction, and perhaps three miles away from the nearest railway station, I had noticed a couple of bungalows by the side of the road. Leaving the nurses bathing in a lovely deep river near Kyaukse, we officers explored near-by roads; but finding nothing we decided to set up at the bungalows—Kume Town.

April 20th—Grindlay was quite friendly this morning. In Maymyo yesterday he discovered his old pal of Chungking, Sergeant Chesley, whom he describes as the only really good laboratory man in the world! He spent a lot of time telling Chesley what a fine bunch of girls our nurses were and how expert they were at their nursing. Chesley, who had seen the smoke screen of profanity that Grindlay had laid over the historic city of Chungking when he received orders to work under an ex-missionary, and who himself was a most confirmed misogynist, laughed in scorn.

Rumors of a break through the Sixth Army at Loikaw came to us this morning, so I impregnated a truck with a jeep, and with a nurse-driver and Bill Brough in his ambulance, we went back to Pyawbwe to get orders direct from General Stilwell as to where the casualties could be found. The general had been working steadily for several days without rest and had just started to take a much needed nap when we arrived. Hearing I was there, he came down, told us where to find the patients, confirmed the news of the Japanese break-through, and had me sworn in as a major in the Medical Corps. I told him that the break-through would negate the value of our Sixth Army unit to a great extent and asked for permission to rush to Loilem at once and bring back five nurses to Kume.

"How do you plan to get to Loilem? By the Maymyo road?"

"No, sir, I prefer to take the direct road through Thazi and Kalaw."

The general's tired face became grim. "If you go by Kalaw you will have to start at once and drive like hell or the Japs will reach Hopong before you!"

"I am starting at once, sir."

"Good-by, Major." Gosh! was I really a United States major?

That pregnant truck certainly covered the ground!

While we were driving along tonight I kept thinking of the way General Stilwell came down to see me today. It was the same way the first time I met him. Someone introduced me to Colonel Dorn, explaining about our work with the Sixth Army. Colonel Dorn went into the general's room, and almost immediately he came out and shook hands, asked a lot of friendly questions and then was very apologetic because some Chinese generals had come in for a big banquet and he couldn't continue his conversation with me. Some bootlickers that I knew tried to act as though they had known the general all their lives and didn't even get a "good morning." They say that he turns down invitations at important places right and left because "there is a war on," and yet he always has time for anyone who is trying to do a good job. Bill Cummings also got to see him, and the general spent a long time talking with him. He is most fun of all when you are talking business with him for he gets the point before you are half through with your sentence and his decision is as quick as lightning. You certainly get the idea right away that it wouldn't pay to start any bootlicking. He had a big laugh today when I told him our unit had three gears forward and only one in reverse! Even the nurses see through him. This morning before I left several of them told me to give their love to "Granddaddy Joe."

"Why, who on earth is 'Grandaddy Joe'?" I asked.

"Why, General Stilwell, of course."

"I suppose you have a name for Colonel Williams, too?"

"Yes, he is our *dooteah* daddy'—'second daddy.'"

Thinking of Stilwell made me think of Fogarty. That grand fellow is dead. The plane that was taking him to Chungking crashed and he got a compound fracture of the thigh, dying some time later.

April 23rd—At midnight Bill Cummings turned up with Kaw Naw whom he had picked up in Lashio. This morning we had a powwow with the nurses.

"The 'son-in-law' says that today is the last day cars can get back to Hsipaw and Lashio," I said. "We are not going to be able to get out of Burma through Namkham as we planned. When we go, we will undoubtedly follow the general up the west bank of the Irrawaddy, and we may have to walk out into Assam. If any of you girls want to quit and go

75

back to your people to hide out with them until the war is over, you will have to go now. If you go along with us into India, you will have to count on a lot of hard and perhaps disagreeable work in a strange country for nobody knows how long! Nobody will say or think anything unkind about you if you stop now, and I will furnish you transportation back to Namkham. Stick up your hands if you want to leave."

Not a nurse moved. Only my Lahu orderly wanted to return to rescue his wife and child.

"Well, Bill," I said, "I guess they really mean it! I will have to leave the Namkham-Hsipaw groups entirely in your hands. Let any of the girls leave that want to join their families. Dispose, as you see fit, of all our Namkham equipment and medicines, and the trucks and jeeps of the Sixth Army crowd. If you can get out to Myitkyina, perhaps we may meet you there."

Amid a shower of tears the "son-in-law" disappeared around the bend in the road.

Bombers bombed the Kume Road station today, and the Friends picked up a few casualties. Right behind them came General Sibert. The Jap machine-gun bullets had just missed him. There is another one of those rumors running around to the effect that there is a regiment of Japs, on the other side of the river, which has been lost sight of. If anyone who knows his map of Burma wants to figure out what the Japs are up to, all he has to do is make up his mind what the meanest move in a certain area would be, and a few days later news arrives that the Japs have done just that thing. In this case they are undoubtedly heading for the Chindwin to cut off retreat into Assam by the southern route.

April 24th—While we were eating dinner last night, patients began to arrive from Yamethin. In all there were eighty-five of them. We finished operating at seven-thirty this morning, and after two hours of sleep I began again. Grindlay has a ureteral stone which began to torture him during the night. He has spent most of the day in the bathtub, soaking. Later a real cyclone came on. Could hardly breathe for dust before the rain finally arrived. The wind blew our stuff all around the house, and we had only begun to straighten things up when a truckload of British troops were brought in. The sergeant said they had been traveling in convoy up the Myingyan road when the storm broke and a tree crashed down on their truck. Several of the cases were horribly injured. It was odd to have the men lie quiet on our six operating tables, each waiting his turn. One of the men had his scalp torn off. Another's skull had cracked like an eggshell. Of the sixteen British, only three had relatively minor injuries.

April 25th—They woke me at night for sixty more Chinese. Grindlay insisted on helping with a few, though he could hardly stand. Worked all night, using two shifts of nurses as we did the night before. The girls are so tired that two of them dropped asleep on their feet, and then cried when I ordered them off to bed.

Sagaing, April 26th—About five o'clock yesterday afternoon we received orders to move to Sagaing at once. We were packed up and off by nine, weaving in and out of columns of British trucks and tanks that had been using the road all day. Case has joined our party. We nearly missed the turn to the Ava Bridge in the traffic jam. It was long after midnight when we located the A.B.M. compound at Sagaing. The only empty building was the church, and most of the girls slept on the pews. I slept on the front seat of my truck. Soon after dawn a lot of Japanese bombers flew over and bombed Mandalay and the bridge, and for the first time I heard the sound of antiaircraft guns. Nobody hit anything. Beyond Sagaing the road was jammed with British and Indian troops. I kept my eyes peeled for some decent place for us to set up, and just happened to see a lovely bungalow, half a mile away from the road, almost completely hidden by pride of India trees and palms. It would certainly be invisible from the air. We settled down for some rest. All of us are pleased. There is a large irrigation canal beside us with a high dike that jeeps can travel on very nicely. There is only one fault to find with the place—the well water is full of alkali and has a ghastly taste! Spoils the coffee!

April 27th—Grindlay, Bill Brough, and O'Hara went off to the general's new headquarters at Shwebo, twelve miles away. They saw General Stilwell sitting on the verandah looking terribly tired. No one knew what the next move would be, nor will they until orders come in from Washington and Chungking. No further resistance is being given to the Japanese, except for a few Chinese troops that are in danger of being cut off. Everyone is talking about the action in which the company of General Sun's troops cut through

77

the Japanese lines north of Yenangyaung and rescued a regiment of British. General Stilwell sent for Grindlay to have a friendly talk, and outlined plans for dumping our comparatively useless stuff. The next move will be toward India. Grindlay heard that Major Wilson was killed yesterday in the Mandalay bombing. First American casualty!

While the boys were at headquarters I took the girls for a shopping expedition.

When we got back to our charming bungalow we found that the surgical team of the Friends Ambulance Unit, China Convoy, had arrived. I will never be able to understand why these men came down. By the time they reached Lashio the Battle of Burma was over. We were doing no surgery now. They had come through, knowing that bridges were to be blown up behind them. Peter Tennant, their boss, was with them, and he had brought with him Lu Shang, one of their Chinese interpreters, the only F.A.U. man we did not like. However, the surgeon, Handley Laycock, is the sort of man one ought to have a chance to meet: conscientious objector? Yes. But any sensible man objects to the things he objected to. He certainly never objected to war because of fear, nor through dread of hardship.

Tonight the Friends had a big powwow. Tennant doesn't want them to remain with us. The Friends who have been with us don't want to be taken away. Bill Brough finally got permission for them to remain. Williams has suggested that Laycock and his surgical team join the British on their trek out, while we go along with the Americans. I think that is the best solution. There are so few doctors that it seems useless to keep so many in the same place.

April 29th—I went into Shwebo with Grindlay today to see if Colonel Williams had any orders for us. We are not getting any casualties, except for an occasional man that jumps out of his truck when he sees our flag by the side of the road and comes in for treatment. I met Grindlay's friend, Sergeant Chesley. While we were talking to him the bombers came over again. We started back as soon as the bombers disappeared, finding the whole town burning, trees across the road, electric mains torn and impeding our way. We wove in and out through the streets looking for casualties, but there were none. None of the natives had remained in the town; they had too much sense!

April 30th—Terribly hot again. We had a few minor casual-

78

ties. Brian and Kenneth drove in toward Mandalay for some stuff, but couldn't get there. There was some rain, and Brian was driving like mad, as usual. He skidded, turned over, and now has a broken collarbone. Bill Brough is down with severe dysentery. Tennant has ordered them off to Myitkyina by train, as soon as the railway line is cleared, and they are to be flown to Calcutta. How on earth will we get along without them? This talk of our tramping out of Burma has me worried. It has been a long, long time since I have had to do much foot work in the jungles, and I feel much older than forty-five with this confounded malaria that keeps returning. And no treatment of any sort helps these four sores on my feet. The only thing that gives me hope that I may be able to make it over the mountains is that the Friends brought me a pair of English Army Issue boots today. They are as heavy as lead, but they permit me to wear two pairs of thick woolen socks, and that ought to pad my sores! Plans for evacuation change daily. We understand the idea at the moment is for us to go to Myitkyina by truck. Unless the government has been rushing construction of new roads that I don't know about, we will have ourselves a real trip.

8 RETREAT!

May 1st—Colonel Williams was downstairs in his jeep just as we woke up. Somewhere north of Mandalay is a regiment of Chinese who couldn't get across the Ava bridge. Colonel Williams wanted Grindlay, a couple of Friends, Lieng Sing, and Low Wang to go east to Kyaukmyaung, where one takes the ferry for the Mogok Ruby Mines, and set up a surgical station there to take care of casualties when this regiment arrives. The rest of us were to go north to Zigon. We hurriedly selected a lot of equipment for Grindlay and loaded it on a separate truck, and they set off with the truck and a jeep. Grindlay is afraid this means he is going to be permanently separated from our unit, which makes him swear as badly as he did when he was first ordered to join us! The rest of us started north. We have enough men to drive all our trucks and jeeps except for one jeep, and Big Bawk is driving that one. The road north of Shwebo is nothing but a graveled dike along the canal and so narrow that you can hardly pass anyone else, so it takes hours to cover a few miles.

General Stilwell has set up three miles beyond us on the "Mu" River. Since there is nothing further to do until tomorrow, I am going back to Kyaukmyaung to see how Grindlay is getting along. Maybe we can contact Colonel Williams again. He has remained in Shwebo.

May 2nd—We got to Kyaukmyaung about nine last night. Eric was beside the road looking for me. Told me Grindlay was down at the river since there was a lot of trouble about steamers. Only available ones had no crew. Kyaukmyaung had been bombed the day before, and everything was in a turmoil. Eric had a lot of cold rice and sardines and—of all things—real American coffee! Grindlay came in stomping angrily. He had to go right in to Shwebo and contact my old friend General Martin and have the English cough up some steamer crews, or the Chinese Army would not be able to get across the river. The Japanese are already at Kalewa, and that means that all these English troops that are trying to get out of Burma by the "comfortable" southern route will have to cut their way through. As I thought, that is where that "lost battalion" of the Japs was heading for all this time.

We went back together in our jeeps. General Martin is nothing but a walking skeleton. Still calls me Colonel! There is no way he can find crews, so we went on and found Colonel Williams still up. He had been burning everything at headquarters. When he heard Grindlay's story he decided it was a useless gesture to send him back on the original mission, to wait with his arms folded until the Japs surrounded and killed him; so the captain left at once to pick up the truck and his personnel and rejoin us at dawn. When the colonel heard that I knew where the new general headquarters were, he decided to come along with me. Not all of the general's papers had been destroyed yet, so he got rid of them all—plus the house—by means of a tin of gas and a judicious match. I got him to headquarters at four-thirty, and, after contacting the general, got orders for our unit to fall in line at dawn when the general's echelon passed us. I got fifteen minutes' sleep while our boys and the girls loaded up. Grindlay, the old truck driver, got to camp just as we were pulling out. Three Anglo-Indian refugees hitched themselves onto us at the last moment. I am sure I will get into trouble about their being along. Never should have been given a commission in this man's Army. I am not tough enough; but there is hope. I am getting tougher and tougher every day!

Who told Big Bawk to lead our echelon, I don't know, and

I don't want to find out, for I wouldn't have time to repair his shattered jaw. Just beyond the road's end we had to drive across the bed of a stream and then up a sharply sloping bank onto the dike again. Bawk is a wonderful driver, but she had not had enough experience to know there would be less chance of tipping over if she attacked the bank at right angles; so her jeep rolled over. None of the girls was hurt. The officers wanted me to take the jeep away from her, but I refused, and told Bawk to get back in and drive. She has guts, all right! The road from that point on was ghastly; nothing but cart track here and there, and occasionally nothing but a blazed trail through the jungle where the general's advance guard had chopped down small trees to open up a path.

Stopped at dusk at Pintha, a town with the expressive name of "beautiful fanny." There was a well across the railway line, and we had a gorgeous time washing off dirt. Grindlay began to bathe after the nurses had left and, thinking himself alone, did it in the nude. He could not reach the caked dust and sweat on his back so he yelled, "Hey, somebody, come and scrub my back." Little Bawk heard him and, quite unselfconsciously, went over and began to scrub. As soon as Grindlay could get the soap out of his eyes he looked around to see who was obliging him, and there was General Stilwell standing near, chuckling!

May 3rd—We followed the general out at dawn. Traveled all day, but only managed to cover about forty miles. What imitation bamboo bridges there were had been crushed by the Chinese six-wheelers ahead of us. Tennant, who is supposed to be an English racing-car driver, distinguished himself by getting embedded in the sand of a river bank and holding up the procession for hours in the awful heat. My years of misery on these Burma roads are coming in handy now.

One of General Stilwell's cars caught fire. Of course, it was the one with a lot of small-arms ammunition on board. We had to cut a new road around it to avoid the popping shells. Sometime during the day we must have circled that town of Zigon which we were supposed to reach the day before yesterday. In the afternoon there was a twelve-mile stretch of fairly good road leading into Wuntho. Actually sped up to thirty-five miles an hour. Before, we had had miles of rice fields and their dikes to negotiate. I kept awake by clowning around with the truck, and talking Shan at the top of my voice. The natives thought I was drunk!

Martin got fed up with the broken jeep he was dragging

along, so we had a grand time burning it up. We dragged it off into the woods a hundred yards from the road and built a little fire a yard away from it and then I blew a hole in the gas tank with my revolver. Only time I can remember hitting what I was aiming at! The Japanese will never be able to use that jeep. Martin loaded all the spare tires onto my truck. I still have a couple of roof trusses left. That is more than the other truck drivers can say.

May 4th—We lost the whole morning waiting around for orders. Japs are reported to have taken Wanting. That means they are in Namkham right now looting the house and hospital and nurses' home. Why have I worked so hard all these years to build up that plant? I shall never be able to do it again, old and tired as I am. Well, I have had me a darned happy time out of it! I still keep on thinking there must have been some PLAN behind it all. If all that background of mine has molded this unit into the sort of machine that can do the special sort of nasty tasks that General Stilwell needs to have done, I won't shed any tears!

We are to try to get through to Myitkyina. Colonel Williams drove up to order us to be ready to leave at four.

May 5th—We started off at four in three echelons. General Stilwell commanded the first, Colonel St. John the second, and Captain Grindlay the third. I brought up the rear, determined to see that none of our crowd was left behind. I was a minute late getting started and took the wrong turn in town and then had a hell of a time catching up with the others. We had a graveled road for a while but went past the north turn and would have been at the Irrawaddy again in no time if Case had not interrogated some Burmans. The road north was one of those things. Some government official had existed in this district with the vision to know that if the Japs attacked Burma, it would be advisable, even this far north, to have means of communication available to replace the railroad when it was cut. The road began all of a sudden at the boundary line of his district. We got lost trying to find it, but the general's luck held, for he discovered, near the turn, the man who had built the road. We backed up in the dark and got onto the road. Even then it was not easy, for there were bits of elephant roads and paved roads here and there leading off into the jungle. With the guide, we managed fairly well. At every crossing the general left some officer behind to direct the traffic, and we carried him along with us in our truck. There was one place where the general did not feel it necessary to leave a traffic cop; but Tennant, who had gotten to the van of our group, somehow, decided to leave Ruby there so the rest of us wouldn't get lost. Famed tiger country! But Ruby got down meekly and stood there in the dark, directing traffic, until Grindlay came along. "Oh, uncle," said Ruby, "I am so glad to see you! I have been expecting a tiger on my back any minute." Grindlay cursed and swore and picked her up. The rest of us might get lost if we didn't have any damned sense, but that girl was not to be left on traffic-cop duty in the middle of a jungle!

The general found a forest bungalow about midnight. We have three hours here to get some food and sleep. All the food we have time for is rice and sardines. All the other pews are occupied so I am going to relax on the roof of my cab.

Off again on the dot of three. Same kind of roads as yesterday! Grindlay was so sleepy he decided to wake himself up by scaring the sleep out of O'Hara. On a little strip of good road he sped up to sixty miles an hour, sweeping past O'Hara and bumping him over toward the other side of the road. The ruse was very effective. O'Hara will never get sleepy again when Grindlay's jeep is behind him! At dawn we got to the Maza River near Naba. The big railway bridge was right beside us, and we had to wait there for hours because a Chinese six-wheeler had broken through the flimsy bamboo bridge. We went swimming while Chinese repaired the bridge under Colonel Holcombe's direction. General Stilwell promised the men he would give them a hundred rupees if they had the bridge ready under three hours.

Between that bridge and Indaw many of the villages are deserted. We had a long wait in one of them while the general went into Indaw for information. Rumor says the Japs will be in Myitkyina tomorrow, so we are cut off. We were ordered to start west from Indaw to take the middle route into Assam. A group of British joined us.

Indaw was jammed with refugees, and the road, ankle deep in dust, was so crowded that we had to do a great deal of it in low to keep from hitting someone. Those poor people! Mothers trudging along, pregnant, but carrying children on their backs. Blind people. Lame and wounded soldiers—saw and recognized a few of the Chinese casualties we had operated on. Children and ancients walking along hand in hand. Punjabi cavalrymen on lovely horses. British officers on foot with their men. Chin soldiers of the Burma Rifles walking home with their families, looking as though they had been discharged from their regiments. Easy to see that the road into Assam is going to be lined with graves—or, more probably, skeletons—soon!

Fifteen miles of this, and then we had to ford streams. Paul's truck sank in up to the hubs in the first ford and something went wrong with General Stilwell's own car. The general must have heard some bad news in Indaw, because he has ordered us to move forward continually at all costs, abandoning vehicles at once if anything goes wrong. He abandoned his own car there, and we hurriedly salvaged our surgical instruments out of Paul's truck and went on. At the next ford they ordered Lilly, the American Technical Group man with the powerful thumbs and leather stomach, to drive the trucks across so there would be no more mired down. Tun Shein forgot to tell him that his truck had trick brakes, so when Lilly got across the other side and jammed down on the brakes the truck plunged into the body of the one in front and crushed the radiator. We had to abandon it also. Mine was the only one of the original trucks of our unit that got through.

May 6th—We passed through a big Hkamti Shan village called Mansi, and, five miles farther along, the road ended at a flimsy bridge which nothing but a jeep could negotiate. The general got us all together around him and made us a speech. All the different groups were to turn in their food supplies into a pool, then abandon everything they had except what they felt they would be able to carry themselves. I got the nurses together, after that, and told them the Chin Hills and Naga Hills which our trail would cross were famous for their steepness and therefore they certainly could not carry so much stuff as to make them lag on the march. We must vindicate ourselves by covering the ground as fast and as far as the long-legged Americans. Furthermore, we would certainly be called on to care for the sick en route; so each girl must take a little first-aid kit, with the drugs for malaria, dysentery, headaches, etc. My speech was very effective; for tonight I find the silly girls threw away their blankets and have only enough for one to every group of three.

While the Americans were shuttling back and forth to the end of the jeep road eight miles away, transporting the food supplies, we set out on foot. I find my feet don't hurt much if the ground is fairly smooth and I can set my feet down squarely. It is this ghastly heat! After four miles I was exhausted and lay down for a half hour under a mango tree and soothed my parched tongue with green mangoes. There is no shade, but at least we did not have to climb mountains. That guy Grindlay has got guts. He carried Ruby's pack as well as his own. Colonel Williams did this trip on foot with us, though he could have hopped one of the food-carrying jeeps. He seemed to have made up his mind to take things the hard way with his medical unit. He is ten years older than I am, but he can walk circles all around me.

May 7th—Up at dawn, but the Chinese muleteers, as usual, took an extra hour or more to get the loads tied on the saddles; so the sun was fairly high when we started. We followed a path that passed through jungle crossing a stream they call the Chaunggyi several times until we came to a sort of gorge; and then there was no road at all. The general and his Hkamti Shan guide led us splashing right down the stream bed. The general sets the pace and is followed by the American officers; then comes a small group of heterogeneous officers; then the English; then our group; and finally the general's Chinese bodyguard. The general has been carrying one of the tommyguns. From ten minutes to until the hour we have a rest, and then fifty minutes of marching.

We are all worried about Than Shwe and how she can stand the trip. It is less than a year since I opened her abdomen for appendicitis symptoms and discovered the peritoneal cavity full of tuberculosis and the appendix tight to the horn of the uterus. She looks well and is carrying absolutely no pack at all. About ten o'clock one of the Friends saw a rubber air mattress that had been discarded by an officer, inflated it, put Than Shwe on board, and dragged her along. As soon as the girls got tired they began to sing. I was scared that the general might think this a breach of discipline, but no bullets hit me from his tommygun and their singing put new life into me, as it always does, so I let them go to it. About noon Colonel Holcombe, who has been ill for weeks, had a heat stroke, and they brought him down slowly behind us. About a mile farther on Major Merrill fainted from the heat right in front of Bawk and me, and we fell out of line of march with Colonel Dorn and gave him first aid. He should not have had such a heavy pack! Than Shwe and her air mattress gave me a sudden inspiration. When Merrill's condition improved, Bawk and I hurried on to send Paul and Tom back with it. They dragged Merrill into our noon camp where the general was having two small bamboo rafts built while we

85

were cooking. Colonel Dorn has given us permission to cook our own mess separately from the officers, as the girls like chillies and things in their food that the Americans can't eat. I had an hour's sleep until the ants biting me had had a good meal, and then we all had a bath. I asked the general for permission for four of our Friends Ambulance men to drag the hospital rafts down the river. Colonel Williams has assigned Than Shwe to ride on Colonel Holcombe's raft, and a Chinese lieutenant, who also collapsed with the heat, to Major Merrill's. It was dark before we stopped for the night.

May 8th—Grindlay has been detailed to bring up the rear with the sick who are to travel at their own rate of speed. The river is running in a sort of gorge. On some of the sandbanks there is tiger spoor. Some group of refugees had driven jeeps down the river but gave up and abandoned them. We stopped for our noon meal on a high bank above the river, where there were some big trees and shade. Bawk spread out a rubber sheet she is lugging along so I could lie down and get some rest; but the shade moved away from me so fast that I had to get up and move every few minutes. Thorns were everywhere, and the girls kept picking them out of their bare feet. But the ants were positively vicious! Grindlay didn't turn up until we had finished our food, really delicious with some wild gooseberrylike fruit and some boiled wild greens that Tun Shein recognized. We are all vegetable hungry. We are camped for the night by a big Hkamti village on the river bank. It took Tun Shein about fifteen minutes to make the villagers fall in love with him and cook us a dinner.

May 9th—The coolies the general secured to carry stuff at the first village refused to go any farther, so Case had to round up a new group. Took us that much longer to get started. Some of our packs are being carried and we distribute the rest around so that each person's load is fairly light. The Friends' packs are still rather heavy, but they are the type we all really need—they hang from the shoulders without constricting the chest. The rest of us have the ordinary Kachin and Shan bags and their straps make it hard to breathe.

May 10th—They say it is Sunday again, but you can't prove it by me! The general had secured three large rafts and one small one, and we are to float down the Uru to the Chindwin. Each of the rafts consists of three sections fastened together with rattan. The Burmese had several hours' more work to do on one of the rafts, so we had a long wait ahead of us. The sight of those bare bamboo rafts worried me, for I hate the hot sun, and there were occasional dark clouds that looked like rain in the offing. Tun Shein scouted around and found a lot of thatch piled up under a native house, so I went over and stood near the general until he noticed me.

"Sir," I said, "if we may have your permission, our nurses will build shelters of thatch on each of those rafts to protect the whole group from sun and rain. We can complete them by the time the last raft is ready."

"O.K., get going!"

The Friends and orderlies split bamboos, some of the nurses cut rattan into twine and others wove framework under Tun Shein's direction. As the shelter went up some of the American officers got interested, watching the way the girls twisted the rattan knots, and then began to help. We did our raft last, putting on the thatch after we had begun floating down the river. The raft assigned to us was the largest and had been tied nearest the bank. As the other groups loaded supplies onto their rafts, they had to carry heavy loads across ours and many of the rotten bamboos had broken before we started our historic trip. The small raft with Colonels McCabe, St. John, Wyman and Major Merrill went first, with orders to explore Homalin for Japanese. The Americans went next, then the English, and finally our group. Grindlay is with us as my second in command.

The first hours were easy. We had a Hkamti captain at the bow and a helmsman at the stern. We men only had to jump to action when we got into shallow water. The Hkamti have taught us to be patient and not try to pole faster than the current, for when we pole too rapidly, the several sections of the raft tend to pull apart. We had to pull them together once during the morning and attach them with reinforcements of full-thickness rattan. An hour before sunset we caught up with the general who had stopped at a sandy bank to cook dinner. The minute the girls set foot on land they scattered into the jungle. This time they were unusually successful and came back with five different wild vegetables. The variety of which they had secured the most was a tender leaf with a slightly sour taste. I took some of it to Colonel Dorn.

"Have a taste, Colonel," I invited. "Tun Shein guarantees that it is edible and the nurses have brought in far too much for us to eat. How about boiling some up like spinach for the general's mess?"

Colonel Dorn took a taste, decided the leaves had possibilities, and gave instructions to the cooks. He told me later that they had really enjoyed it. It was something like spinach with the vinegar already added.

Since we always make a point of it, we were done with dinner and ready to move before the others were, so we sat around and sang while the others ate. It was dark when we started off again. We arranged shifts of two men each, since we were to travel all night and our Hkamti friends were tired. Grindlay and I took the first shift, I on the bow and he on the stern. The batteries in my flashlight were almost gone, and we kept grazing snags that appeared out of nowhere. I could have done a better job of it also if there had been anything for me to stand on. There were only one or two sound bamboos left at the bow. I couldn't keep my shoes on for fear of slipping into the water, and as I moved from port to starboard and back again with my long bamboo pole, those confounded broken bamboos kept piercing my feet and often they ran right into those blasted sores of mine.

After three hours of cussing I turned my pole over to Paul with a sigh of relief. I found my bed was partly under water, so I moved over to a six-inch-wide stretch between a couples of nurses on the other side and went to sleep.

May 11th—Tun Shein cooked us some red sticky rice for breakfast. We caught up with the other rafts at ten. Even with the extra food that Tun Shein wangles out of the natives we are still half starved. I don't know how the others stand it! Soon after we caught up with them a bomber flew over us and swerved back and down toward us again. We expected to be machine-gunned any minute, till someone spotted the English insignia. When only a hundred feet off the ground the plane began to drop bags on the sandbank and we all plunged overboard, General Stilwell included, and raced for the sacks. Natives of the near-by village also were racing, but aside from a sack or two we got the whole shipment. Inside the sacks were bully beef, many of the tins cracked, ration biscuits, and cigarettes. The general carried back his own sack. The beef in the cracked tins had to be eaten immediately, so for once we had our fill.

May 12th—The raft broke away again. The front and center sections held together by only one bamboo. It began to pour rain, but I was sopping wet as it was, the place where

I lay being six inches under water. From then till dawn all we could do was let the raft take its own course while we tried to keep the various sections somewhere near one another. As soon as there was light enough Tun Shein got some more rattan and tied us together again. Then it was a question whether the raft would stay afloat long enough for us to catch up with the general, who had vanished during the night. It rained again this morning and we had a time trying to get our clothes dry. The funniest thing that happened the whole trip was when we came around a bend and found Lieutenant Belknap sitting on a snag right in the middle of the stream hoping someone would find him! He had started off across country with the mule caravan, but his feet were so covered with sores he couldn't make it in to Homalin. Tun Shein found some potatoes and cooked them for breakfast—one tiny potato each!

Just before three this afternoon we found the other rafts tied up to the bank behind a huge boat with high carved teak stern. The officers on the scout raft and those with the mule train had explored Homalin and had found no Japanese there. While we were eating some bully beef and the biscuits, I heard there were some shops still open in Homalin, so, with the general's permission, sent Tun Shein, Grindlay, Martin, and Eric on ahead to try to buy shoes for the nurses. When they got to Homalin everything was closed; but Tun Shein started kidding the Burmese until he got them laughing, and then one of them admitted he had some shoes for sale. They bought ten pairs of tennis shoes and two pairs of oxfords, a lot of cigarettes, and some flashlight batteries. By this time the Burmese had fallen so much in love with Tun Shein that they invited the party into the headman's house and gave them tea. They were drinking the tea as we marched through. The rest of the party is sleeping the night in a Buddhist monastery and our unit is in the "nunnery." The floor is full of holes. Grindlay distributed the shoes, and all were fits except Ruby's. Her feet are as big as a man's and we had to cut holes for her big toes.

9   OVER THE MOUNTAINS

May 13th—Off at daybreak, marching north two and a half miles to the Chindwin. Over to the west were the terrible mountains to be marched over. The top of the range was wreathed in clouds. We had to cross a half-mile of deep sand before we got to the river itself. There were only two or three small dugouts available for the crossing when we arrived. The nurses crossed over in one of these, crouching on the bottom and balancing carefully to keep the thing from rolling over. Later, larger dugouts came along and one Burmese cabin boat with a hold and everything. Someone had found a little pony for the sick men to ride, and the general ordered me to swim him over. I held on the stern as the boat started off, leading the pony by the bridle. At first the animal went willingly, being used to fording small streams; but when he got tired and saw no farther bank in sight he got wild and tried to swim back. For ten minutes the boatmen could make no progress at all and then, catching a glimpse of the bank, the pony became docile again.

There was a good trail through teak forest. As we climbed the ridge we saw our first Chins, villagers with heavy loads of thatch grass they had been ordered to produce for construction of shacks for refugees. They are quite like the Kachins and some of their words have a resemblance. After only a short march we passed a burned village and descended to a small stream whose banks were very rocky. We found enough patches of sand for us all to have just enough room for a small bed. The water is very cold and very refreshing after the awful heat we have been through. My sores are much worse. While we were bathing, a tremendous storm blew up and we could see rain pouring down all around us. It missed us completely, much to everyone's delight, for there was no possible shelter for us and we would have been set for a cold wet night. The nurses burst forth into song again. They say we made only ten miles today.

May 14th—Case had to get a lot of Chin carriers to replace the Hkamti, and so, since Chins carry their loads suspended from their foreheads and not on yokes like Hkamti, there was a lot of repacking to do. The road today was steep from the start, and the swarms of monkeys everywhere kept laughing at us as we panted and sweated. Our noon camp was by a clear mountain stream rushing madly over gigantic boulders. I had a malarial chill while the boys were cooking and the nurses fixed me a place where I could stretch out in a sort of arbor and rolled me up in a blanket. Of course, the general had to catch me at it just as the chill passed off.

"What's the matter, Seagrave, got fever?"

"No, sir, I got wet and felt a little cold so was warming up."

"How are your feet?"

"Better, sir."

"You are lying."

"Yes, sir."

The general laughed and walked off to give orders to start. There is supposed to be only one more day's march before we reach the top. The afternoon climb was worse than the morning one. I got so angry with the girls for singing and talking at the tops of their voices as we climbed. Couldn't stand the idea of anyone wasting breath while I was dying on my feet, as it seemed to me. I asked them to confine their singing to the few slopes down. Maran Lu wouldn't listen to me and I had to give her a direct order. The last hour the road was horribly steep and a drenching rain came on. My morale was at very low ebb. We finally reached some half-finished grass shacks at an elevation of thirty-nine hundred feet. That means that we have climbed three thousand feet today, for Homalin is only four hundred and fifty feet and we went down almost as much yesterday as we climbed up. A Mr. Sharpe, secretary to the maharajah of Manipur, was waiting in camp. He was sent out by the government of India to meet General Stilwell. He has a few ponies here and about a hundred Naga coolies. There are more ponies and anything up to four hundred more coolies a few miles farther on. Now, at least, we won't have to carry our packs any farther. The sick are to ride the ponies. The party brought large quantities of food with them and we have to be on half rations no longer. There are only five to eight more days of travel ahead of us, depending on how fast we travel. The general knows the rains are due to break suddenly and effectively soon, and he has rightly determined to push us along to the limit of our endurance. It would be terrible to have to climb these mountains if we had rain all day long, and the Assam rainfall is so heavy they measure it in feet and not in inches.

May 15th—We were up at dawn but couldn't get off till seven-thirty as the loads all had to be arranged again to suit the Naga carrying customs. Colonel Williams ordered me to take command of the sick cavalcade. Lord, what a break! I honestly don't think I could have taken another step. There were only eight ponies at the start but I managed to wangle two of them for Than Shwe and Esther. Grindlay now commands our unit. He will not ride a pony and yet I have seen his feet and they are a terrible sight. He insists he is younger than I, and that, of course, is a self-evident fact.

91

The trail was very steep and hard on the ponies. There was no shade from the hot sun and the heat was damp. We covered only six miles before the noon halt, where our meal consisted of tin willie and biscuits. We had tea, though, and that washes anything down! Had to climb another two thousand feet in the afternoon to the border ridge at an elevation of six thousand feet. During all this latter part we could look back and see across the entire country that we had taken seven days to cross spread out in panorama below us. On the horizon were the low hills of the jungle where we had abandoned our trucks and supplies. We passed a border pillar and the girls burst into song again as they crossed into India. Clouds came up from the west, and then as the rain broke, we had a last glimpse of the Chindwin before we plunged down into the valley. There were now twenty-eight ponies, but only eighteen were usable. Many had no saddles. Most of the saddles were in pretty poor condition, without decent girths or stirrup leathers, and my stirrups today were so narrow I could just get the tips of my Army boots into them and no more. I am glad Than Shwe and Esther had a chance to ride up the steep section. Going down in the rain we had to lead our ponies and walk a good bit of the way. The Naga village where we are spending the night is back in Burma again! There is only one hut for us and we had to dry out our clothes. Maran Lu is completely all in and in a rotten humor and acts like a cat. Grindlay says she insisted on talking and singing all by herself while they were climbing the worst stretch. Now she and all the rest of us have to pay for it. Several of the girls are distinctly pooped. The ones who usually take care of me could do nothing but change into drier clothes and drop down on the floor, so I have been trying to dry their wet things, holding them in my hands over the fire.

May 16th—Up at 4:00 A.M. and off at 5:30 to the sound of a wild elephant trumpeting in the distance. I made Koi and Bawk ride with me today and they kept me busy answering all sorts of fool questions. I wish I had a phonograph record with me to say, "*Nga m'thi, nga m'thi.* I don't know, I don't know." Maran Lu had to ride, too, but she is still provoked with me and didn't say a thing. We went over a mountain shoulder with gorgeous scenery—just like the woods in Ohio —and then down a deep chasm, losing most of the height we struggled so hard to gain yesterday. Why did I put my movie camera onto the mules? The road up the other side of the chasm wound back and forth on the face of the precipices and the whole line of march was spread out in front of us, certainly a full mile in length. This was the first very steep climb since the last group of Nagas joined us, so I heard something new and very impressive. The Nagas travel in groups from the same village, keeping step as they walk in single file. At every step one or another lets out a grunt, each grunt in a different key, up and down the line until each has had his grunt, and the leader begins again. It makes a weird tune something like this:

Leader	Unnhh
No. 7	Hump
No. 3	Ugh
No. 8	Heep
No. 2	Hic
No. 5	Hah
No. 6	Ho
Nos. 4 & 9	Hay

Not a chance of our riding the ponies up that stretch! We had to get off and lead them. At the top of the precipice I found several of the girls and a couple of men waiting. Grindlay had ordered them to wait for me and have a ride because they had been on the verge of collapse. We hitchhiked from there on. The grades were not quite so steep but they were enough. Thank goodness it was not much farther till we came to the little village where the general had set up the noon camp! Red-blanketed chiefs carrying rifles met us there with their formal present of rice wine. The blankets and rifles are a gift from the government and are the royal marks of the chief. Nobody has any trouble persuading the Nagas to carry his rifle or tommygun. The Naga lucky enough to carry one is the envy of the whole tribe for the day! We left at two this afternoon and walked downhill for a couple of hours.

We stopped for the night by another rushing mountain stream. Our whole crowd had to get into one narrow hut. I made the nurses spread out a single layer of blanket on the top of the rough saplings that the floor of the hut is made of, and we are all going to sleep in the one huge bed. I was selfish and picked my spot at the farther end where various portions of my anatomy can bulge out of the side wall of thatch if I don't have enough room—and provided it doesn't continue to rain! All the menfolks dropped down to rest, but those silly girls rushed off to the river, bathed, washed their own and our clothes, came back and have been powdering their noses and even putting on a touch of rouge! Now they are singing as they serve up our food! All sorts of fellow sufferers have been coming to us for dressings for their feet, and the adhesive is running short; but I overheard two girls laughingly tell each other that they each had a roll hidden out, which I wasn't to be told about until I had gotten properly frantic!

May 17th—General Sibert rode with us today. One of my stirrup leathers was very short and the other long and there was nothing to be done about it. I dangled my feet most of the time. The road was so narrow we could hardly pass the carriers. We climbed steadily for hours. Veins of coal had been exposed everywhere cutting the road. First we went through a forest of firs and then, near the top, came to pines. This, they said, was the real top. I don't believe them. I got permission from General Sibert to remain behind at "the top" with the two nurses who were riding until the lost ponies turned up. Our ponies had a chance to graze and we found a hut where we could stretch out on a couple of banana leaves. Colonel St. John and Major Barton caught up with us there with the whole mule team and they straightened out the *syces* so we could have decent saddles at least.

The rest of the party was an hour ahead of us on the trail, but the road now was smooth and comfortably wide and so well graded that we made wonderful speed, even running and trotting in spots! We got to the afternoon camp just five minutes after the others. General Sibert is fed up with his pony and would rather walk no matter how sick he is. The nurses were laughing about how on the way down they took the wrong turn onto a path that turned out to be a short cut, and the first thing they knew, they were ahead of the general! There was an occasional drizzle. One thing that impressed me today, as we passed through the Naga villages, was the absence of women anywhere near the road. We made eighteen miles today, pushing on after lunch to a Naga village of fourteen houses built of heavy planks carved with all sorts of figures. There were totem poles here and there with the mounded graves of the dead in front of the houses. The houses are decorated with miffin skulls instead of the human skulls of not so long ago. There are pigs and dogs everywhere. All this in an alpine setting. We were given one of the Naga houses to sleep in. The front room had a nicely packed floor covered with straw, and it looked so inviting that our three refugee parasites were, of course, already parked there when we looked for a place to sleep. Five of us have found a sloping platform of planks in a corner just about big enough for us if we don't try to turn over. It is clear and cold. While the boys were cooking dinner we had our usual foot clinic, treating each other's sores and then the sore feet of others of the party.

May 18th—Got up in the dark and were off by 5:15. It wasn't hard to get up. Everyone but myself had been chewed all night by innumerable dog fleas! While the darn things never bit me I was having my own troubles, for I was on the highest edge of the sloping platform and had to cling to the edge with my fingers and toes to keep from rolling the others off onto the ground.

Today the hills were drier and there were fewer streams. The valleys were a bit wider and there were terraced paddy fields here and there. I knew they were lying to us yesterday when they said we had reached the real top, for we climbed up again until we went over a pass seventy-five hundred feet high, where there was a very strong breeze and we had to get off and walk, sick and sore-footed though we were, to keep warm. The rainfall here when the season starts must be very heavy, for the trees are shaggy with orchids, lichens, and moss and parasites of all sorts. Ghostly appearance! We had tea and biscuits for lunch at a camp in the next valley. That was the most wonderful valley of all, for around the camp were six brand new latrines—the only ones on this whole trip. The nurses were so pleased that they practically lived in them! From that camp on we had glimpses of Ukhrul, the town on the top of the distant ridge to which all the mile posts of the past four days had been pointing. When we started to climb again we came to a village with a church in it. Gosh, are there still things like churches in this God-forsaken world? A Naga chief who was walking beside me and knew a few words of English pointed to it and said, "American Baptist Mission." Well, we certainly were reaching civilization again!

As we climbed up to Ukhrul I chatted quite a bit with the British officers who had been assigned to my sick caval-cade for the day. They had held various civil and military positions in Burma and had actually heard about me and about Namkham! I didn't feel quite so lonely—no, I think I felt more lonely as my mind went back to Namkham again: Namhkham in the hands of the Japs! Where was Bill Cummings? Where were the nurses?

95

May 19th—They say we made twenty-one miles yesterday. I certainly felt like it, and yet I had that pony! How do the others stand it?

Grindlay looks just what he says he is: absolutely exhausted. Yet he won't ride my pony. He is so afraid that he will lose one of the nurses that he walks backward at every corner counting them! In the state of half coma we are all in, it isn't possible to tell, except by counting, that anyone is missing. That darned jackass, Maran Lu, was demon-possessed again today and went off into the jungle saying she was going to hide out there till the end of the war!

My saddle kept slipping off as I went down that last awful descent. Finally the pony put his foot in a deep hole and fell just as the saddle slipped up on his neck and made me turn a full somersault on the rocks. Then I got mad and finished the trip on foot! We got into camp late. Colonel Williams met us at a narrow suspension bridge beyond which was the motor road into Imphal, and informed me that the general had ordered our unit to set up in Imphal and help the government with the refugee problem until he had another job ready for us. Near the general's camp was a shack occupied by refugees. They were a healthy lot—probably the last healthy lot to come through—so they moved out quite willingly when they heard there were a bunch of nurses who needed shelter for the night. Maybe you can call it shelter! Grindlay had his hands full, for he had been ordered to leave our unit and remain with the other American officers. His friends, Sergeant Chesley and Colonel St. John, had arrived in camp with high fever, and Grindlay hadn't the slightest idea how to treat malaria.

Sometime after dark Colonel Eckert and Lieutenant Arnold arrived in a jeep to meet the general. We were all ordered into the bungalow to listen to the news. Tokio, Colonel Eckert said, had been bombed by the United States Air Force. Well, we can stand anything now!

May 20th—We slept late this morning. Didn't get off until 7:30! We were quite ready to leave, for it had poured all night, the roof of our shack had not been repaired for years, and we were all sopping wet. To make matters worse, when the rain began to pour, refugees had all pushed back into the hut and lay in the aisle and on top of our feet. The government sent out a number of trucks and ambulances to fetch us. In my ambulance we had Colonel St. John and Sergeant Chesley, both looking more dead than alive,

Oldest building. This was the only hospital building when Dr. Seagrave
and his wife arrived in Namkham in 1922

Dr. and Mrs.
Seagrave with their
two young boys

Nurses' home, built in
1936. This building was
only slightly damaged
during the war

In the Bazaar at Namkham

Scene on the Burma Road

Chit Sein "Miss Burma, 1942"
Bill Cummings

Committee on Buddhist affairs

Grandma Naomi
Bill Duncumb

Nurses resting
Bill Duncumb

Dr. Silgardo and
Dr. Ba Saw

Pansy Po, center, and
her two Buddhist
friends

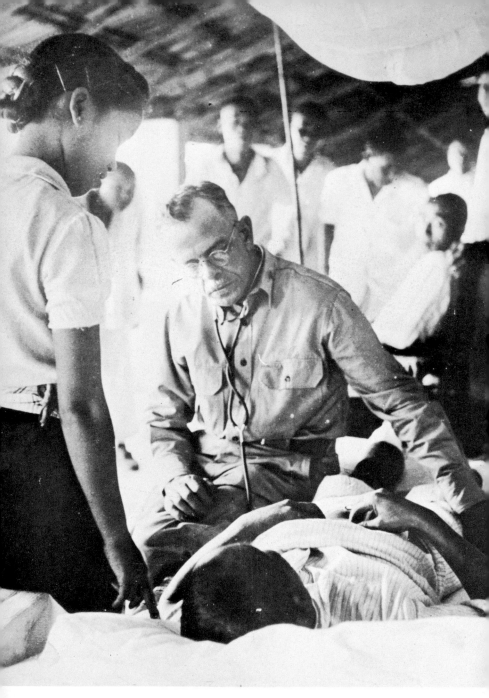

Dr. Seagrave attending wounded Chinese soldier

Making raft shelters on
the retreat
Photo by Colonel Williams

General Stilwell
leads off

Burmese nurses on the
Irrawaddi Ferry
Bill Duncumb

Little Bawk prepares a
meal while Naga Boy
looks on
Signal Corps Photo

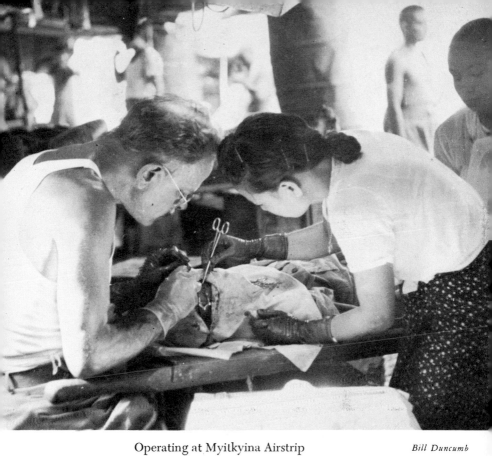

Operating at Myitkyina Airstrip

Bill Duncumb

A casualty is brought in

Intravenous department

Bill Duncumb

Burma Surgeon is joyously welcomed back to Namkham

Dr. Seagrave sits near the ruins of his hospital to watch the celebration in honor of his return to Namkham

Dr. Seagrave giving informal lecture

Nurse Esther Po
administering anesthesia

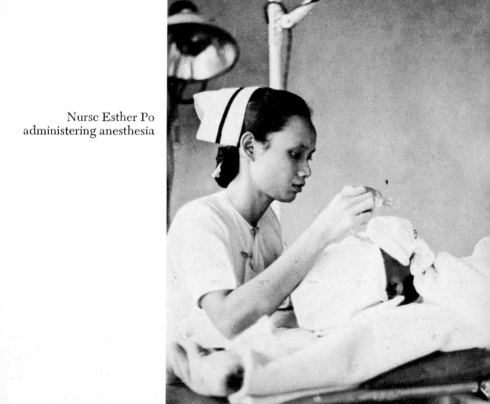

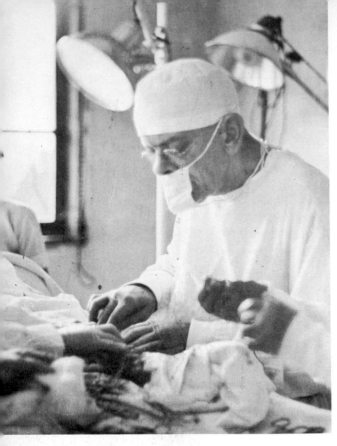

Dr. Seagrave operating

Two operations at onc

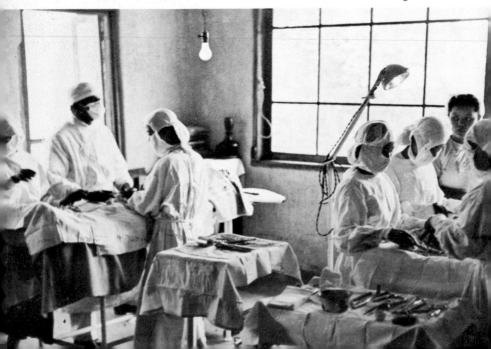

though their high fever had temporarily subsided. As soon as we left the mountains and started across the huge Imphal plain we began to have difficulty with mud. There was no gravel on the road and the trucks had ploughed deep ruts. Our ambulance had huge desert tires and they would not fit into the ruts of the trucks ahead, causing us to skid more than ever. Every time we slipped off the road it was a case of all hands getting out in the mud to push. The cars all had to be hauled across a detour, necessitated by a broken bridge, and General Stilwell pulled just like the other officers. There were sixteen miles of this and then ten miles of graveled road into Imphal. Our ambulance pulled in last after the nurses had disappeared, so leaving Grindlay at the old fort, built in memory of British officers and men massacred during the early years of British rule, we began to explore the town. There were bomb holes everywhere, the tiny ones caused by antipersonnel bombs. Not a shop was open. Aside from troops there were no inhabitants to be seen.

I finally located the nurses and Friends in the English Casualty Clearing Station. There were beds there, and mattresses! How many weeks is it since I last slept on a bed?

With a sigh of relief I pulled off my boots for the last time and started soaking my feet in the puddles of rain water, when suddenly one of the nurses let out an awful scream.

"Mr. Cummings! Mr. Cummings!"

There was Bill coming on the run, tears streaming down his cheeks! What a bedlam broke loose, sobs and cheers, tears and laughter. The girls threw themselves on him and fairly mauled him, firing questions at him so rapidly he had no chance to answer. They would have torn him apart if the food ordered for us had not that minute arrived. The nurses were so starved they finally consented to pack their mouths with rice and dal and give Bill a chance to answer my questions. Gurney had brought out fourteen nurses with him, traveling by plane from Loiwing to Dinjan. Several of our orderlies had also come by plane, among them Theodore and Judson. Bill, Graham, Whittington, Ba Saw, and Bella had driven to Kunming in trucks and jeeps and had then flown to Dinjan. They located Dr. Gurney's crowd at Jorhat in the A.B.M. hospital where the crazy girls were already attending classes in the nurses' training school and trying to help on the wards. While they were worrying about what had happened to us, Bill bumped into my old friend Colo-

nel Ottaway, who used to be a tin-mine manager near Tavoy.
Ottaway told him he had been supplying food-stuffs to R.A.F.
planes to be dropped to General Stilwell and that the general
would probably reach Imphal in another three days.

Bill and Ted Gurney talked over the new information with
Colonel Ottaway, and they decided that if our unit had
come out with General Stilwell, Gauhati would be the logical place to wait for us. Ted would take the nurses there by
train while Bill rode in Ottaway's jeep to Imphal. Kyang
Tswi was afraid Bill would slip away in the jeep without
her, so she hid all his clothes and Bill had to leave in the
things he stood up in! They drove all day and all night and
got to Imphal yesterday. Just a few minutes ago Bill, wandering hopelessly around, had bumped into Colonel McCabe
and learned we had arrived!

10 ASSIGNMENT IN ASSAM

THAT EVENING Bill and I had a chance to talk. He told me
quite a tale:

After leaving us in Kume, Bill traveled back to Hsipaw,
seeing no sign of a stand being made against the Jap advance
which could cut them off on either of the two roads from
the south. There was nothing to do but evacuate Gurney
and the nurses, who had been operating steadily, to Namkham. After they were safely off, Bill commandeered a
Chinese Red Cross truck and followed with the rest of our
equipment. A few miles along, he met a puzzled Colonel
Boatner who wanted to know where the hell that damned
bridge was that General Stilwell had ordered him to blow
up! Bill stopped a minute to enlighten him, made it into
Lashio at midnight, and then, with breakfast at Kutkai,
managed to reach Namkham at noon. Next morning Ted insisted on going back to Kutkai with four nurses to set up,
but they found Major Lindsay already there doing what little
there was to do, so they rushed back to salvage Namkham.
At Kutkai they heard that our base hospital at Loilem had
received a present of twenty-eight bombs the morning
after we left, and Hsipaw also had been plastered.

Dr. Richards of the A.V.G. went back to Namkham with
Bill and was presented with one of our trucks, two of my
sterilizers, my Oldsmobile sedan, and all the medicines he
could carry. He took some of our surgical instruments, too.
Then Bill went over to the nurses' home and discovered

that the Shans had stolen most of the suitcases that the nurses had left ready packed for Bill to put on his truck. Bill doesn't get profane very often!

That historic afternoon Dr. Tu and Nang Leng found a few minutes to get married. Bill pleaded with E Hla to go along with him, but her mother refused to budge and E Hla had to stay behind. What do you suppose the Japs have done to that charming girl and her baby?

Bill called in all the mission staff and paid them three months' salary in advance. To E Hla he gave six months' salary—God bless him!—and huge quantities of salt, kerosene, rice, and sesamine oil. Koi's poor old father and mother got the same. Then he had an argument with Ba Saw.

"What is the advantage of my going with you?" asked Ba Saw.

"If you stick out this thing with Dr. Seagrave, then, at the end of the war, you can build up the Namkham hospital again while he goes home to America for money."

"O.K. I'm going."

Ba Saw arranged to meet Bill at Kyuhkok on the border that night and hurried off in a jeep to get Bella and the baby and return by the road on the other side of the river. Graham, Whittington, and Bill left Namkham in relays as they got their trucks loaded. Bill thought the others had salvaged my clothes and more precious possessions, so he brought along only my family photographs. Somehow or other he didn't find the Kaisar-i-Hind medal the viceroy gave me. When he left, the Shans were waiting to loot our entire setup. Myers of the American Red Cross came through Namkham the next night and went to our bungalow for a couple of hours of sleep and found everything looted and no bed to lie on. At the hospital, also, everything had been stolen. The Japs appeared a few hours later at the precise time that Bill had predicted, one party on each side of the Shweli suspension bridge, surprising and shooting the British captain and men detailed to destroy the bridge.

Bill's memory of the once great Burma Road was of one long, continuous traffic jam. It took him six hours to get from one side of Chefang Town to the other. He refused to sleep in Paoshan because it looked ripe for a bombing; and, sure enough, it was plastered the next morning. A spring on the ambulance that Nang Leng was driving broke, and Bill repaired it with a rear jeep spring, filing extra threads on the shackle bolts, and making a lot of washers out of a biscuit tin. At the side of the road they passed my Olds-mobile, abandoned because of a broken axle shaft; and there was the end of another of my dreams.

White rhododendrons were blooming along the road as if there were no war on; but war traffic jams lengthened the time for the trip to ten days. Casualties on the road asked for treatment when they saw the ambulance, and Dr. Ba Saw and Dr. Tu cared for them.

At Kunming, Nang Leng and Tu went off to his relatives, keeping the ambulance to help them set up in a new practice. One of our trucks Bill gave to the Friends Ambulance, and then turned the rest of them and the jeeps over to the United States Army. A.V.G. influence got them passage by plane to Dinjan the next morning.

May 21st—This place is lousy with mosquitoes. Worst we have seen. The Casualty Clearing Station captain has produced some mosquito nets for us today and a few extra blankets, but last night was pretty bad. This morning I went up to see Grindlay and O'Hara at the fort, and the general was there looking quite fresh. I believe he stood the trip better, tired as he was, than any of us. He could have made much better time if others had been as capable of marching as he. He appointed a board of three colonels to meet with me at two o'clock and decide rate of salaries for each of the groups of nurses and orderlies.

The three officers who appeared were our old friends Colonel Holcombe, Colonel McCabe, and Colonel Williams, who had more firsthand information with regard to the build-up of our unit than the other officers. The policy approved by the board was not to attempt to pay the girls on the same basis as American Army nurses, because of the difference in living standards, but to pay them sufficiently large salaries to cover the cost of messing and refit, and leave enough over to permit them to save against the very rainy days that would come to Burma in the postwar period. While discussions were going on, Colonel Holcombe began to have a malarial chill, and we put him to bed in one of our new wards. Colonel St. John and Sergeant Chesley were already in the wards with three Chinese, for, aside from myself, none of the American medical officers was prepared to take care of malaria patients. Two nurses went on day duty at once, and two more are on night duty now. Sergeant Chesley was so nauseated that we had to give him his medicine by hypo; and Colonel St. John, besides the nausea he is suffering from,

100

is sensitive to both quinine and atabrine. I have decided to treat him with only one dose of five grains of quinine given very accurately at the time he feels the chill begin to come on. He is so fed up with being ill that he co-operates wonderfully.

I reminded General Stilwell of the wide latitude he had given me in Burma in the selection of locations for our unit and asked for permission now to choose the spot in Assam where we could really accomplish the purpose of his orders. He agreed immediately.

After twenty-four hours' separation from us, Grindlay walked down this afternoon to say good-by, for he follows the general to Delhi tomorrow and won't see us again unless our roads lead to the same place after our Assam assignment has been carried out. The nurses spotted him as he entered our compound and, yelling "Uncle Grindlay, Uncle Grindlay," rushed on him and flung their arms around whatever part of him they could reach. Grindlay had tears streaming down his cheeks and the nurses were sobbing quite openly. That fellow has made himself so essential a part of our unit that it is going to be pretty hard to get along without him; but with Gurney and Ba Saw to help me I had no argument wherewith to ask Colonel Williams to continue to detail him to service with us in Assam. I have learned a lot during these twenty years. If you want the confidence of your superiors so that they will give you what you need, you always ask for the very least that you can possibly get along with. If you find out later that you asked for too little, you go to town and turn out the best job you can anyway.

My fever came back on me again this evening and the nice Casualty Clearing Station captain came over and gave me an intravenous injection of quinine. We have just enough ampoules left to get Colonel St. John safely to Delhi.

May 22nd—Off early this morning. There were car wrecks everywhere and a lot of trucks had been bombed by the Japs. The nurses tried to sing, but the rough road jolted the songs out of them and they quit. Grindlay told me yesterday afternoon that General Stilwell said that the singing and laughter of the nurses on the trek out was the most marvelous morale-boosting device he had ever come across. We turned our patients over to Colonel Williams in Manipur Road. Chesley had got over his misogyny. He asked permission to send back presents to the nurses from Delhi.

101

May 23rd—It was midnight before we found a camp to stay in at Manipur Road. Everything was crowded. We got two tents finally, with string beds to sleep on. Had less food to eat yesterday than for some time. This morning we all had breakfast in the British officers' mess and ate several times what we should have been allowed. Since we are a United States Army unit the British are more polite and anxious to please than they would be if we were English. I had fever till two this afternoon and then contacted the British colonels in charge of the local C.C.S.'s·They insist that Gauhati is the place for us, for here even they are able to do nothing constructive. Every available foot of ground is covered with patients for whom they cannot furnish tents. The refugee patients are so ill they can't make use of the toilet facilities and the sanitary condition is awful. Nine died on the way down from Imphal yesterday in our truck convoy. They die every night here before they can be put onto the trains. The only thing to do is get them out of this bottleneck and down to Gauhati for real treatment, before sending them on by boat and train to their homes. The officers were convinced that the Army as well as the government would welcome us at Gauhati with open arms. To facilitate our rapid arrival in Gauhati they have given us a third-class coach and one first-class compartment on the hospital train this evening.

May 24th—We slept in the station all night. They say that after the Imphal bombing all the train crews ran away and they are running the train with volunteer crews. Guess that must be right, for we had not covered more than seven miles this morning when, going around a siding, our driver failed to apply brakes, plunged into the train on the main line and derailed our engine and tender. We have been near the tiny station all day. I have slept almost continually, but the nurses have been running around picking flowers. Tun Shein got on the job again, so we have had enough to eat including delicious bananas. We have almost no medicine left. This evening they began to push the cars of our train around to make way for the wrecker train. The English soldiers turned out and so did the nurses and Friends. Maran Lu got off a statement today that will go down into history. "I hope we never have to travel by airplane like the Sixth Army girls," she said. "We traveled by jeep and had to get out and push the jeep. We traveled by truck and pushed the truck, by raft and had to push the raft, by train

102

and had to push the train. I shouldn't like to have to get out and push an airplane!"

May 25th—They finally got the wrecked engine out of the way and we started off after a delay of twenty-four hours. Assam is very much like Burma, though not nearly so rich a country nor so picturesque. Perhaps I am a bit prejudiced. Got to Gauhati just before dusk. I expected a city, but it is nothing but a town. There was just one gharry and one cart available at the station, so we used them for our baggage and marched over in our best manner to the A.B.M. compound. Several Sixth Army girls were walking around in the cool of the evening and stood paralyzed with astonishment for a full minute when they saw us marching in. Then there was a most joyful reunion.

The A.B.M. has a fifty-bed women's hospital here, with one American woman doctor, Dr. Randall, and three American nurses. They say there are two Indian women doctors, too, a lot of staff and pupil nurses. There are three other women missionaries in charge of a high school and orphanage and they have a large dormitory for college girls studying in the local university. They all made us very welcome. The Educational Mission House has taken over the six Friends Ambulance boys and the girls are parked in some of the smaller buildings. Bill and Gurney are in the downstairs part of the medical bungalow. Paul is across town at the evangelistic mission. The ladies have given me a private room in the hospital which has a bath and a lovely bed with inner-spring mattress.

May 26th—This morning I wandered around the compound, making plans. I asked the mission ladies to let us use their college dormitory for cleaner patients and the high-school building for the others. Both these buildings are unused because the school and college have closed down since the Imphal bombing. The ladies were glad to co-operate, for their own civilian work has almost ceased and they have been wanting to get into the very sort of work we are planning. With their permission I drove around to the Casualty Clearing Station to contact Colonel Meneces, informing him of General Stilwell's orders and asking him if he could use us in his refugee program. He was delighted at our arrival, but needed us more in the care of military evacuees at the moment as the other refugees had not yet swamped the hospitals arranged for them by the government. Colonel

Meneces wondered how long it would be before we could accept patients, and I said we would be ready at once if he could find us any medicines. With the mission hospital beside us we could borrow equipment until the supplies Colonel Williams had promised to send us arrived. Meneces took us right over to his stores and told his officer to give us anything up to half his supply of each article we desired. The good Lord has certainly given me some decent men to work with!

Later—That evening the C.C.S. ambulance brought us twelve Indian troops and I put them in the high-school building with nurses from the Sixth Army group on duty, since they had had quite a rest after their easy trip out. The next day some British soldiers arrived and by the third day we had a hundred patients, and the Fifth Army girls were back to work again. By the end of a week we were up to two hundred patients, which was the capacity of the two buildings. It was a relief to have two such hounds for work as Gurney and Ba Saw again with me, for I could not stand on my feet more than half an hour at a time. My room was on the ground floor of the building we were using for British troops, and I spent my days in a large comfortable chair with my feet propped up, at last getting the treatment and rest I needed for a cure. Nurses and doctors came to me for orders and I made rounds of the most seriously ill patients once a day.

About ten days after we arrived one of the Lahu orderlies whom Case had turned over to us came down with a virulent attack of cerebral malaria and died in twenty-four hours. Several nurses also broke down with the disease, one of them having an atabrine psychosis as a result of our needing to use that drug. She had a mania for climbing trees and stayed up in one all one night, singing, praying, and saying naughty things about everyone who came in sight. We have been lucky not to lose any nurses. The troops we have had have been horribly ill with malaria, dysentery, and skin disease acquired on the way out. Many had had to cut their way through the Japs.

June 21st—The evacuation of troops is over and we will have no more admissions. But the government hospitals are now swamped with Indian refugees and they want us to help with them.

104

June 30th—I have never seen anything so pitiful as these poor refugees! They are starved and emaciated and suffering so much from lack of vitamins that they can't swallow. With this starvation background they have picked up the most virulent forms of malaria, amebic and bacillary dysentery. Those who picked up cholera and smallpox died before they got to Manipur Road, so we have had no cases of cholera and only two of smallpox. There have been women dying of puerperal fever as a result of having had abortions on the trip out. It is the most hopeless situation from the medical point of view. We can't get medicines for them for the railway has been washed out in several places and steamers are busy with the transport of reinforcement troops. The supplies Colonel Williams is sending us are still held up. We are trying to treat malaria without atabrine and with very little quinine and our stock of neosalvarsan is almost gone. There is no emetine and almost no stovarsol for amebic dysentery and absolutely no sulfaguanidine for bacillary dysentery. The typhoid cases have done fairly well. But those poor people keep on dying three or four a day.

The dormitory building is screened and we are trying to keep the worst dysenteries there. The other building is not screened and screening is not to be bought; the flies there are impossible to describe. The patients sleep on mats on the floor, which is what they prefer, and in spite of our nurses being on almost full-time duty with flyswatters, in spite of flypaper everywhere, in spite of gallons of Flit, the patients and the floors are black with nasty flies. The flies are all over the patients' faces and even get into their mouths. The dysentery cases are so weak they are incontinent, and that doesn't help matters much! Some of the patients have "Naga sores" which eat down through skin, fascia, and muscle and even into bone, destroying the periosteum. The other day I had to remove the entire femur of a patient with one of these sores. I put him into a cast then, and his temperature immediately dropped to normal and remained normal. The best treatment for the sores seems to be 10 per cent Mag. Sulph. in glycerin after the sloughs have been debrided in the same way we did our war wounds.

July 1st—I can't help but feel that the Japanese were very clever when they decided to let the Indian refugees leave the country. They took pains to see that the refugees would starve by robbing them of their money and food supplies as they went through their lines. One pregnant Indian woman dropped on her knees before the Japanese and begged for the return of just enough money to help her through into India, and she was kicked in the abdomen for her pains. She aborted on the way out and is one of those who died here from puerperal infection. Making starvation en route certain, the Japs thereby also made inevitable the acquisition of the worst forms of contagious disease, and the arrival, in a poorly prepared province of India, of thousands of sick who would each one be a source of contagion to the whole country. It seems like a new variety of bacterial warfare!

Somewhere in India. Later—The newspapers are full of accounts of R.A.F. and United States Air Force activities in Burma, and the nurses, who have seen the destruction the Japanese wreaked on their home towns, are rather depressed at the certain knowledge that the havoc now caused on those same towns by the allied air forces must mean their final disappearance. I have been comforting them by assuring them that their folks are undoubtedly so sensible that they must have taken to the woods, away from Japanese-occupied sections. Today the matter came closer to home in the announcement that the United States Air Force had bombed Japanese barracks at Namkham. We are at work for the Chinese Army again. We don't know where we are going next, but all of us hope it is going to be to a big job! The last time I saw General Stilwell, I told him we all hoped that when new action developed against the Japs he would save out the meanest, nastiest task of all for us. The general turned on me like a flash with a real sparkle in his eye.

"I can certainly promise you that," he said.

It would not take him long to fulfill that promise.

PART THREE: THE LONG ROAD BACK

IN SEVEN *terrible months from December 7, 1941, to June, 1942, Japan had conquered an empire in the Pacific. Her armies overran Malaya, Burma, the Netherlands East Indies, and the Philippines. China was isolated and Australia menaced. Then, in the summer and late fall of 1942, the Japanese advance was halted at Midway, Guadalcanal, Port Moresby, and the gates of India.*

With the main military strength of the United Nations then dedicated to the defeat of Nazi Germany, General Stilwell saw only one possibility of effective action against the Japanese. With Chinese troops trained and conditioned in India, he would reconquer a route into northern Burma. American engineers and service troops would build a road through some of the worst terrain in the world from Ledo in Assam to the old Burma Road and Kunming. This would relieve China's isolation and make it possible to supply her with weapons and equipment for the war against Japan.

It took a long time to nurse back into health the disease-ridden remnants of the Chinese armies which had retreated from Burma into India. It took even longer to train the Chinese soldiers who were flown into India over the Hump. Center for these activities was Ramgarh.

11   RAMGARH TRAINING CENTER

IN JULY, 1942, Stilwell was organizing a training center at Ramgarh to teach the remnants of the Chinese expeditionary force how to use modern weapons to fight an offensive war. Everyone said it couldn't be done, but the general was determined to succeed. We left our work at Assam and went to Ramgarh to open a base hospital. The Burmese girls were at their best then, for they were thrilled at the idea of being allowed to help "Grandaddy" with his job.

The P.O.W. hospital at Ramgarh consisted of twenty-two wards, each in a separate building of brick with tile roof and cement floor, surrounded by double barbed wire barricades. The five wards, operating room, dental clinic, and orderly

107

room that were nearest to our quarters were again separated from the rest of the hospital by double barricades. This was the Italian hospital. The larger group of buildings was for Germans. Outside the barbed wire were three wards for Indian troops, two for "Europeans," and the administration buildings. The central roadway that passed by the office building divided the total area in half. The patients in the P.O.W. hospital had been cared for entirely by medical prisoners of war who had lived in what was now our barracks area; so we, too, were entirely surrounded by barbed wire. The hospital had a total of some seven hundred and fifty beds. It was the intention of the theater surgeon, Colonel R. P. Williams, that we take care of all patients till half the hospital was full; then an American station hospital would be sent in to take over the other half. The necessity for using the entire hospital was considered somewhat remote.

The U.S. Army was, no doubt justifiably, skeptical of my ability to run a G.I. institution. An unorthodox arrangement was decided upon. I was to be in complete charge of the professional work of the hospital, while Major Bevil was to be post surgeon and administer the hospital with a Medical Administrative Corps officer and a group of Medical Department enlisted personnel from a casual detachment. Any extra men from the casuals would be turned over to me for professional work. Majors Grindlay and O'Hara and Lieutenant Chesley were to return to us as chief of the surgical service, chief of the dental service, and chief of laboratories, respectively. Captains William Webb and H. Myles Johnson of the Medical Corps also joined our staff.

With most casual detachments the units who furnished the cadre took the opportunity to get rid of men for whom they had no further use, and this one was no exception. It contained some of the best and some of the worst. Three of the men, Technical Sergeant Emmet T. (Stinky) Davis, Technical Sergeant Mitchell (Puss) Opas, and Staff Sergeant Chester Deaton, were so good we held onto them against all odds and they remained with us till September, 1944, when the two-year rotation scheme sent them back to the States.

The 38th Chinese Division had come out of Burma on the same road to Imphal that Stilwell had used. They were in an awful condition when they reached Ramgarh. In addition to all the diseases the refugees had brought to Assam they had picked up ferocious "Naga sores," ulcers that eat down to and through bone. Luckily the 22nd Chinese Division was only then beginning to reach Ledo over the West

108

Axis or we would have been swamped. We had to open two or three new wards every day. It had been thought we might run slightly over four hundred beds when both divisions were in, but we were already beyond that figure with only the 38th Division.

I had heard of General Sun Li-Jen of the 38th Division in Burma, for it was he who rescued the British from encirclement at Yenangyaung. He had been decorated by both the British and American governments. He came over to us every evening now to check on the physical condition of his men. Sun was a graduate of Virginia Military Institute and spoke superb English. Quite tall and very handsome, he looked much younger than his years.

When General Sun went on rounds in the hospital, he chatted with each patient as if he were one of them, treating the enlisted men much more courteously than their sergeants or lieutenants would have done. As for the soldiers, though they gazed at him with intense respect, they would call to him across the ward to present some gripe or other, more often than not directed against me. Sun always listened patiently, yet usually he did me the honor to recognize the difficulties under which we were trying to give his men adequate attention.

Not all Chinese generals were like General Sun. There was the big shot who came over with General Stilwell one day, apparently determined to criticize Uncle Joe and all his works. Stilwell brought him over to inspect the hospital and Grindlay and I produced our entire bag of tricks trying to get him interested in the welfare of the soldiers. Finally Stilwell nudged me to one side and growled in an undertone, "Don't waste time on that- - - -. He doesn't give a blankety blank about anything worthwhile. Get him through the hospital and out again as fast as you can." Stilwell seldom broke out in profanity. When he did, it was well deserved. I noticed that Chinese generals who didn't care for their men didn't remain very long in command of the armies under Stilwell.

Soon the 22nd Chinese Division began to arrive. They had had a much more ghastly time getting out of Burma than the 38th. At least three truckloads of men, packed like sardines, were brought to the hospital from each train. During the train ride of one group from Ledo to Ramgarh, fifteen men had died and been buried en route. It was common to have three or four men die within a few hours of arrival. One patient, deathly ill with malaria, refused to wait for our enlisted men to carry him to his bed and stumbled from the truck to the ward by himself. He was dead in three hours. I saw that happen many times among the Chinese. We saw it almost two years later at Maingkwan when the 50th Division was flown in direct from China. In this case the man was sitting up in the truck as it came in beside me. I called to our enlisted men to get him first, that he was dying in his seat. He was dead in a half hour. In Myitkyina I saw it again as the Chinese litter bearers carried in a soldier sitting on the stretcher holding several yards of intestine that had escaped from his shell-torn abdomen. No doctor will ever understand the Chinese. They die when a post-mortem discovers no cause of death, but they live for days, still trying to do their stuff, long after the people of any other race would have died.

The U.S. 98th Station Hospital under Major Warrenburg was ordered to come to help us, but by the time they arrived we were up to 1,200 beds and a few days later topped 1,350. And this in a 750-bed hospital! It was lucky that every ward had verandahs on each side running down its length. Aisles and verandahs were now packed and there were patients crowding even the decrepit buildings of the P.O.W. isolation camp.

During all this time the nurses were extremely happy, though they put in many a sixteen-hour working day and occasionally even an eighteen-hour day. My malaria gripped me once more just as Colonel Williams was visiting us and he shipped me off to Darjeeling for a month's rest, together with three nurses who were also breaking down. From that day on I never lost half a day's work from illness. But while we were away, Saw Yin, our chief medical nurse, was taken ill and began to develop tuberculosis in the glands of her neck.

Even though their bodies were beginning to give out, the nurses' morale was very high. Our officers treated them with great courtesy and their work was absorbing enough to keep them from being more than normally homesick.

On his first visit to the hospital General Stilwell called our officers together, explained what he was trying to do, and asked us to support him by getting the sick Chinese well as fast as possible by any means, no matter how unorthodox, so that the soldiers could get into the training school and learn how to fight. Grindlay and I were determined to see the general's orders obeyed and with the help of the entire staff set about finding ways to cut short the number of days lost in the hospital. We were handicapped by lack of medicines and supplies and had to adapt ourselves to the drugs in hand. Thus, with malaria, we had at first nothing but Indian quinine which is far from potent, then nothing but the British imitation of atabrine. We were all willing to try anything once.

Typhoid was another worry. The Chinese would not cooperate by staying still in bed or eating the diet we permitted. Friends brought in all sorts of indigestible Chinese delicacies which the patients devoured, to their great detriment. Since sulfaguanidine and sulfadiazine were coming in from the States, Webb prescribed sulfaguanidine empirically without much success until he used sulfadiazine simultaneously and then his patients began to stop dying. I will admit, for the sake of argument, that American typhoid patients are not benefited by these drugs; but Chinese certainly are. Webb fortified his cases by giving them two large eggnogs a day, each with an ounce of Scotch. We had no trouble making the Chinese drink those eggnogs. Webb lost no more cases except those complicated with intestinal worms.

That we were able to avoid some serious epidemics during our stay at Ramgarh was entirely due to the brilliance of our laboratory chief, Lieutenant Chesley. When typhoid started he made a complete survey of all the Chinese in town and discovered several carriers in the Chinese restaurants. Their removal stopped the epidemic. One day, within twenty-four hours of admission, Chesley diagnosed a patient with atypical symptoms as cholera, much to the disgust of the Public Health officer who said such a diagnosis could not be made in less than three days. We had no more cholera. A patient was admitted with epidemic meningitis, in a coma and incontinent. After a fifteen-minute diagnosis by Chesley, the 98th Station Hospital ward officer gave an intravenous injection of sodium sulfathiazole to start his treatment: the following morning incontinence had ceased, by afternoon the patient was conscious, and the next day a nurse had to be on hand continuously to drag him back to isolation when he started to run away. There was no further meningitis.

Of course, being typical G.I.'s, we griped about our work, and since our work was with the Chinese, we griped about them. Most interracial strife seems to be caused by differences in habits of thinking and acting. In America, men steal. But it is a relatively small per cent who steal and they steal in a big way, wholesale. The Chinese don't steal but they pilfer. It is not stealing to them—if they are not caught. They feel

111

they are salvaging things for their own use. Pilfering is an almost universal Chinese habit, and several good truckloads of stuff could be carried away piecemeal—and there was nothing we could do about it. During his first speech to American officers at the post, General Stilwell had made plain the sensitiveness about loss of face which is a national characteristic of the Chinese race, and he warned us it would be an unforgivable offense for any American to lay hands on a Chinese while under his command. No order Stilwell gave caused more griping among the Americans than this one, chiefly because no similar order appeared to have been given to the Chinese, who frequently laid hands and drew guns on us. But Uncle Joe knew what he was doing. If he hadn't given that order there would have been no fighting against Japs in China-Burma-India. There would have been riots with far more casualties than the Japs caused—riots resulting from paltry, trumped-up misunderstanding of each other's customs and language.

General Boatner, then chief of staff of the Chinese Army in India, pretended to be a very ferocious infidel but he knew enough about Christianity to insist on my "giving till it hurt." First he asked me for Bill Cummings, who was then a second lieutenant in the Medical Administrative Corps. He had known Bill in Burma and his liking for him, as well as his respect for his command of the Burmese language, made him determined to acquire Bill for his own staff. Bill felt that more excitement could be found in this work than in a hospital unit, so we reluctantly let him go. A month later Bill and the general drove to the hospital in a jeep and asked to see me. Bill fidgeted around and couldn't look me in the eye. The general just hemmed and hawed.

"All right, all right. I know what you want, sir," I said. "You want Tun Shein."

"Yes, I do," the general admitted. He had all the arguments on his side and I could do nothing but let Tun Shein go too, though he had been invaluable to us as a supply officer. Later the general wheedled me into letting him have Saw Judson, my other Burmese supply officer, and finally even took away my Lahu boy Aishuri to work with Brayton Case in supervising the truck gardens he was persuading the Chinese Army to develop—Brayton Case who practically single-handed had fed the Chinese Fifth Army during the first campaign.

When the last of the 38th and 22nd divisions' battle

112

casualties had been discharged to duty, our hospital census dropped rapidly to about seven hundred. Then my real troubles with the nurses began. During our first busy months they hadn't had time to be more than normally homesick. Furthermore, everyone prophesied that General Stilwell's return would begin in November, 1942. But Stilwell hadn't been given the wherewithal in 1942 and the sudden disappointment, coming at the same time as the decrease in pressure of work, was more than the girls could bear. At first they found a great deal of pleasure in the recreation hall we opened, where they could gather together in the evenings with the enlisted men and play games. Then the Special Service officer brought over officers twice a week to teach the girls to dance. But the girls weren't accustomed to mixed dancing and didn't enjoy it. Paul Geren proposed that we learn Gilbert and Sullivan's *Mikado* and put on a G.I. show of our own, but just as things were becoming interesting, the male soloists in the Friends Ambulance Unit were transferred to China and with them went our pianist. So that plan also failed.

Then I made a bad mistake. I bought the girls two guitars, a mandolin, and a ukulele. Thereupon they gathered four or five to a room of an evening, strumming and humming the songs they used to sing in Burma. Someone would make a nostalgic remark; someone else would add another; a third would voice her sense of frustration at the postponement of the return to Burma, and the whole party would forthwith dissolve in tears.

The nurses' psychology was much like that of other exiled persons. They had voluntarily left their country in order to share in the task of liberation. Now the return seemed indefinitely postponed. It was impossible to reach their people by mail; and though their families were probably unharmed they had heard so many true accounts of Japanese atrocities that they knew that some, at least, had suffered. Poverty was rife in Burma, foodstuffs being commandeered by the Japs and clothing material completely unavailable. The fact that the nurses were rapidly banking funds to help their families only made matters more difficult since they had no way of sending the money to them. Many of the families in Burma didn't know that their daughters were safe with me in India, and the girls were sick at the thought that their families might be despairing of ever seeing them again. As a climax to their other worries, they realized with dread that with our return, cities and towns would have

113

to be razed to the ground and thousands of civilians unintentionally killed. What was to prevent their own people being of this number?

American troops found it hard to endure separation from their families while on garrison duty in a foreign country even though they knew their families were safe from enemy attack and could exchange frequent letters with them. My own position was halfway between the American soldiers and the girl refugees. I could hear weekly from Tiny, get frequent letters from the two older children and an occasional one from the two little boys. I knew they were out of harm's way. I was homesick but I had resources to combat my feelings which the nurses did not have. They had no Burmese books to read, no magazines, no newspapers. And the language in English books and periodicals was so difficult for all but a few that they could get no enjoyment from them.

Lacking my forms of self-anesthesia the girls tried to develop some of their own. A movie theater had been opened with three-fifths of the seats assigned to the Chinese and the rest to Americans. Both Chinese and American units rotated on assigned days. The nurses greatly delighted in these movies and to my utter astonishment began to imitate various actresses, as their tastes dictated. Big Bawk fell for an actress in one of the musicals who talked with a resonant, singing tone even when she wasn't supposed to be singing. For months Bawk concentrated on her own voice, developing its naturally lovely, sweet tones until every word she said rang like a chime through the entire area. By the time we reached Myitkyina she was more expert than the screen star. We were then operating on some of the ghastliest casualties I had ever seen and under tremendous strain. To have Bawk, at the instrument table, sing out in her wonderful, resonant voice, "Okay, retractors coming up! Abdominal gauze? Right away!" would jerk me out of my operating trance and irritate me more than the shells that whistled over us.

But of most absorbing interest to them were the love scenes and especially American love words. They were learning English very rapidly of necessity and there is no better place for a foreigner to learn English than at the movies. Practicing love words on each other didn't have quite enough spice in it for them. Besides, the feminine nature is extraordinarily possessive. They had to "own" someone, and God help the person who said more than three words or looked more than twice at their "property." Each girl had at least one other girl who was her personal property already.

114

Now she set about looking for some male to call her own. That was not so very difficult. There were plenty of volunteers among the Americans, both officers and enlisted men, and it was seldom that the girls made a mistake in the men selected.

In the contest of wits that continued throughout the campaign, the boys definitely came out second best. I knew this, for I censored the girls' letters. The boys never caught on to the fact that they were being used as foils to satisfy female possessiveness or as a help in the practice of English. The girls wrote incredible letters, full of an extraordinary variety of love words and phrases picked up hit or miss at the movies and thrown hit or miss into the "sugar reports." One phrase would be used over and over until the little Burmese girl felt she had mastered it—then she would start on another. Fortunately sugar reports didn't have to be grammatical. The boys used slightly better grammar, but as for spelling, the girls won hands down. Being Americans, the boys never thought to use a dictionary. Being Burmese, the girls always did—either the dictionary or the old man. One of the girls went so far as to make me write her sugar reports for her. She would bring paper and pencil, ask me how one said this or that endearing phrase in English, get the spelling right, and then copy it. I often wondered how much her various boy friends would have enjoyed those love letters if they had known that they had been written by the old man.

Another morale-boosting—and, incidentally, work-saving —device was introduced by Sergeant Opas. He pretended that he couldn't tell the Burmese girls apart and that even when he could, he couldn't pronounce their names. So he nicknamed them all Susy. There was Susy No. 1, Susy No. 2, Susy No. 3, and so on. He himself became just plain Susy to all of them. The result was that when something had to be done in a hurry, Opas had only to shout "Susy" and everyone on the operating-room staff jumped to attention. There was so much laughter and delight over this in the operating room that the 98th Station Hospital surgeons couldn't think and we had to ask the girls to laugh in whispers.

From then on nicknames were given all around, some of them most appropriate. Ma Kai delighted in the name of Tugboat Annie, which, considering her shape and her winning ways, was most apt. Hla Sein became Chow-hound No. 1 and Lulu, Chow-hound No. 2. Nang Aung could

115

speak Chinese so fluently and with such a perfect accent that even the Chinese were mistaken in her ancestry and called her Miss Wang.

But nicknames were soon to be far from our thoughts, and problems of morale would again be second in importance to problems of survival.

12   THE TRAIL OF THE REFUGEES

EARLY IN 1943, General Stilwell was ready to begin an operation that many observers regarded as impossible.

It was March and Burmese refugees were at last on their way back into Burma. At any rate a small group of us were on our way: twelve of the Burmese nurses, Lieutenant Harris of Washington, D.C., and myself. Bill Cummings was our escort.

It had not been easy for us to obtain permission to start back so soon. All of "Uncle Joe" Stilwell's plans for an early return had been given up for lack of support from home. Uncle Joe was XYZ on the priorities list in those days. All the supplies and troops America had were pre-empted for what the world—but not the G.I.'s of China-Burma-India or the Burmese refugees—considered the really important theaters. And that meant every other theater except C.-B.-I. We could get along on a face-saving shoestring to make the Chinese remain in the war until we conquered all enemies but hers. Then we would begin to rescue China in earnest.

General Stilwell couldn't have been very pleased by the meagerness of the resources allotted to him, but distress was never visible in his face or actions. Give him little or give him nothing, he had promised to return the "hell of a licking" the Japs had given him, and he went about his "impossible" task with determination and no complaints. Already his few colored engineers had bulldozed a road from Ledo in Northeast Assam to the Burma border in the Pangsau Pass. Now the road was going down into Burma itself—if you can call the Naga Hills and the Hukawng Valley "Burma." But though the boys were working at all hours, with rifles and tommy guns strapped to their backs, Stilwell knew they would accomplish more if the Chinese troops he had trained for eight months at Ramgarh were to do their share in opening the Ledo Road to China by throwing a screen in front of the road builders. So the Chinese were on their way and we after them.

116

It was good luck that had secured the assignment for us. Uncle Joe had been on an inspection trip to Ramgarh and asked me, as usual, to tell him what we needed.

"Sir," I said, "since we came to Ramgarh last July we have had no complete set of surgical instruments. I understand that at Ledo there are large stocks of surgical instruments in China Defense Supplies destined for China. Since our hospital is working for Chinese troops, may I have your permission to go to Ledo and select instruments both for the Ramgarh hospital and for our unit to use when we finally return to Burma?"

"You're not planning a one-man expedition into Burma, are you?" the general asked with a twinkle in his eyes.

"No, sir," I replied with a grin. "I promise not to go beyond the border." Granddaddy was acquainted with my slippery ways.

"My plane starts for Delhi in the morning and then we'll go on to Ledo," the general said. "Be at my headquarters an hour ahead of time."

I was not late for that appointment.

We drove to the airport in Ranchi and took off in "Uncle Joe's Chariot."

At Ledo I found my friend Lieutenant Colonel Victor Haas who once told me in Lashio that no matter how good a teacher I was I would never make a decent nurse out of a Kachin.

Later Haas came to Ramgarh to visit me. "When I was flown out to India," he said on that occasion, "they asked me what famous historical sights I intended to visit and I told them there were only two famous things I wanted to see in India: the Taj Mahal and Seagrave's Burmese nurses. Now let's see them!" At the end of the inspection Haas had to admit that Kachins could be made into wonderful nurses.

Haas was now surgeon of S.O.S. in Ledo. He not only secured my instruments for me but drove me to "Hellgate" in sight of the Pangsau Pass and then back to my assigned quarters at Chih-Hui-Pu. To my delight one of our unit's best friends, Lieutenant Colonel McNally, was in command. Mac was in perfect condition, griping in his best manner at what was going to happen to his Chinese troops when they established their advance screen in the Naga Hills.

"It's ghastly country, littered with the bones of the refugees," he said. "There is malaria everywhere and the streams must be still swarming with the cholera, typhoid, and dysentery that killed the refugees by the thousands. In two weeks I

117

have to send Chinese troops down to Tagap and Punyang and there isn't a medic around to go with them."

"There's me," I said, ungrammatically.

"If I had a chance to see General Stilwell I'd jolly well ask for you. But what would happen to Ramgarh?"

"My executive officer, Major Crew, is a better army officer than I'll ever be," I said. "Besides, there are only about seven hundred patients left in Ramgarh instead of twelve hundred. They could spare a couple of surgical teams from our unit and never miss us, and," I added out of the corner of my mouth, "General Stilwell is in Chabua. I rode up in his plane."

Colonel McNally jumped up and reached for his hat. A few seconds later his jeep vanished around the corner.

Back at Ramgarh Lieutenant Harris and Stinky Davis wanted to go along if my Ledo *coup* produced results. It did. General Stilwell radioed orders for two surgical teams of the Seagrave Unit to report to Ledo for orders.

Captain Webb headed the smaller group—Stinky, four nurses, and my Lahu boy Aishuri—while Lieutenant Harris and I led the larger group of twelve nurses and Judson, my Burmese supply officer. I discussed the question of Chinese orderlies with General Boatner, and he ordered me to select thirty Chinese sailors and soldiers from our wards and take them along. These sailors had had a hard life. Removed months before from interned ships at Calcutta, they had been a constant headache to the British who gladly dumped them in the lap of the Chinese Army when it reached Ramgarh. The Chinese could think of nothing to do with them except put them in a concentration camp, where they became an American headache. General Boatner cured the headache by turning them over to me to use as orderlies and cooks in the hospital. Having spent their lives on occidental ships, they were the perfect servants.

"But, General," I said, "what if they desert as we pass through Calcutta?"

"You won't be held responsible," he replied.

The thirty men—there were six soldiers among them—were suspiciously eager to go with us.

On the seventeenth of March, we were at the great jumping-off place for Stilwell's return to Burma—Ledo. We parked the girls at the 20th General Hospital and took up our quarters in a tent at Chih-Hui-Pu.

In the excitement of moving I was sure the nurses had forgotten my birthday, but at five next morning the entire Chih-Hui-Pu staff, Chinese and American, was astounded to

118

hear "Happy Birthday to You" pour from female throats right in the middle of a male camp. The girls had carried presents for me all the way from Ramgarh. Later I learned that the girls in Ramgarh had also thrown a party in honor of my birthday.

That afternoon, as we were repacking our equipment into forty-pound porter loads, Colonel McNally asked me to take a look at Colonel Rothwell Brown of the tanks who had just returned from a trip to Shingbwiyang in the Hukawng Valley. The climax of their trip had come when, at the foot of the incredible climb up to Ngalang, Brown had come down with a terrific chill and a temperature of 106°. But he marched on into Ngalang, 106° and all. Now a shadow of his former self, he was worrying Mac to death insisting that I treat his malaria "on the hoof."

McNally asked Colonel Tate of the colored engineers to get me a hundred porters for our trip. The colonel claimed it couldn't be done, and then promptly went ahead and did it. Stilwell and his men only enjoyed life when they were doing the impossible. So Mac put us all into two Chinese six by six trucks and started us off for Hellgate where the porters would be waiting for us.

How the girls enjoyed the trip! They gurgled with laughter at the signs the colored engineers had stuck up along their "Ledo-Tokyo Road": "DON'T TEAR ME UP, ROLL ME DOWN!" I'M YOUR BEST FRIEND; DON'T RUIN ME!" "HEADQUARTERS FIRST BATTALION, HAIRY EARS." "TATE DAM. HOT DAMN, WHAT A DAM!" And later, "WELCOME TO BURMA. THIS WAY TO TOKYO!"

Soon we began to pass groups of colored boys at work. One stepped back wearily with his spade, took one look at us, threw his hat in the air, and screamed, "My God! WOMEN!" The girls became a bit scared as they recalled some of the things they had heard about the way American Negroes treat women. They recovered soon enough as they became acquainted at close hand with our colored soldiers. Let me say here, for the record, that though an occasional American white enlisted man or officer and an occasional Chinese soldier or officer had been known to offer insult to our Burmese nurses, not one single colored soldier ever treated them with anything but respect. The girls often recalled with misty eyes the colored soldiers they came to know so well.

When we reached Hellgate—Chinese drivers were not permitted to go farther—we expected to sleep in some of the coolie huts. But Colonel Tate had sent word to the captain

119

of engineers that we were coming, and the captain met us and escorted us to his own camp, where he turned over the newly completed messhall to the nurses and gave me General Wheeler's bed—the only time I ever had the honor to sleep in a major general's bed. I begged the captain to let the girls cook their own Burmese food since they were so fed up with American meals, and much against his sense of hospitality he permitted them to do so. It was the first time the girls had cooked for themselves for many months and the dinner was delicious.

The next morning some colored boys drove us up the mountain until they bogged down in the mud just before reaching the Pangsau Pass. We had been surprised at how good our Chinese drivers had been after their Ramgarh training—we remembered well how they had driven on the Burma Road! But these colored boys could really drive. Even when the fresh earth of the road shoulders slid away they performed miracles getting their trucks back onto solid ground again. We stepped out into the deep mud, when the trucks finally bogged down, and began to march. Almost immediately Sein Bwint's flimsy shoe was sucked off in the mud. We hadn't been able to buy one pair of stout shoes in all India that would fit the girls, and G.I. shoes, three sizes too large, were so ungainly that I never dreamed the girls could use them. Captain Webb, however, thought differently, and the girls clattered around delightedly all day long in their huge oversize G.I. shoes.

As we passed the "WELCOME TO BURMA" sign at the top of the pass the girls began to laugh and sing and trot downhill, though the rain was drenching and cold. They were on their way now, back to Burma and home and parents. That night we slept, still drenched, in three little huts in Nawngyang—the returning refugees' first night in Burma! To our astonishment we were serenaded. "Silent Night," "The Spacious Firmament," "All Hail the Power," and other favorite hymns swelled forth in exquisite harmony from the hundred throats of our Garo porters.

I was proud of the noble work of our Assam colleagues of the American Baptist Mission among these wild Garo tribesmen of southwestern Assam. All our porters were Christian. Garos take their time when portering but they stole none of our goods and they are the only race I have yet found in India that knows how to give out with a belly laugh. On contract to the British Government and under command of American missionaries, they did almost all the portering for the U.S. Army as far south as Tagap. Later they worked southward as far as Shingbwiyang, the first "town" in the Hukawng Valley. They know their jungle. One group of G.I.'s was astonished to see the Garos suddenly get excited and

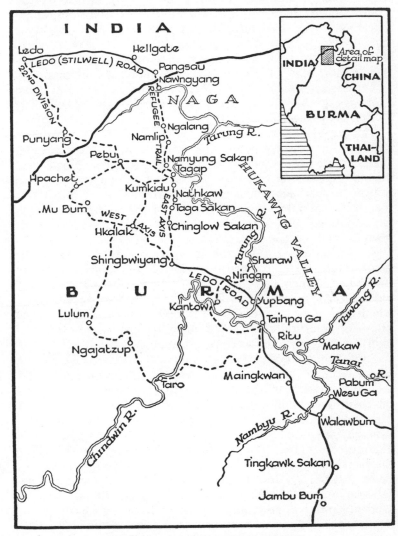

NAGA HILLS AND HUKAWNG VALLEY

begin splitting a hollow tree trunk. They were still more astonished to see them start pulling from the tree trunk, foot by foot, an enormous twenty-foot python. Their astonishment knew no bounds when the Garos immediately cooked and ate the huge snake.

Garos will not set out on a journey before seven in the morning. I was worried about how six-foot-two, spindle-legged Lieutenant Harris would stand the trip up the terrible ranges ahead. How a man from the most notorious chair-warming city in the world, Washington, D.C., could negotiate these hills on high was a mystery, until he acknowledged that his Washington address was a temporary one and that during most of his life he had been a Tennessee mountaineer.

I was curious about this Refugee Trail which ran from Mogaung on the railway near Myitkyina through the Hukawng Valley and Naga Hills to Ledo.

The Naga Hills were famous for their head-hunting tribes. The British never entered this route unless backed by a small army. I was curious to see these frightful Nagas and compare them with those we met on our retreat with General Stilwell a year before on the Indaw-Imphal trail, much farther south. Would we meet the famous tribe whose women wore nothing before marriage but a tiny apron on their behinds and swung it around to the front after?

As we marched along the trail, we soon found that the people were no man's people. I could see Kachin blood in the shape of their faces and stopped to pass the time of day with them in Kachin. Thank God we were back in a country where we could converse with people without using several relays of interpreters! I asked them whether they were Kachins or Nagas. "Neither," they said. "We are Chins." People the whites called Nagas called themselves Chins but spoke Kachin. Along the East Axis, as the army called the Refugee Trail, all the Nagas called themselves Chins—which they decidedly were not. They were hybrids. All sorts of conquests and migrations had occurred along the axis through the years. We saw natives with unmistakable Shan, Hkamti, Burmese, Kachin, or Naga physiognomies calling themselves Chin, but there was no pure blood of any of these races. In a few more years people still calling themselves Chin will have American, English, Indian, Negro, Garo, Nepali, Chinese, and Japanese features as well!

We soon found that it was also a no man's land with regard to climate. Assam has the world's heaviest rainfall but at least the rain has sense enough to fall in season. Burma weather is beautifully regular. But that of Hukawng follows no rules whatsoever. It makes all its own climate, every bit of it wrong. July was supposed to be the rainy season, so we had weeks of beautiful weather. We shivered in Tagap in the hot season. As we marched along it was the middle of the dry season, so it poured steadily for a month. This was the country through which Stilwell's engineers had to build their road from Ledo to China, and build it without hard rock with which to surface it—nothing but clay and soft river rock.

Through these torrents of rain the Chinese had marched down the Refugee Trail two days ahead of us and with animal transport. As a result we were continually to our knees in mud even when going up the steepest of hills. At every step you had to yank your leg out of the mud with an angry suck and sink it in to the knee again as you put it down. Stilwell's pace, with a ten-minute rest every hour, had to be abandoned at once. Ground leeches were everywhere. I had always thought people were exaggerating when they claimed the leeches could suck a man to death, but I'm sure that many of the refugees must finally have succumbed to leeches.

Certainly they had succumbed! From the first day on we passed skeletons in ever increasing numbers, yet we could see evidences of camps where, by setting fire to the shacks, hundreds of skeletons had been destroyed en masse. There were skeletons around every water hole, lying sprawled out where the refugees had collapsed. At the foot of every ascent were the bones of those who had died rather than attempt one more climb, and all up the hill were the bones of those who had died trying. Still standing along the road were some extremely crude shacks, each with its ten to twenty skeletons of those who couldn't get up when a new day came. In one shallow stream we were horrified to find that the Chinese had placed a long row of skulls to be used as stepping-stones. Sex and age and even race could be noted, not by such elusive clues as surgeons use but by rotting clothes. Looking at the skeletons of little boys in khaki shorts, I realized they might have been John or Sterling. There were men, women, and children of every race and age, their hair white, gray, brown, and black, still lying beside the whitened skulls; there were English, Anglo-Burmese, and Indians—civilian and military.

And yet in spite of the hundreds and hundreds of skeletons we saw, we didn't see half of those who had died on the Refugee Trail, for English and Indian and Chinese burial and cremating squads had been at work. A few months later only a few scattered skulls were left to mark the trail of the refugees. Now we were the first of the refugees to return.

As we reached our second night's camp we began to get a foretaste of what was to hound us for the entire year to come. There were officers in the area who knew not "Joseph and his daughters" and supposed these girls "couldn't take it." We were told that officers up ahead were horrified at the speed of our advance and were rushing to get proper camps built for the nurses. We were not to proceed until all camps were completed. We halted for Sunday since the coolies were tired and, as Christians, entitled by contract to one day off per week. Then, too, the girls had worn out their first pairs of shoes and were beginning to develop sores on their feet. But by Sunday evening everyone was so restless to get on that we resumed our march the following morning.

On that day we had the worst climb of all—uphill hour after hour, pulling ourselves up out of mud by the roots of trees. On the slippery stretches I stamped my G.I. heels as deeply as possible at each step, hoping the nurses might catch toe holds. Each of us carried a long strong cane to push ourselves along and help us keep erect. But at almost every step one or the other would go down, to the uproarious delight of the rest of the party. Cheers always burst forth when the old man himself went down. And so on, up and up to unbelievable heights, till at last we came onto the air-drop field at Ngalang. There the enlisted men at the radio station made us completely at home in a spare shack, while they prepared for us the kind of meal only our air force units could produce.

Travel the next day was much easier and brought us to a camp delightfully situated near a rushing stream. The shack was only just building but by night there was a thatched roof over our heads, and what more could returning refugees want?

At no time did we cover more than eight miles in one day, although without a heavy pack sixteen miles a day is quite possible in those hills if it has to be done. We got a big laugh when we read long after an article in a States-side magazine about the Signal Corps man who "taught himself to walk five miles a day" in the head-hunting Naga Hills. We purposely took it easy on this trip because we had no idea how soon the Chinese would begin to have casualties, and the girls had to be ready for them.

Nowhere along the road was there a single native village. Even "fierce Naga head-hunters" could not understand the tragedy of the refugees except as the act of one of their mysterious gods, and they had moved away, as far as they could from the haunted and accursed trail. Even at Tagap there was nothing left of the village that formerly housed the tribal chief.

Airplanes were dropping food and ammunition as we reached a knoll in front of Tagap. We watched them free-drop sacks of rice and then parachute down sacks of canned goods and ammunition. It was impossible to cross the field as long as the planes continued to circle and drop. Finally, as American Quartermaster boys began to gather in the day's haul, we pushed on to the coolie camp beyond the Chinese troops. We were at Tagap Ga—the base for our work.

Major General Wheeler of S.O.S., a day behind us on the trail, reached Tagap in the early morning. His first action was to ask Major Peng, the Chinese commandant, whether he had yet sent forward the company of troops that had been ordered on patrol. Peng had not. Wheeler ordered them off at once. Finally a patrol of one platoon set off and had proceeded only a mile beyond Kumkidu, with a Kachin scout a hundred yards ahead of them, when they bumped smack into a Japanese patrol. Machine-gun bullets tore up the earth around the Kachin scout. The Kachin slipped into the dense jungle and circled back to the Chinese who were frantically deploying to return the Japanese fire. The first engagement of the new Burma campaign was joined within twenty-four hours of our arrival.

The first casualty was, of course, an abdominal case. We had not set up yet. The few available transport planes were bringing in higher priority stuff than tarpaulins. We would have to build thatched bamboo shacks and that would take time. So we borrowed the Signal Corps messhall and did the operation on their dinner table. The intestine had been badly torn and, as in the case of so many Chinese, roundworms were escaping from the various rents and exploring the abdomen on their own. One was actually lying in the abdominal wound, its body cut in two by the bullet. By the light of one gasoline lamp and several flashlights we resected the torn intestine, and made an end to end anastomosis. A respectable number of my abdominal cases had been known to live, but not one where roundworms filled the abdominal cavity. This patient lasted twenty-four hours.

While our own Chinese battalion was successfully holding the Japanese, Bill Cummings was ordered to proceed with a Kachin patrol down the Salt Springs Trail that connected the East and West Axes and find out what had happened to

125

the British troops when garrisoning Hkalak at the entrance to the West Axis. The garrison consisted of Indian and Kachin troops officered by former British tea planters of Assam. There was also a radio team of American enlisted men at Hkalak. Bill made a forced march of twenty miles and when he reached the middle trail toward Pebu bumped into the force retreating to Pebu on the double quick. Attacked by an "overwhelming force of two hundred Japs," they had barely had time to fire their supplies and run. The American boys, ordered to retreat, had scattered their radio equipment in the jungle. Bill about-faced and marched back over that ghastly trail without rest to report to General Wheeler.

The retreat of the Hkalak garrison, before the arrival of Chinese troops down the center trail, laid Tagap wide open to Japanese encirclement and General Wheeler ordered us to pack up and be ready for immediate evacuation—if the Chinese had to fight their way out of the encirclement. The same old story of the first campaign in Burma: the Japs attack with a party of ten or two hundred, it doesn't matter which; the colonial troops retreat at the drop of a hat, convinced that they will not be able to resist successfully; the Chinese have to retreat or be surrounded; and commanding generals have to start worrying about the safety of American medical units. Was the new campaign to be tainted with the same defeatism? Had no one the guts to make a real stand? What would Stilwell say if we all started running again?

General Wheeler was busy sending out radio messages, but twice that day I snared him and pled with him.

"Sir," I said, "the Chinese have so far not discovered much reason to trust the United States fully. They have no proof that we also are not going to run away and leave them holding the bag the minute they come up against danger. During the first campaign General Stilwell kept our unit well out of harm's way and always warned us in time of an imminent Chinese retreat. The general was certainly justified because at that time we were the only surgical unit he had for the entire Chinese Army. That situation has changed. There are all sorts of American medical units now in the theater. If anything happened to us we wouldn't be missed. These nurses are Burmese girls of the country for which we are fighting. They aren't going to gripe if they die for their country."

"Naturally not," interpolated the general.

"Furthermore," I resumed, after the laughter that this outburst provoked had subsided, "nothing would please the

126

Chinese more than to have a high-ranking American officer stick it out with them. If, in addition, that officer is an American officer with a detachment of nurses who have the guts to stay, their morale will be enormously improved. As for myself, I had a hard trip here, marching forward over those hills. I know I can't go up them backward!"

The general was noncommittal, so I saluted and left.

Next morning, scouts reported that the Chinese advance patrol at Pebu had thrust south below the entrance of the Salt Springs Trail and had dug in there while the colonials continued to retreat. Colonel Brown was with them. Captain Webb and his nurses had arrived at Ledo, minus twenty sailors who had slipped away as they came through Calcutta, and were marching in to Punyang on the West Axis. Judson, whom I had left behind to escort Webb into the jungles, was with them. Our own Chinese were holding at Kumkidu and "had inflicted many casualties on the enemy." General Wheeler, greatly relieved at the stabilizing of the line, permitted us to go ahead with our plans and build the hospital.

Our Garo porters cleared the bamboo jungle and erected wards, a supply shack, an operating room, and, finally, several little bamboo houses with bamboo floors and bamboo beds thatched with bamboo leaves. There was a cottage for every four nurses, one for Harris and any guest who might appear, and one for me. Some Nagas built us a pipeline of bamboos which carried water from a stream nearby right through the hospital grounds to the operating room. As soon as the supply building had been built we moved into it and put up a combined messhall and kitchen. That day there was another casualty whom we placed in the messhall since the wards were not quite ready.

About ten that night there was a tremendous burst of machine-gun and tommy-gun fire and bullets whizzed over us. Everyone supposed the Japanese were making a fierce attack and I expected casualties before morning so ordered all the nurses to bed while I went on sentry duty beside our patient.

In the morning we discovered that the great battle was caused by the appearance not of Japs but of a herd of large monkeys which swarm all over the Naga Hills. A few days later a Chinese patrol found that the Japanese had retreated. It was discovered a month later that not more than ten or twenty Japanese troops had caused the rout of the colonials at Hkalak.

While the 38th Chinese Division was moving to Hkalak to replace the colonials, a battalion was ordered to guard the flank of the West Axis at Hpachet Hi. Captain Webb's hospital group was ordered forward from Punyang with this battalion. There was a lateral road connecting the two axes running from Tagap to Pebu to Hpachet. Since it was necessary for Webb's group to pass through Pebu, I arranged to meet them there and see personally to the establishment of the new hospital. I had a secondary thought in this plan. Perhaps if I were away from Tagap for two weeks it would be good for the girls there and, again, I might be good medicine for Webb's nurses who had already driven that long-suffering hero almost out of his wits.

From Tagap one drops back to the Namyung River on the Refugee Trail and then goes up the river, crossing from one side to the other some fifteen times in the first twelve miles. There had been leeches on the wide Refugee Trail—lots, we had thought, compared to anything we had ever seen in Burma. But at that time I hadn't seen the Pebu Trail. This must have been the birthplace and ancestral home of the leech. There were three species, all of them of the "ground leech" type, an inch or so long when hungry, as opposed to the "water leech" or "buffalo leech," some three inches long before it gets to work. The brown ones were on the ground or in the damp grass waiting, so close together that your eyes had to be focused on the ground at your feet to find a place where you could step without landing on several of them. The red variety kept out of the mud on the stems of the elephant grass or small plants, and the green ones on branches about shoulder height from the ground. All three kinds fastened themselves on you as you went by. They seemed to direct themselves by a sense of smell. Poised on the small sucker at the base, the big sucker at the head end waved in the air leaning directly toward you. If you suddenly moved a yard to another position, the leech would immediately sway like a compass needle and still keep pointed right at you.

Every ten or twelve steps my Naga porters stopped and cut leeches off their feet with their long dahs. I had a pocket knife and tried cutting my leeches in two after I scraped them off. Then I was astonished to see both halves come for me. I tried flicking them off with thumb and middle finger. I soon found you couldn't budge them if you snapped at them while the head sucker was attached. But they would fly off into the bushes at once if you flicked just as the head sucker was about to take over from the tail sucker. This was a pretty lesson in timing. The flick had to be correct to the split second or you could flick in vain all day.

At our first and second ten-minute rest periods I took off my leggings, socks, and shoes and burned off about thirty leeches that had squirmed through my defenses. Remembering experiences in Namkham with patients who had leeches in the nose, throat, and urethra, I finally compromised with the leeches of the Pebu Trail, letting them get their fill elsewhere so long as they kept away from my face and the fly of my trousers. All in all I tried all the routines: brushing the pests off with sacks of wet salt and tobacco, burning them off with matches. I found that nothing compared with Skat. If you soak the fly of your trousers and your socks with Skat, tuck your trousers into your socks and smear Skat all over the exposed parts of your body, the leeches take one suck and quit. But on this trip I had no Skat. When I reached Pebu I made a fire and cremated some seventy beautifully gorged specimens and then bled so much all night that my sheets were covered with blood.

I also had nightmares all night long, for two miles short of Pebu I had suddenly ceased looking for leeches at my feet and glanced upward to see a long green snake hanging by his tail from a branch, his head on a level with mine and his beady eyes staring inquiringly at me. People had been telling me that there were no snakes in the Naga Hills. On their trip from Tagap to Hkalak months later Grindlay and Chesley killed three: a cobra, a krait, and a Russell's viper, the big three of poisonous snakedom.

The air supply dropping ground at Pebu was on the top of the mountain behind the camp. On Sunday afternoon I climbed up, both to meet the colored Quartermaster boys and their lieutenant and to meet Webb's detachment if it came in. Nobody turned up. So I loafed in camp until Thursday, when I again walked to the top of the mountain; just as I reached the brow, down tumbled the nurses of Webb's unit on top of me, clattering along in the huge G.I. shoes Webb had secured for them.

That night was the worst I ever spent anywhere for insects. There is no place in the Naga Hills that is not infested with one or another insect plague. In Hkalak it was a small black fly, which cuts a clean hole in your skin and then injects a drop of a horrible itch-producing poison. They bite only in the daytime, but you don't know they're biting or even that they're on you until the poison has been injected, and then it's too late to do more than squeeze out the poisoned blood and hope for the best. At this camp, too, there were literally clouds of buffalo flies, insects so tiny that they can hardly be seen. They bite only at night and swarm through the meshes of the mosquito net. A single bite doesn't itch nearly so much as that of the black fly, but when myriads of them bite at once it is more than the nervous system can endure. I may have slept a total of two hours that night. Our huts were horrible old coolie shacks with roofs of dried withered leaves, and it poured rain all night. We fastened our ground sheets over our mosquito nets. I didn't seem to be very expert at that. During the first half of the night the head end of the ground sheet gave way repeatedly and then the foot end fell down and buckets of water poured in on me.

The next day's trip into Hpachet, a large village full of pigs, chickens, cattle, buffaloes, and dogs, was almost entirely uphill but the country was so pretty and the villages so interesting—Hpachet is on the edge of real Naga country— that we didn't mind too much the steepness of the road; and the natives hadn't run away from the West Axis.

Building materials were very scanty about Hpachet and it was several days before we could get our quarters and a small hospital built between the Americans and the Chinese. The camp was so high that there were few insects and the scenery was beautiful. But because of the height, there was almost no water—just a trickle from a spring. Bathing was next to impossible and I could feel the forthcoming gloom. You can deprive nurses of almost anything and they will smile, but not if you deprive them of their baths.

General Boatner was now in command at Ledo. While I was in Hpachet a radio came in from him: "Your mission is first to furnish hospitalization for all Chinese troops south of the line Tagap-Pebu-Hpachet; second, to give medical attention to all porters in the employ of the U.S. Army; third, to furnish medical attention to the natives as far as practicable in order to obtain their friendship for the U.S. Army."

It was the end of May. During the week at Hpachet the weather had been delightful, but it couldn't last. If I didn't hurry back to Tagap before the rains finally broke in earnest I wouldn't be able to use the "leech trail" but would have to strike for the mountains. I would rather have the leeches than the mountains any day.

I arrived back at Tagap in time for another "battle." The shooting began at Nathkaw, several miles south, where a patrol of Japs had been reported trying to outflank our outpost. The outpost at Kumkidu heard the shooting and opened fire and then Tagap itself threw in everything it had. We kept ducking as all sorts of missiles whistled over us. Bill Cummings was a bit skeptical of there being any Japs near us so he set off with another officer to investigate while the nurses and I cut several American-made bullets out of Chinese bodies. On his return Bill told us that there hadn't been a single footprint in the valley through which "the Japs" passed. Bill had asked the Chinese captain which direction he had been firing.

"Sir," the captain had replied with much dignity, "we fired in *every* direction!"

Grindlay's detachment was now due to arrive and we all decided to go meet them. Knowing that the rains would make the Namyung River unfordable, American engineers had had cables dropped by air, dragged them to the site by elephant, and built a suspension bridge across the Namyung gorge. There was a new road to this bridge and Bill Cummings claimed he knew where it was. Thinking we might have a long wait, we took our swimming suits and some hand grenades and a picnic lunch so we could enjoy ourselves while waiting. Our stomachs already rebelled at canned corned beef.

But Bill had been too enthusiastic about his knowledge of the right turnoff. He led us on the wrong path and we finally arrived at a river that was not the Namyung at all. We agreed we'd have plenty of time for a good swim, fishing, a picnic lunch and still be able to return to the Refugee Trail to meet Grindlay. So we cast all care aside, put on our swimming suits, and had a really good time. It was the first time the girls had worn occidental swimming suits instead of *longyis* and they were quite shy at first, though the suits were extremely becoming.

Bill went upstream to a deep hole under an overhanging cliff and threw in a grenade. Fish of all sizes up to eighteen inches floated down, and men and women went wild grabbing at them. Bill and my Chinese orderly Pang Tze (Fatty) got the biggest fish, but Chit Sein and Little Bawk won on total number, though Bawk was just learning to swim. Chit Sein, born on the banks of Inle Lake, the largest lake in Burma, could swim like a fish. Grabbing fish right and left and diving into the deep water for them, she thrust them into the bosom of her swimming suit and piled them into the tiny apron, came out of the water after each dive bulging in all the wrong places, rid herself of her fish on shore, and dived back in again.

I managed to catch one small fish.

When our three grenades were used up and we had caught enough fish to furnish the whole unit with a big meal, we started a fire, made coffee, ate our picnic lunch, then hurried back up the hill. As usual Grindlay was ahead of schedule and we found the crowd had just passed by. They were still getting out of wet clothes when we arrived back at the hospital.

For days, while we waited for permission to push on to Hkalak, everyone was busy and happy. Squads of nurses hoed and planted a large garden with the type of vegetables that could be eaten as they grew. There is hardly a green thing Burmese girls don't love to eat; they eat pea vines, for instance, long before the peas flower and pod.

To prepare Hkalak for us, Dr. San Yee, two nurses, and a Chinese boy had gone on ahead. Now they radioed that quarters were built and medical work was increasing rapidly, so I set out with seven nurses and Pang Tze. Of the three Chinese garrisons, Tagap was the largest and Hpachet the smallest. Hkalak, of medium size, was farthest forward, and about twenty-five miles from Hkalak was Shingbwiyang, still in the hands of the Japs. Since Captain Webb and Captain Johnson were friends, I detailed Johnson to join Webb at Hpachet. Grindlay always got mad if he didn't have enough medicine and surgery, so I left him in charge at Tagap with Gurney, who now had his commission as captain, and Ba Saw. At Hkalak I would be farthest forward and in an intermediate position between our two other stations.

The road from Tagap was west along the Salt Springs Trail, down, down, down, crossing two large streams like millraces to a broken-down coolie camp at the Salt Springs. If we had only known it, we could have gone four miles farther to a lovely little camp that had just been built. Anyway, we spread our ground sheets over the broken-down roof and slept on the broken bamboo floor. From there, the next morning, we walked many miles continually uphill over an unconscionably miserable excuse for a trail. In many places we had to guess where the trail was supposed to be. There were innumerable fallen trees over which we had to

132

scramble, some of them four feet in diameter. We evolved a special technique with these: one, look for leeches; two, turn your back to the tree; three, push yourself up to a sitting position on the top; four, swing your legs over in an arc; five, pray silently that your knees can take it; six, drop down on the other side.

Halfway up the huge mountain, the strong wind had blown down bamboos, forming arches about four feet high across the trail. It began to rain and we had to stoop under the bamboo arches and claw ourselves to a stop with our fingernails when we started to slip back. About three in the afternoon we came to a shoulder of the mountain that we thought must be the top and, therefore, near our next proposed camp. The nurses were hungry and cast eager eyes at bamboo shoots, the first we had seen in two years, so we stopped every few rods and cut the shoots to carry with us. The wind was very strong now and made us shiver in our wet clothes as we climbed. The top was still a long way off.

When we finally reached the camp there was nothing left of it but a few scattered bamboos. We were tired out but the girls managed to put up a framework to support our ground sheets and a lot of leafy branches. We stuffed ourselves on rice and fried bamboo and got what sleep we could between the attacks of buffalo flies.

Our third day out of Tagap was much easier. The road was as much down as up. Then after one last horribly cold damp night beside a stream with still more buffalo flies, we were over the range and moving down into the camp we had left at Hkalak.

Instead of waiting for me to check in with him, the liaison officer, Lieutenant Stewart, came over to check in with me. Not far behind him was the Chinese battalion commander. I knew at once that there was to be one more fly in the Hkalak ointment. In my time I have come to know many officers, good and bad, in many different armies. I cannot permit myself to state my feelings with regard to Major X, except to say that he would disgrace an army in Hades, where he undoubtedly is now roaming restlessly around. The major's first act was to try to force me to "pull my rank" on Lieutenant Wallace, the Quartermaster, and compel him to issue American rations to his troops instead of the Chinese rations to which they were entitled by order of Chungking. When I refused, he tried to force me, "for safety's sake," to move the hospital into a hollow in the center of the Chinese camp.

133

After my experience with trigger-happy troops at Tagap, I knew we would be safer outside the Chinese lines.

The night of our arrival, Wallace and his colored boys came over to give us a welcome concert.

I was always greatly impressed by all the dealings between our enlisted men, both white and colored, and the natives throughout Burma. I wonder why psychological studies are not made on different races based on the dozen or so words each race will pick as the most essential to teach to foreigners or to learn from foreigners. With the English, the words of Hindustani deemed most essential are those for "Get out!" "Go!" "Stop!" "Left!" "Right!" For the Indian the most essential words are "No papa, no mama, no brother, no sister—backsheesh!" In Chinese the words necessary for Americans are "Hao bu hao? Ding hao, bu hao!"—Good or bad? Very good, no good! The many Burmese languages are too much for the Americans, but what they teach the natives is "Okay. Come on, let's go!" whereat everyone digs in with a laugh and the job is promptly done.

It's the "Let's go" that spells the difference between the American and the colonial Englishman because it indicates the truth: that the American intends to work along with the natives and sweat the job out with them. It is therefore not surprising to hear natives everywhere say of the four races: "We fear and detest the Japs. We are afraid of the Chinese. We respect the British. But we love the Americans, especially when they leave our women alone."

During our first two months at Hkalak, Major X forced his battalion to perform a prodigious amount of labor in building a most elaborate system of defenses. He was obviously planning to remain at Hkalak for the duration. Now his defenses were complete and he planned an inspection of three days to be performed by me, of all people, and Lieutenant Wallace who was now liaison officer as well as Quartermaster. Since I wasn't busy medically, and couldn't think of a valid excuse, I spent three of the unhappiest days of my life inspecting every trench, every foxhole, every dugout and pillbox, not only in the main camp but in the outposts as well. Wallace was a canny southerner and stood around looking at the scenery and, taking notes, pretending to be mapping the defenses, while I jumped in and out of trenches and foxholes, exclaiming about their individual "merits"—each was really worse than the last—gasping in astonishment at the marvelous intricacies of each dugout and

134

pillbox. The climax came when Major X took me into the top story of his own pillbox. "This pillbox," he said proudly, "being my own command post for the day the Japs attack us, is, of course, the best of them all!" He leaned against the center post which promptly fell with a clatter to the floor.

Informers began to bring in reports that the Japanese were opening a series of supply bases on a line from Taro, outflanking us, and on to a point within twenty air miles of Ledo. General Boatner radioed that General Sun was ordering Major X to send a platoon to cut this supply line and ambush the Japanese. I was ordered to furnish two first-aid men to accompany the expedition. I had only two men, Sergeant Deaton and Chiou Seing, a former officer of the Chinese Army who was working with me. Neither of these men had seen action—and when anyone in my unit was to see action for the first time, I wanted to lead him into it—not drive him. I promptly radioed Boatner for permission to go. In the morning, back came Boatner's message addressed to all American liaison officers in the Naga Hills: "Any American who catches Seagrave more than five miles in any direction from Hkalak is hereby ordered to shoot him. Seagrave is not, repeat not, allowed to go on this expedition." Boatner told me later that General Stilwell came into his office just after the message had been sent and that he showed the general a copy.

"Change it," Stilwell growled, "change it to one hundred yards!" So I sat and cussed and cussed.

Letters reached me from Tagap saying that Pearl, E Kya-ing, and Louise wanted to take a vacation at Calcutta, and I was in trouble again. These girls hadn't had a vacation for two years. Perhaps I was all wrong. Looking at the matter now I know I was wrong, for I had put the success of our job first in importance, the integrity of the unit second, and personalities third. When we first went to Ramgarh there hadn't been time for vacations, so only the sick were permitted them. About the time the work began to decrease we were unofficially alerted for a campaign to begin in November or December, 1942, so we only arranged for a rest camp in the mountains near Ramgarh. The girls had wanted to tour India. Then the campaign was postponed till mid-February and I sent off one party of nurses on a vacation to Agra and Delhi. If line officers would only give medical officers definite information, which they never do, I would have had no difficulty, for our work was easy and I could have sent off large groups of nurses at any time.

135

Now in the middle of the Naga Hills in the latter part of the rainy season, with our unit newly alerted for action supposed to begin the first week of October, three of the girls wanted a vacation. I wrote back advising against it because, first, a total of twelve days' marching through deep mud would not make fourteen days in Calcutta a very successful vacation and because, second, we were alerted for a day earlier than they could possibly return; but I left the decision up to them. They decided to let the vacation go. But then girls who had not asked for leave began to gripe verbally and in letters, until I dreaded to see the mail runner arrive.

Then General Boatner ordered me to Ledo to discuss plans for the medical setup for the coming campaign. He had suggested by radio that he place three new portable surgical hospitals, fresh from the States, under my command and the 25th Field Hospital in close liaison so I could integrate the medical work of the entire front and, as he put it, get the new units away from the Park Avenue methods of running hospitals and get them used to the woods. Grindlay came to Hkalak to hold the fort during my absence.

At Ledo, I discovered that Colonel Vernon W. Petersen, M.C., had arrived the day before, assigned to combat headquarters. Boatner's plans were therefore automatically canceled and I had made the trip for nothing. Petersen not only outranked me but was a splendid officer of many years' experience in the army. They didn't need me any longer. The whole theater was lousy with medical units, and with many more on the way.

But my troubles weren't over. General Boatner ordered me off on a month's vacation.

So there I was, off for a month's vacation I didn't want, after having requested the Tagap nurses not to insist on theirs. On top of everything else, that was too much for them, and I wasn't surprised when I returned to Tagap to find that the girls had no further use for me.

In 1943, forces of the United Nations climbed up the ladder of the Solomons. Early in 1944 they invaded the Gilberts and Marshalls and leapfrogged up the coast of New Guinea. Simultaneously a campaign for the control of the Hukawng and Mogaung valleys in Burma was fought by Chinese, British, and a small force of American troops. Fighting and cutting their way through the hills and jungles, the Chinese and Americans advanced toward the strategically important

136

town of Myitkyina which the Japanese defended until August 3, 1944.

While the campaign for the Hukawng and Mogaung valleys was being fought, the Japanese launched two offensives on the Arakan and Manipur fronts in an effort to cut the Bengal-Assam railway to Ledo. Had they succeeded, the communication lines of the Chinese and American forces in northern Burma would have been severed. The repulse of the Japanese by the British Fourteenth Army at Kohima and Imphal—and the capture of Myitkyina—assured the eventual realization of General Stilwell's plan for the conquest and construction of a relief route to China.

13 THE FIRST OFFENSIVES

AFTER my unfortunate vacation I returned to Ledo four days late for the job at hand. The Chinese had been ordered forward in three columns. The first, from Hkalak, was to secure the right flank at Taro, then held by the Japanese. A detachment of our unit, minus nurses, was to proceed with them and serve that flank until replaced by a surgical team of the U.S. 151st Medical Battalion. The second column of Chinese would advance from Tagap to secure the left flank at Sharaw down the Tarung Valley. Another detachment of our unit, also minus nurses, was ordered to proceed with them. The third and main column would then advance directly south to Shingbwiyang and continue up the Hukawng Valley until stopped by the enemy. The main group of our unit, with our nurses, would follow this center thrust in three echelons. I assigned Captain Johnson and three Burmese technicians to the Sharaw flank—Major Grindlay, Major O'Hara, Lieutenant Chesley, and Dr. Ba Saw to the center. If I made a forced march of double stages, I could reach Hkalak in time to head that detachment with Dr. San Yee and three men. Captain Gurney and the nurses would remain at Hkalak until relieved there. Captain Webb's transfer from our unit to another assignment was a terrible blow, but he was being replaced by Lieutenant Antonellis already on his way to join Grindlay at Tagap.

Harris and Pang Tze were willing to undertake the double-stage forced march, so we set off with as small a kit as possible. When we reached Namlip Sakan we came upon Antonellis whose knees had soured on him. He had planned to rest there a day but decided to go on with us if we would let him take his time. I could well sympathize with him, for

137

my own knees had squeaked for three days after we first reached Tagap, for a week after I made the Hpachet trip, and for a month after we went to Hkalak.

At Tagap we left Antonellis for a few days of rest and started on for Hkalak. Reinforcements for Major X were on the road, sick and weary from their long march. One poor soldier with a high temperature was helping himself down from rock to rock in a part sitting, part crawling posture. We knew he could make that last mile to our hospital so hurried on by. It was wonderful to have the Hkalak girls come running to meet us with the old-style enthusiasms we had grown so to depend on. The Quartermaster boys came over immediately to give us a welcome concert.

One day late already, we hurried on the next morning and by nightfall caught up half a day on Major X's troops. Two of my men were with him so that there was no further necessity for me to hurry. It was known that there were no Japanese north of Ngajatzup. If I arrived at the village two miles north of Ngajatzup the day the Chinese contacted the Japs, I would still be in plenty of time.

The second day out of Hkalak, Harris broke down. I didn't wish Harris any bad luck but I was quite proud of the fact that the old man had outlasted the young infantryman from the mountains of Tennessee. Stinky Davis was waiting at this camp with a fever casualty whom he turned over to Harris and then he went on with me.

After two more days we reached a little deserted village behind the lines and were eating our third meal of baked beans for the day when our first casualties arrived. One of them was a lieutenant who had a shattered thigh with a three-inch overriding of the bone ends. No forward unit had even an imitation fracture table, so it was up to me to arrange some sort of traction apparatus. It might be weeks before the lieutenant could be evacuated, so we had to give definite treatment in the jungle. We set up on the dirt floor of the verandah of an abandoned Naga house in the midst of buffaloes and their dung. Naga houses have enormous posts and girders. Our parachute air-drop canvas bags were reinforced with two-inch-wide straps. We ripped off these straps and, fastening them to the girders above, suspended our lieutenant by the hips and shoulders a foot above the bamboo operating table. With cuffs of strapping around ankles and armpits and a lot of rope, we secured traction and countertraction on our patient by pulling against the posts of the house. The knee and thigh were held in the cor-

rect amount of flexion and abduction by additional straps
fastened to the roof. It was then easy to put the patient in a
plaster cast which incorporated the straps. The "fracture
table" was such a success that I decided to patent it, though
a Naga house might prove difficult to transport all over the
jungle.

We didn't have a good night's sleep in that old house, for
it was already far too well "occupied." In the morning we
picked out two newer shacks, much smaller but cleaner, at
the other end of the village. The village was built in a semi-
circle around the crown of a little hill, and the Air Corps
transport planes were using this thirty-by-eighty-yard area as
a dropping field. It was the first time our transports had
dropped so close to the Japanese lines and the pilots were
probably a bit nervous. They were also new to air-dropping
so they were very erratic. Already we had lost one Chinese
whose skull had been cracked like an eggshell when a sack
of rice hit him. Now, all day long, we had to dodge as they
threw rice, corned beef, baked beans, mortar shells, and
small-arms ammunition at us.

The third morning a plane came over whose pilot had
gone completely haywire. Without the usual warning he
buzzed down the length of the field and dropped about fifteen sacks of rice within a very few yards of where I was
standing beside our hospital. Very well, I thought. If he's
going to drop lengthwise I'll step over behind that house
twenty-five yards to the side. Back circled the pilot. This
time he shifted his axis thirty degrees and again the sacks
came straight for me. I moved over another twenty-five
yards but he came straight for me again. He was shooting
pretty close. He must be trying to get me, I thought. Okay,
I'll move once more. There was a tree behind which I had
stood during previous droppings. It had a trunk nine inches
thick. If the pilot threw them at me there, it would mean
he was dropping on an axis exactly ninety degrees from his
first throw. I stood a foot from the tree and peered out to
watch. He was heading straight for me. Just as the sacks
tumbled out I drew my body erect and turned sideways behind the tree. Sacks fanned my back and one struck squarely
in the fork of the tree beside my head. The tree bent with
the shock, hitting me on the point of my shoulder and frac-
turing the coracoid process of my scapula.

The pilot must have seen me tumbling down the hill,
for he didn't change his axis again. Chinese soldiers grabbed
me and put me in their trench while they stood guard over

me. This would have been little protection if the transport had "bombed" us again, but the soldiers seemed to think it more important for their *Lao E Guan* (old doc) to be safe than for themselves to keep out of harm's way.

A half hour after the bombing the medical detachment of the 151st Medical Battalion arrived. I had been worried about how to keep people from finding out about my shoulder. If I had to operate in the next few days some American might see something peculiar about the movements of my left shoulder and report me. Then brass hats would order me back to Ledo just as the campaign was getting under way. The arrival of the 151st boys meant I could use the ten days of marching back to Hkalak and Shingbwiyang in teaching myself how to handle that shoulder. I took the captain into my confidence and he strapped it into position with adhesive tape so I wouldn't be tempted to swing my arm as we marched. The next day went well. I had dreaded the climb up the precipice to Lulum but even here I had no trouble, for Pang Tze pushed me all the way to the top.

Traveling by double stages again, we reached Hkalak and found that Gurney and the girls there thought I had been wounded. They were more gently exuberant over my return than ever before. If I'd thought it would have the same effect on the nurses at Tagap, I'd have stayed out in the open and let the "bomber" pilot have one more chance at me!

It was hard leaving Hkalak and the Quartermaster boys. We had had happy times there. The boys came down to give us a farewell concert and of course they ended with their "masterpiece."

> High above the Chindwin River,
> Near the Taga Hka,
> Stands our dear old Alma Mater,
> Hail to Hkalak Ga!

And now the refugees were leaving the Naga Hills and going down into the famous Hukawng Valley for the real test as to whether or not Stilwell had been able to teach the Chinese to fight an offensive war to win. The colonials had reported few Japanese in the valley. It was thought a few battalions of the 38th would have no difficulty in pushing the Japs over the Tarung to the Tanai in a matter of three weeks. And certainly from what we heard at Shingbwiyang things seemed to be going according to plan, for the Chinese already had driven the Japs beyond Ningam to Yupbang. Grindlay had moved on to Ningam Sakan, and with my knees and shoulder it looked as if I would never catch up with him. Our morale was wonderful! Perhaps our return to Burma would take no longer and be no more difficult than our trek out with Stilwell!

But Grindlay was still at Ningam when we got there on November 11, 1943. Things had been moving so fast that we medics, at least, were certain we'd be marching on any day for Yupbang, Taihpa Ga, Maingkwan, and points southeast. Myitkyina by February, 1944, did not seem impossible at all. Since we were not going to be in Ningam long there was no use building new quarters. We used sheds with tarpaulin roofs and bamboo floors.

Grindlay had put up parachute tepees for an operating room and there were already three wards full of patients, for the unit had been quite busy during the first week in Ningam. The front line was in Yupbang about eight miles away. The road was not bad for foot travel. Evacuation of casualties from the front to Ningam was by regimental litter bearers. At Ningam we were to act both as a surgical hospital and as a clearing station, evacuating the most serious cases to the 151st Medical Battalion at Shingbwiyang by litter bearers of the Chinese Transport Company under Major Thrailkill. The litter bearers from the front did their work most efficiently; our patients reached us from three to five hours after being wounded. In front of us were no American medical personnel. The Chinese battalion medical officers gave excellent first aid and sent the patients back to us at once.

One of my first duties at Ningam was to build a fracture table and, since I had been unable to bring my Naga house along, to modify it so it could be made entirely out of bamboo. This proved quite successful, since it was possible to move the bamboos around to suit the patient rather than move the patient around to fit the posts and girders of the Naga house.

We had no electricity. Our Storm King gasoline lamps were of India make and cracked on their first lighting. We had six kerosene wick lanterns and some flashlights, but we could spare no personnel to hold the flashlights. However, in actual combat the U.S. Army was a huge family. Stationed in Ningam were a company of antiaircraft men and a company of airborne engineers, as well as a few Quartermaster and Signal Corps men. We didn't have to wait for a nurse to

141

notify us that a casualty had arrived. The American boys would spot a casualty a hundred yards away and come thundering in to hold flashlights, act as litter bearers, orderlies, or what not.

It now became known that the Japanese had many more troops in the area than the Chinese. Both sides were sparring for time. The fighting was not continuous and some days there were only six or seven casualties. We had plenty of time for relaxation and good fellowship. We swam in a little stream that ran by the hospital and sometimes grenaded for fish. All this, together with the success of the campaign to date, made us feel so cheerful that our previous misunderstandings were being ironed out and in another month we would all have been ourselves again.

And then the blow fell.

In his firm determination to be nowhere near the Chinese camp, Grindlay had chosen a site for the hospital downstream and completely outside the Chinese perimeter of defense. While the hospital was in this defenseless position a small Japanese patrol broke through between Yupbang and Kantow. The Japanese patrol was less than a mile from the hospital when intercepted by a Chinese patrol. Major Boag, the American liaison officer, promptly radioed General Boatner begging him to order the Burmese women to the rear, which General Boatner immediately did. The nurses realized that without their help we wouldn't be able to carry out our assignment and ten of the Hkalak girls begged the general to permit them to remain. Their request was granted, but the remainder marched back to Shingbwiyang.

Thus within a month of the actual beginning of the second Battle of Burma the nurses were as much as told that they weren't needed, that they couldn't be counted on to work under danger, and that in all probability the second campaign would be full of retreats like the first. So I was not surprised when at the end of December fourteen of the girls resigned from the unit and went back to India as refugees.

Losses never come singly. O'Hara had been refused a deserved promotion to a lieutenant colonelcy simply because our unit wasn't big enough to merit two lieutenant colonels. I had protested the fact that a superior officer like O'Hara should be penalized for being a member of a small unit. The army was O'Hara's career and he ought to have gotten his promotion even if it meant our losing him. Now his promotion came through. At the same time Major Grindlay and Lieutenant Chesley were transferred to Ledo, and later, because of long service in the theater, sent back to the States. To replace them we were given Major Milton A. Dushkin and Captain Bachmann; but the unit wasn't the same any more.

A peculiar thing was now holding up the Chinese attack: lack of cough medicine. The floor of the Hukawng Valley is less than a thousand feet above sea level, but it is a hundred air miles or more north of the Tropic of Cancer and there is a heavy damp fog blanket over the valley until late in the morning. The Chinese, never heavily clothed, in muddy cold trenches all night and day, suffered from bronchitis almost to the last man. By their incessant coughing they gave themselves and the Chinese positions away to the Japanese. Gallons and gallons of cough mixture—goodness only knows what the mixture contained—were finally issued and the situation improved rapidly.

And then General Stilwell himself came to town, and wherever Stilwell went something happened. In a very few days the Chinese began again to attack.

With Stilwell's arrival the triangle between Sharaw, Yupbang, and Ningam was cleared permanently of the enemy. Almost simultaneously the 22nd Division pulled a surprise encirclement on the Japs at Taro and wiped out the garrison. Annoyed that the 22nd had beat him to it, General Sun threw his men of the 38th Division into a final assault at Yupbang and captured that town. Many Americans wondered why the Battle of Yupbang was considered so important. It was not that the Chinese had demonstrated their ability to fight a prolonged offensive campaign at Yupbang. They had not. It took Taihpa Ga, Maingkwan, Mogaung, and Kamaing to do that. But to us Yupbang was important because here the Chinese passed their final examinations and graduated from the course of instruction Stilwell had begun for them at Ramgarh.

From Taihpa to Shaduzup, the Chinese would be having their postgraduate "internship," with the assistance of General Merrill and his famous Marauders. Then at Mogaung and with other engagements north of Mogaung, Colonel Lee and several other distinguished Chinese regimental commanders demonstrated conclusively that they had become expert tacticians. They proved, as Stilwell always claimed, that with proper food, training, and sufficient weapons the Chinese could really lick their weight in Japs.

143

I don't pose as a military genius. Whenever I'd say a word about military matters in General Boatner's hearing he'd burst into loud laughter and proclaim Doc Seagrave the world's worst strategist. Wherever in this book I make references to maneuvers of any sort, they must be understood for what they are: a doctor's ideas about a campaign he happened to take part in. And more, they are the ideas of a doctor to whom, aside from General Ted Wessels at Myitkyina, not one line officer ever told a single fact about what the blazes was going on.

In the fall of 1943 a swarm of unattached medical officers appeared in the theater unannounced, assigned by combat headquarters. Not knowing what to do with some of them at that time, General Boatner asked me how many I could use.

"Sir," I explained, "our nursing personnel is only sufficient to handle the work for the medical officers we now have. We can use as many more officers as you care to assign—providing you can give us ten enlisted men for each new officer."

General Boatner and Colonel Petersen undertook to find out whether we might be given the Table of Organization of a clearing company. In the meantime he sent us some fifteen men, many of whom had been with us in Ramgarh.

As these men came in, hitchhiking over the Refugee Trail, their barracks bags were free-dropped by airplane at Ningam. Air-dropping could be very funny. The parachutes on cases of corned beef and Spam never failed to open. But those on cases of peaches or coffee or milk frequently remained closed or their shroud lines ripped off and the supplies would come hurtling and crashing down. This had already happened to much of our stuff. Parachutes didn't open when they dropped the nurses' suitcases at Tagap. The shroud lines gave way on my own suitcase at Tagap, so on my vacation I invested in a new high-priced one and filled it with my most valuable stuff. When it was dropped at Hkalak the unopened parachute came down with it as a little packet, and the Quartermaster boys picked up my stuff from all over the field. A pressure sterilizer dropped at Tagap came down the same way, and it took Colonel O'Hara a month to fix it so it would hold steam. To see three shipments of canned beer free-dropped to the enlisted men at Tagap and Hkalak had been an experience, for the cans exploded and foamy beer fountained into the air and flowed off in tiny streams. Now our men's barracks bags were being dropped quite expertly—into the river.

Almost at the moment of losing the fourteen nurses, we discovered two of our other old girls, one in India and one in China. Naomi had come for training to Namkham in 1932. She was a Taungthu girl with a fine sense of humor, a born mimic; she was also the best educated girl I had trained. She remained in Namkham as head nurse for two years after graduation. But she had several younger brothers and sisters, one of whom was Nang Aung (Miss Wang), who needed education, and she left our Namkham hospital to work in the civil hospital at Taunggyi where the government paid her more than twice what I could afford.

When the British evacuated Taunggyi they gave Naomi twenty-four hours to bid her folks goodbye. She hurried to her home village only to find that her father and mother were away on a visit so, without seeing them, she was flown from Shwebo to Calcutta, and later was evacuated to the Punjab where she lived a completely humdrum existence on a small pittance from the Burmese Government. One day, languidly turning the pages of a London illustrated weekly, she was startled to see pictures of myself and the nurses at work "somewhere in India." For months she searched for an American officer who could tell her where we were. Finally, long after we had left Ramgarh she was given the Ramgarh address.

And now in January, 1944, we had her back as chief nurse. Like a good chief nurse, Naomi watched quietly for several weeks, relearning our American ways and studying the psychology of the younger nurses. She was intensely annoyed at the trifling complaints of the nurses who had left, because she knew what real trouble was. She was some six or eight years older than the other nurses, and when she had them diagnosed she began to win their friendship by displaying her old sense of humor, mimicking everyone in sight. The girls began to call her Grandma.

One day when a younger girl was nearing the ragged edge of control and in a few more minutes would have had a tempest well organized in her teapot, Grandma Naomi suddenly exploded with a gruff "*S'taing ga!*"

"What do you mean?" the girl asked, startled.

"*S'taing ga!* You're posing!"

The girl thought it over, recognized the correctness of the diagnosis, laughed, and it was all over.

145

S'taing is the Burmese transliteration of our word "style." To the occidental, style is important. It changes every year or every month and one must change with it. In other words, one must pose as everyone else is posing at the moment. To the oriental mind, style, which is a temporary custom, is perfectly ridiculous and something to be embarrassed about. Custom, the custom of your ancestors for generations, which the Burmese and every other race in Burma call *htonzan*, is everything. To give up the *htonzans* of centuries for the *s'taing* of the moment is disgusting or at the very least laughable. *S'taing ga!* from now on became a byword of the unit. The enlisted men used it as well as the nurses and officers. Everyone's delinquency, from that of the old man down, was recognized as a pose and laughed off.

The other girl to come back was Wasay, who entered training four years later than Grandma Naomi. A Karen girl of strong physique, almost never ill, priding herself on being able to stand as much as a man any day, Wasay had been in charge of my Kokang hospital on the east of the Salween River, the largest of my branch hospitals. When the Japanese attacked Rangoon in 1942, she stayed with her job till she heard that the Japs had broken through the Chinese Sixth Army and were on their way to Lashio. Then she set off on foot hoping to join me at Namkham ahead of the Japs.

When she reached the Salween crossing at Kunlong she found, to her dismay, that the Japanese were already on the other side of the river—so she hurried back to Kokang, hastily collected the most important drugs still in her possession, and, with her assistant nurse and the Karen pastor and his family, hurried out to the Lisu Mountains just as the enemy pulled in.

Finally in December, 1943, an American liaison officer discovered Wasay and, through Colonel Condon and General Dorn, radioed me asking if I wanted her. I replied that I certainly did. Wasay found a horse, rode many days until she reached the Burma Road east of Paoshan and was given a jeep ride to Kunming to catch a plane for Shingbwiyang. She was rather ragged when she arrived and it took about three months to get her over her experiences, but as assistant chief nurse she became most useful.

During the cold season the Hukawng Valley is very cold and very wet at night. A fairly large number of casualties occurred during the battle that resulted in the final capture of Yupbang. Shock had reached alarming proportions by the time casualties reached us. We now had a new operating shed, covered by a forty-foot-square tarpaulin, in which were six operating tables. We built four more shock tables with very low head ends in front of the operating room. On these tables the casualties were given plasma and other treatments for shock before being taken to the operating tables. One of our boys put up a smaller tarpaulin in the form of a tent heated by a gasoline stove, where our blankets were hung and brought out warm to cover the chilled bodies of the casualties. A small-power light unit reached us, and the boys made blackout shades out of empty No. 10 cans. My third "Hukawng Model" fracture table was more of a success than the earlier models, but the American boys immediately introduced some improvements of their own. Tired of continually running after the *hkai shwei* (hot water) which the Chinese demanded all day and all night, the nurses filled empty plasma bottles or enema cans with water and hung them to the roof beside each patient, with the rubber tube within easy reach of his mouth so that he could suck to his heart's content.

With the Japanese wiped out at Sharaw, Yupbang, and Taro, the next objective was the triangular area of ground between the Tarung and the Tanai, which form the Chindwin River, and the village of Taihpa Ga, which guards the motor-road crossing of the Tanai. So far the Japanese hadn't worried much about Stilwell's Chinese accomplishing more than a pinprick. Now they threw in a good part of the Japanese 18th Division, which had helped capture Singapore, and pulled up some 150-mm. guns.

The entire Chinese 38th Division was now in the main Hukawng thrust and officers were busy training new replacements from China. One regiment was in garrison at Ningam, one began the sweep down the triangle from the Sharaw-Yupbang line toward Taihpa Ga, and the third was ordered to cross the Chindwin at Kantow to outflank the Japanese in the Taihpa area. A detachment of our unit was ordered to accompany these troops in the Kantow flank. Captain Gurney and Captain Antonellis, Dr. Ba Saw and Dr. Taubenfliegl went on this mission with our enlisted men. On the arrival of Major Royster from the 20th General Hospital, the command of the group was turned over to him. Not only was Royster a great surgeon; he was a born teacher as well. In their six weeks of surgery with Royster, Antonellis and Ba Saw learned more surgery than they'd thought it possible to know. Royster made himself the "assistant" and the young men the "great surgeons" and their self-confidence increased immeasurably.

Dr. Taubenfliegl was a Polish contract surgeon. At the beginning of the war in Spain he joined a medical unit with the Republican Army and served till the end of the war, after which, with other foreign doctors, German, Czechoslovakian, and Polish, he was evacuated to China. There the group spent troublous years serving the Chinese armies, with little or nothing in the way of equipment and medical supplies. All spoke Chinese well and had learned how to live with the Chinese and like it. Under Stilwell they had been transferred to Ramgarh to work as liaison officers with the Chinese regiments. Taubenfliegl was a grand person to have around. Although he had taken punishment the like of which few American officers have ever experienced, he was never known to complain and had a sense of humor that was leaven to the whole group. At Myitkyina when Colonel Petersen offered me my choice of any liaison medical officer as a permanent addition to our unit I chose Taubenfliegl.

The remainder of our unit continued to run the clearing station at Ningam until the first echelon of the 25th Field Hospital could set up a semipermanent hospital there. A surgical unit of the 25th was hurried forward to newly captured Yupbang. Major Thrailkill, post commandant at Ningam, thought that this team, setting up for the first time in the jungle, might be saved a great deal of trouble if one of my officers were to go along with them in an advisory capacity. I selected my executive officer, Major Dushkin, a fire-eater who seemed determined to take vengeance on the Japanese for all the sins of the Axis against the Hebrew race.

Dushkin and Bill Brough reported to Thrailkill the next morning and started off with the detachment.

The Japanese seemed determined to keep them from building anything permanent. Howitzer shells came over at regular intervals. Dushkin and his men got underground in short order and had enough dugouts to accommodate us all by the time we arrived. For the first and only time in the war we lived underground with sand in our hair for days, while we built wards and bamboo shacks. Since it was most painful and most un-American to the entire army for me to have no fancy domicile in which to live, Pang Tze and the Burmese boys built me another charming twelve-foot-square bungalow.

Pushed across the Tanai at Taihpa Ga by the 38th Division,

148

the Japs now began to run, and not till the Battle of Myit-kyina did any semipermanent medical installation catch up with Stilwell's front line.

Even Dushkin wasn't convinced that the 150's were gone for good. He found a stray bulldozer wandering down the road one day and borrowed it to scoop out a huge underground ward. The bulldozer did its work in a day and Dushkin threw his hundred Chinese labor corpsmen into the job of roofing it. They had it half finished when we were ordered on. The men couldn't decide what the major had built, a garage, a ward, a swimming pool, or a garbage pit. Whatever it was, it was gorgeous. We named it Dushkin's Folly.

The name Brambrang stands out in my memory as the place where our unit's basic equipment finally caught up with us. Colonel Williams, the theater surgeon, had ordered a clearing company minus personnel in August, 1942. We were told the equipment had left the States in October. In February, 1943, we learned the ship had been sunk and that Williams had ordered us another complete outfit. At long last, our equipment rolled into Brambrang, but almost immediately the men of the unit were ordered on flank moves and had no chance to use the equipment or ride in the vehicles—and the main unit went into an eclipse that lasted for two months.

For the Battle of Taihpa Ga was over. The Japanese had been thrown back on Maingkwan, capital of the Hukawng. From now on the 22nd Division would be responsible for the main drive down the valley, reinforced by Colonel Rothwell Brown's tanks, while the 38th Division, spearheaded by General Merrill's Marauders, took responsibility for the wide left flank and its encircling moves. We turned over our hospital to the 25th Field Hospital and moved to the south bank of the Tanai to vegetate.

Our unit sat on the Tanai with the war going by all around us and with not a thing to do. I sent off six girls at a time for a two weeks' rest in Calcutta. With San Yee, Antonellis, and Dr. Kish, another contract surgeon, to help me, I would still have a powerhouse to go into action if and when I could persuade someone somewhere to want us.

Our supreme commander, Admiral Lord Louis Mount-batten, put on a little show for us, one day, coming personally to inspect what Stilwell was doing. Lord Louis hinted that before long the British would be giving Stilwell the support he deserved.

Next morning I was standing bored and despondent at

149

the entrance to our area when Stilwell's aide, Captain Young, drove a jeep in; and there was a patient for me, Lord Louis himself! He had been driving when a bamboo had sprung loose and struck him across the left eye. Examination showed a hemorrhage in the anterior chamber of the eye. Here was real trouble. Stilwell had long waited for the admiral to come and watch the Chinese in action, travel over the Ledo Road, and see how well the Americans had accomplished the "impossible." And now, before the admiral could see either the Chinese or the road, it was my certain duty either to send him back to Ledo by air to Captain Scheie, the ophthalmologist at the 20th General Hospital, or else be responsible for the loss of the eye. There was no question at all that Lord Louis was as unhappy to be sent back as I was to send him. But the nurses were thrilled at having a chance, however slight, to serve a cousin of their king.

One noon a radio message arrived: Merrill's Marauders had captured Walawbum on the motor road fifteen miles beyond Maingkwan, only thirty minutes behind schedule. About a mile east of Walawbum the Americans had come to the edge of a rice field across which the Japanese were entrenched. The Marauders were not green troops. They set up machine guns, screamed tauntingly, "Tojo eat ——! Tojo eat ——!" and mowed down the Japs as they sprang to the defense of Tojo's lost reputation.

With the establishment of Merrill's roadblock, the Chinese 22nd Division rushed into action spearheaded by Rothwell Brown's tanks, and for the first time in Burma the Japanese were massacred. Headquarters moved immediately to Maingkwan and I obtained permission to move forward to a new bivouac on the Nambyu River near Walawbum. My first act was to put up a sign, "SEAGRAVE UNIT," hoping that the powers that be might see it and give us a job.

Our new bivouac area was as nice as a bivouac area *can* be. The Nambyu is a medium-sized stream, clear, fresh, and deep enough to provide good swimming. We were on an old village site. No houses remained but there was a parade ground, almost like a lawn, where we played baseball. Orchids were in bloom and the girls brought in lovely clusters of gold and purple ones that would have been worth a fortune in the United States. The country was beginning to look a bit like Burma at last. There were actually a few fruit trees, mangoes, lemons, and pomelos, even raspberries and a few poor-quality plantains. These, together with fresh fish, when

150

we could beg a grenade from someone, gave us a welcome change from corned beef and Spam.

There was always plenty for me to think about in the Nambyu bivouac, even though a feeling of helpless uselessness is not conducive to constructive thinking. Pamphlets kept coming to me continually from the government of Burma at Simla containing charming pictures of prewar Burma and the government's idea of the kind of propaganda against the Japs worthy of being distributed to the Burmese refugees. The pictures, presenting as they did scenes that will never be the same again, brought an unbearable nostalgia. The publishers undoubtedly realized the scenes would never be the same, for the theme of the pictures was, "Look what the Japs are desecrating!" And how did they happen to be desecrating Burma? It takes two parties for an invasion to be successful: a strong invader and a weak, unprepared defender. The invader is wicked in sins of commission but the weak defender is wicked in sins of omission.

My unhappy thoughts at the Nambyu bivouac were not entirely caused by the apparent determination of the Burmese Government to learn nothing from the "hell of a licking" given them by the Japs.

Letters began to come from good Baptists back home in America who were very shocked that a few cusswords had been reported in my book, *Burma Surgeon*.

It seems to me that swearing is sometimes a very excellent safety valve and keeps one sane and on the job. At other times it amounts to a prayer and I am convinced God recognizes many oaths as such. If one couldn't see God in that story of mine he wouldn't believe me if I'd protested on every page. Somehow it never seemed to me that a man proved his real Christianity just by proclaiming it to the world in a loud voice.

In Namkham we had Bible study out of school hours and many Buddhist children came early just to be present. If no one wanted to be converted I didn't care, for we were thinking in terms of generations. I don't love people who become "Christian" too easily. I never required any of my Buddhist nurses to go to our religious services. As a result they went to all of them.

While all these things were going through my mind, the Chinese Army gave Stilwell a birthday present of the Jambu Bum Pass into the Mogaung Valley, and headquarters moved to Tingkawk Sakan. The battle of the Hukawng was over; the

151

armies were at last in real Burma, but we, the refugees, were left stranded in the horrible, dark, foul, stinking no man's land they call the Hukawng.

"Girls," I said, "we are nothing but a bastard unit now: no papa, no mama, no brother, no sister, no friends—backsheesh!"

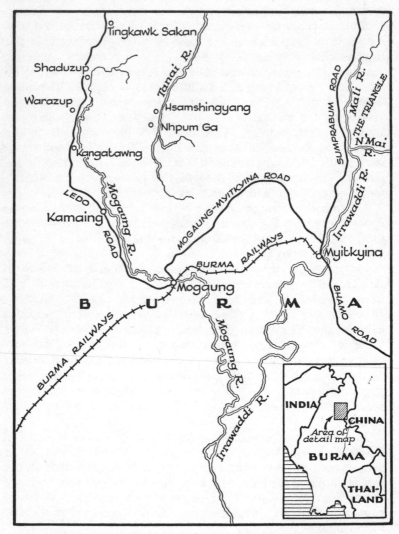

LEDO ROAD FROM TINGKAWK SAKAN TO MYITKYINA

14 MYITKYINA! MYITKYINA!

I HAD another birthday at the Nambyu River. Our Special Service radio was working for once and gave me a most wonderful birthday present: news of the airborne landings of General Wingate's Chindits behind the Japanese lines in Burma. Lord Louis had kept his promise. Stilwell was receiving a bit of support at last.

I was worried about rumors that Stilwell was flying in some new Chinese divisions. It would have been entirely in keeping with army thought at that time to push me back to process those divisions rather than give the Burmese girls a combat assignment. So I pretended that our unit would remain assigned to the 38th Division and went forward to contact Dushkin and select a site.

Walking up a tributary of the Mogaung River I bumped into Dushkin.

"I thought you'd be coming after us!" he said. Never have I been paid a better compliment.

I took Dushkin back with me, arranging to send back transportation for our men the following day. At Tingkawk I reported to Colonel Petersen, realizing that I was in for it.

"The 50th Chinese Division is being flown into Maingkwan this week," he said. "The Seagrave Unit will proceed to Maingkwan at once and open up a hospital for them."

That meant we had to retreat again, this time twenty miles.

"It's your own fault," Dushkin said. "You said in your book that you asked Stilwell to give you the nastiest jobs he had."

"Okay," I said. "I'll shut up."

God bless those girls! They could see that the old man was heartbroken about it and not one of them griped. Their co-operation at Maingkwan was immense. From that point on our unit perhaps proved itself worthy of General Stilwell's tolerance of us. We had lost fourteen of our girls, but from Maingkwan on we turned out a bigger job than we ever did with the original unit except during the first two months at Ramgarh.

It was plain that Stilwell wanted us to do as we had at Ramgarh: get the sick into wards as rapidly as possible, cure them, and rush them out again for combat. We couldn't do this effectively unless we held sick call ourselves. Holding sick call would be a horrible job for our few officers and nurses in addition to ward work, but if we had been chosen because the job was important to Uncle Joe, extra work was nothing to complain about. Only one officer did complain. I added insult to injury by sending our trucks to the Chinese camp to pick up outpatients. That was a bit of shrewd psychology because these were Chinese who had seldom seen or ridden in a truck and lots of patients came with minor complaints just for the ride. The doctors sorted them out rapidly until we had three hundred beds filled, the number I had calculated a new Chinese division would need. There were an additional three hundred in sick call every day.

More than a hundred of our worst cases had very severe relapsing fever. Since the Chinese had been deloused in Chabua as they changed planes, we had the perfect chance to wipe out relapsing fever immediately, before the Chinese again acquired lice and spread the disease among Stilwell's fighting troops. The relapsing fever was the worst I'd seen, and there was a small epidemic of pneumonia also acquired by troops in a weakened condition flying over the Hump. We cured the two diseases when they occurred separately but lost a dozen cases that had both diseases simultaneously. Malaria wasn't too bad. Beriberi was present even in April, two months before the beriberi season, for these troops were half starved. Many of the beriberi cases were partly paralyzed. Luckily for them we had secured a large shipment of thiamine which resulted in visible improvement daily, while thousands of multiple vitamin tablets soon wiped out the rest of the beriberi. During the real season for the disease at Myitkyina we had only a few of the minor cases and no severe beriberi.

The new Chinese needed Indian-type typhoid and cholera vaccines as well as smallpox. Liaison officers lined the men up by the regiment and we went to town in the old Namkham way. As we gave the shots we found no plump Chinese but many emaciated ones. After one week of good and oversufficient food the Chinese came back for their second injections without that starved look. In the wards it was the same as at Ramgarh. Patients fattened so rapidly that their intestines didn't have sufficient room to circulate freely in their abdomens and they were continually whining about abdominal pain. Apparently none of Stilwell's new Chinese had had full bellies on consecutive days since birth. Now their abdominal weight increased more rapidly than that of a woman during pregnancy.

Just after we passed our peak Colonel Petersen came to visit us. Merrill's Marauders were crossing the range to attack Myitkyina from the north. They were to be supported by a regiment of the 30th Division of Ramgarh-trained Chinese, with whom he was sending the U.S. 42 Portable Surgical Hospital, as well as by a regiment of the 50th Division, with whom I was ordered to send a medical detachment from our unit, composed of men only. As we polished off the 50th Division, I was to evacuate the chronics and bivouac until Colonel Petersen found something for us to do. Dreading another bivouac I begged for permission to hold onto our chronics so we might have something to do. Petersen agreed, but warned me that he might have to order us to move suddenly. Sudden moves didn't frighten me; what did were sudden and prolonged sits.

Early on the morning of May 17, 1944, as I was tossing sleeplessly on my bed wishing it were time to get up and that there were something special to do when I did get up, one of those incredible hunches hit me. Something was cooking. I hustled the boys out of bed and ordered them to evacuate all our remaining patients to the Chinese regimental hospital. While they emptied the wards, the nurses, our few Chinese, our Burmese boys, and I pulled the tents down and rolled them up. When the trucks returned we loaded them with equipment for a surgical hospital. Everyone thought the old man had gone mad.

After breakfast the following morning I sat waiting for the telephone to ring. It rang at eight-fifteen. On the other end of the wire was Colonel Petersen.

"How long will it take you to evacuate your patients?"

"I evacuated them all yesterday, sir."

"How soon can you start for the airfield at Maingkwan?"

"In an hour!"

"Hurry down there. Three C-47's have been assigned to pick you up."

"Yes, sir. Goodbye!"

"One suitcase and one bedroll each," I shouted. "We leave at once."

I was the last to be ready and even then a couple of the girls had to help me. Fifty-five minutes after the telephone rang we were at the field. Hour after hour passed. Planes were darkening the sky and a few landed on our field but

155

they were on other missions. They had never heard of Seagrave. At noon the boys we were leaving behind with our equipment and vehicles brought us down a hot meal.

A liaison plane flew in and circled to land. "That's Colonel Petersen," I said to one of the boys. "Meet him and show him where we are." Those were my psychic days.

"What made you think it was I?" the colonel asked.

"I know you fairly well, sir. I knew you would come if you could steal a plane."

"That's just what I had to do. Yesterday Merrill's men took the Myitkyina airfield. You will report to Colonel Hunter."

"Yes, sir. Will I have to radio you for instructions as to evacuations and so forth?"

"Whatever medical measures need to be taken in the Myitkyina area will be determined by you," the colonel replied. "You are to arrange the entire medical setup with Colonel Hunter."

"Yes, sir."

"The planes seem to be held up. Medical needs are third priority today. I will have to return this stolen plane at once."

"Lieutenant Harris will telephone you when we leave, sir."

The boys played horseshoes. The girls fluttered around here and there looking for fruit. I sat. I had sat so many months I felt I could tolerate a bit more without going mad, for Myitkyina—Myitkyina!—was at the end of this wait.

Out of a jeep climbed a Chinese in an American uniform, covered with dust that had caked with his sweat.

"Are you Colonel Seagrave, sir?" he asked.

"Yes."

"I'm Corporal Wing, sir. Medical Department. Colonel Breidster assigned me to your unit and I have just come in from Ledo."

"Are you an American-Chinese?"

"Yes, sir."

"You're Cantonese, aren't you?"

"Yes, sir."

"Then you don't speak Mandarin?"

"Yes, I do, sir."

"You don't write Chinese, do you?"

"Yes, I do, sir."

"Somebody catch me while I faint! Where's your barracks bag?"

"Here, sir."

156

"Stick around. We're leaving for Myitkyina any moment. What do you know about medicine?"

"I'm a dental technician, sir."

"You aren't any longer. You're registration clerk to the Seagrave unit. God help you. I'm going to work you to death. A Chinese-American who speaks Mandarin and Cantonese and writes Chinese as well! God is good! God is good!"

Little Bawk had too much thyroid secretion for her own good. About four o'clock she came to me for the umpteenth time.

"Darn it, Daddy, why don't the planes come?"

"I don't know, I tell you. Listen, woman. Everything that's happened during the last two days shows that the good Lord is at last taking an interest in us again. I don't like to wait any more than you do, but I'm willing to bet you real money that when we get to Myitkyina we'll find that it was a good thing we didn't get there any sooner."

A C-47 circled in to land. After it had taken off again one of the Signal Corps boys from Hkalak sauntered over.

"Sir," he said, "the radio reporter on that plane says the Japanese bombed and strafed the Myitkyina field a little while ago. An American casualty that was being put on the hospital plane was killed and an American nurse shot in the leg."

"Bawk," I yelled, "just listen to this!"

We didn't have much longer to wait. A plane landed and the pilot admitted that he had heard of Seagrave. A third of the nurses, a third of the Burmese boys, a third of the supplies, and I got on board. Johnson, Ba Saw, and San Yee would come in the other two planes.

I looked down on those awful hills as we crossed the Chindwin-Irrawaddi divide: the hills that our men had negotiated on foot. Then I felt my still-creaking knee joints. And I thought the Lord didn't care about me any more, I thought, shamefacedly.

A railroad. The Burma Railways. The Irrawaddi again. Myitkyina. Myitkyina airfield from which half the unit had taken off for India two years before. The refugees are back again in real Burma. God is good!

We circled the field. What if a Jap sniper did hit us now? We were in Burma. I had always wanted to die in Burma.

A smashed C-47: was anyone hurt? Several crushed gliders: I hoped the passengers weren't killed. A Zero half buried in the ground: our boys got to work in a hurry.

157

We landed. Burma at last. Burma. Burma!

"Where will I find Colonel Hunter?" I asked a nonchalant American soldier.

"Across the field, sir," he said, pointing.

Hunter was minus a front tooth and wasn't ashamed of it. He was a real American officer who cared about nothing but the job in hand.

"Lieutenant Colonel Seagrave reporting, sir. Seagrave Hospital Unit. Four medical officers and eighteen Burmese nurses. Where do you want us to set up, sir?"

"My God! Women!"

How often I had heard that phrase shouted in joy! But Colonel Hunter's tone was one of complete disgust: hadn't he had enough trouble?

"We ask for no special security, sir," I said.

"Go over to the revetment next to the first-aid station across the field. I suppose you want rations. I haven't had enough food for seven days."

"We have three days' rations with us, sir," I said. "We shall be glad to share them with you."

"No, thanks. We'll get along."

"Yes, sir," I saluted and took my leave.

It was about four hundred yards from our plane to the revetment that Colonel Hunter had assigned us.

Ba Saw's and Johnson's planes parked near our revetment. The airstrip was lit up by flares, for planes were coming in all night. Snipers' bullets whizzed over us as we carried our equipment down the field piece by piece but the refugees didn't care. They were back in real Burma at last. We laid a tarpaulin over some upright litters and crawled in. Only two casualties came in during the night and they were dead on arrival.

Our first task was to boil our instruments and set up operating tables for casualties. Anything approximating an operating room was out of the question. There wasn't a bamboo or a stick anywhere to support a tarpaulin. We set packing cases up with litters across them for operating tables and were soon ready to go. Before long the Chinese found us, and Ba Saw, San Yee, Johnson, and I were busy. At noon Dushkin and Gurney arrived with their detachment, the thinnest, dirtiest, weariest bunch of men I'd seen for a long time. The sun was blistering hot and our skins began to burn, for we were naked to the waist. Then a squall of rain blew up and a nurse held an umbrella over the operative field while I removed a man's shattered spleen.

Dushkin immediately began acting as triage officer, and Gurney and Antonellis, tired as they were, set up two more litters and joined in. Our men stretched electric wire over upright litters, cut holes in empty No. 10 cans to act as blackout shades and as night fell we had electricity. The men put up several parachute tepees for patients, while they covered others with ground sheets. We operated on one hundred and twenty patients that day and crawled under our tarps with patients all around us.

On our second full day the men put up three operating rooms of triple-layer parachutes and several more tepees for patients. On Sunday evening the Japs began throwing 70-mm. howitzer shells at us. Colonel Hunter thought us too close to the field so on the fifth day we moved two hundred yards nearer town. Here there was a much larger and higher revetment, the best near the field.

The only fault with the revetment lay in the fact that it was on lower ground than the rest of the area. The only drainage was into the huge pits outside, from which earth had been taken to form the revetments. The drainage ditch by the operating tables was continuously running red with blood, and the pits soon became unspeakably foul—so also was the mud we churned up as we operated. On wet days the mud was ankle deep but didn't stink quite so much, while on hot days the mud dried and stank. One night during a heavy downpour a huge ditch in front of us collapsed and all the water from the airfield, instead of being carried away, flowed into our area, filling the pits and our revetment a foot deep. By morning our suitcases and shoes had floated some distance away. But the accident flushed out our stench very properly.

About a week after we reached Myitkyina, Sein Myaing, one of our nurses who lived in that town, heard from her uncle that our unit was back in Burma again. One dawn she made him lead her out from Myitkyina through the Japanese and Chinese lines. I could understand the Japanese letting them through, for at that time they were anxious to get civilians out of the way. But I couldn't understand why the Chinese didn't shoot them down. Sein Myaing's nonchalance was amazing.

When we came out of Burma, Sein Myaing had been a bit fed up with me because I had chosen her as one of those to stay behind and help run the Namkham hospital for a few months rather than go to the front, little realizing that the battle would be over almost as soon as it started. There were other things, too. So when, on my instructions, Bill Cummings told the nurses at Namkham to decide whether they wanted to fly to India or stay in Burma, Sein Myaing decided to stay, and set off for her home in Myitkyina. The first Japanese commander there was a Christian and had enforced order among his troops, treated the people with kindness, and even organized Christian services on Sunday. Sein Myaing had been ordered to serve in a hospital for civilians in town and had been well treated.

After the refugee nurses had almost hugged her to death, Sein Myaing gave us the surprising news that Sein Hla Tha, headmaster of my Anglo-Vernacular Middle School at Namkham, had been in Myitkyina the night before the airfield was taken. Impressed by the Japs to act as interpreter he had come straight up there from Namkham, starting for the south just as the Americans came in. So Sein Myaing was crammed with news of Namkham, and very fresh news, too.

"Your own bungalow is untouched and the Japanese general lives there," she said to me. "One wing of the nurses' home has been hit by a bomb but no bomb has yet touched the hospital. On the other hand, the Japs have torn up floors and wooden walls and doors and windows and have used them for firewood and to build sheds." This after we had obligingly left the Japs more than a hundred cords of firewood conveniently cut and stacked!

Not long after that epidsode, a Kachin scout serving the Americans across the river was flown to us in a liaison plane with a minor injury. As I was treating him I discovered to my astonishment that he was Toi Roi's older brother.

"Doesn't Toi Roi want to come back and work with us?" I asked.

"She will when she learns you're here," he replied.

"Can you get her down to your American officers? If you can they will fly her to us."

"I'll try."

Three days later, in walked Toi Roi. She was pale and thin and told a long story of semistarvation and malaria, with no drugs available for treatment. It was good to see her again. Then one day Nang Seng No. 2 and Nang Seng No. 3 herself appeared together. No. 3, whose husband was in Rangoon studying medicine, was nursing in the government's new hospital for civilians. No. 2 had several children, acquired since she had been forced some years before to stop training and marry a man who didn't want her.

160

I was especially glad to see Nang Seng No. 2. I had a problem to talk over with her.

"The nurses are wasting too much time on jobs that require no skill," I said. "Don't you think you can find some boys and girls who would like to work for us? I'll pay them five rupees more per month than the army pays coolies. They will have good food and a civilized place to sleep and Christian people to work with. If they prove to have the knack of nursing they may go on with us when we leave Myitkyina or stay behind if they choose. Even if they stay with us only while we're in Myitkyina, they'll pick up enough nursing to be a help with their families all their lives."

Not many days later Nang Seng appeared trailing three Karen girls, three Kachin girls, and a couple of Karen boys after her. One of the girls was her own sister, Nang Pri. Soon girls began to trickle in by ones and twos and a few more boys appeared. One day Ohn Hkin's entire family walked in from a village north of town and left Ohn Hkin's younger sister Ohn Yin to work with us. Even Hkawn Tawng turned up, with a sheepish grin on her face for having married the wrong man, and left her twelve-year-old-sister Roi Ji with us. I hardly recognized Roi Ji with her short hair and boy's clothes. Like Hkawn Tawng she had a fascinating smile and a mincing way of walking as if she were wearing high heels. This, in a twelve-year-old, presaged years of heartbreak for the males of her world.

And then a Karen doctor, Mildred Pan Hla, walked in and asked for a job. Working in the government civil hospital at Lashio she had started on the run a few jumps ahead of the Japanese, who caught up with her at Myitkyina. The Japanese refused to recognize her medical degree and orderd her to work as a nurse.

All of our new additions were useful. Having lived through American bombings and shellings they paid no attention whatever to Japanese 70's.

On the day the airfield was captured it seemed that Myitkyina would be ours within a week. We were told on good authority that the Japanese had actually evacuated Myitkyina except for snipers, not knowing just how big a force Stilwell had thrown against them. But Colonel Hunter had only his depleted, weakened Marauders and two regiments of Chinese, who also were not only tired out from their forced march over the mountains but were fighting their first battle. There had not been nearly enough troops to guarantee both airfield and town against unknown odds. Of the two, the airstrip was by far the more important. So while we hurriedly flew in reinforcements, the Japs moved back into Myitkyina and dug in. We had to fight for it, blast and burn the enemy out of their dugouts under road and river embankments and deep under huge banian trees and bamboos.

15   SURGERY AT THE AIRSTRIP

WITH a long battle ahead of us we organized our work to the peak of efficiency possible in the jungle. Two operating tables for each officer cut down the time lag for surgeons, until they had time for only half a cigarette between operations, during which they had to write up the previous case on the inevitable toilet paper to send back to base with the patient the next day. To make our surgical instruments go further and save time of nursing personnel, we set up one large instrument table at the angle of the V-shaped operating room, like the serving counter of a huge restaurant, from which "short orders" were served out at a moment's notice to the first assistants of the surgeons at all tables. Two nurses were on full-time duty with plasma and glucose, getting shocked pattients into condition for operation and keeping them alive as we operated on them. One Chinese sailor ran the autoclave all day, sterilizing linen washed free of blood by two of our soldier-orderlies. Two other Chinese orderlies were continually hauling water to keep our G.I. cans filled. Two nurses injected each new arrival with morphine, atropine, and tetanus antitoxin, reporting the nature of wounds and the patient's general condition to Major Dushkin, who acted as triage officer and assigned cases to the individual surgeon's tables. Nurses who were not assigned elsewhere cut and folded gauze into sponges. At least we didn't have to wash out and use again the blood-soaked gauze, as we did in the first campaign. Sergeants Probst and Stolec organized the men into the "Myitkyina Plasterers' Union," and soon they were putting on plaster casts most efficiently, with only an occasional glance from the surgeon. This proved its value one day when there were fifteen hip spicas to be put on men with badly shattered thighs. Two men with hand brushes and basins of soap and water rushed from table to table as patients were anesthetized, scrubbing out the wounds and cleaning skins of the mud and grime of war. Then nurses applied

162

alcohol and iodine, draped towels, and the surgeons began to cut.

And up and down the operating room were cries for "Grandma. Grandma!" "Pang Tze. Pang Tze. Pang Tze!" "Wing. Wing. Corporal Wing. G.I. Wing!" as the three most essential people in the unit were called to straighten out difficulties everywhere at once. Grandma Naomi, unruffled, calm, efficient, pulling wisecracks in two or three languages, stood in the angle of the V, supervising the cleaning and re-sterilization of instruments, assigning nurses and American, English, Burmese, and Chinese technicians to scrub up as operative assistants or to anesthetize patients, smoothing ruf-fled feelings, and always casting a critical eye around to spot some gross break in technique on the part of the younger personnel.

"Pang Tze, get this patient off the table for me and bring me another, will you?" "Pang Tze, scrub!" "Pang Tze, hold this leg for me!" "Pang Tze, *tang cha ping* [litter bearers], *tang cha ping!*" "Pang Tze, I want a box to sit on. My back is breaking!" And again and again, "Pang Tze, what the Sam Hill was the number of that last patient I operated on?" And Pang Tze, running for a look at the strip of adhesive glued to the patient's forehead, would shout back, *"Sickasa fifa tree!"* or, *"Nina sickasati pour!"* Poor Pang Tze's hard-earned fat began to melt out of his pores and he hitched his belt a quarter of an inch tighter every day.

Wing was the only person we'd ever had in the unit who could write Chinese. Until he came we'd never tried to get the patient's name for our records. We'd tried it at Ram-garh, spelling out the name as best we could in English, but no two people spelled the names the same way, and no mat-ter who had written the name, the patient wouldn't recog-nize it when read back to him. But Wing took over our admission clerk's work and wrote the names in Chinese, and his records were a pleasure to work with. If he'd been a lesser man he'd have gone insane those weeks at the field. While admitting one patient or preparing him for evacua-tion, other casualties would come in behind his back. Be-cause the surgeons could allow no time lag before beginning the operation, Wing was in continual demand.

Two nights after we moved to the larger revetment, we had just crawled into bed when an incredible storm of wind and rain hit us and nearly blew away our tents. Every bit of starlight was blotted out of the sky. Suddenly, as the storm swept past, there was a tremendous burst of machine-gun

163

fire all around us, the lighter, snappier noise of the Japanese small-calibered weapons. Then the clatter of the heavier American-made weapons replied, as the Americans and Chinese opened fire. Even the machine guns of the English antiaircraft battery just across the way from the open, unprotected side of our revetment began to blaze away, and we knew it was the real thing and not hysteria. These English were old-timers who had seen action all over the world. Tracers streaked over us from all directions. One Japanese machine-gun squad had sneaked up under cover of the storm and was located between us and the landing strip.

But there was no panic. Dushkin quickly assigned men to sentry positions and to barricades of packing cases at the entrance to the revetment, while the nurses crowded around me for whispered instructions. "Get down flat on your beds at this end of your tent," I ordered. "No lights, no talking. Two girls on each cot."

Hours later, when the shooting had died away, I told the girls to climb back into their own beds. As Ruby and Louise brushed past me I noticed they were sopping wet and muddy and shaking with cold.

"What on earth happened to you?" I asked.

"You told us to get down flat, so we did—under the other girls' cots!"

Soon there was shuffling and a muttered curse that sounded like Chinese, then a fierce challenge in Chinese from Bill Brough. If Brough was taking care of them it was all right, for he was a crack shot. We breathed easily again. Minutes later Bill crawled under the tent wall. "Chinese litter bearers with a casualty," he said. "I thought they might be masquerading Japanese so I asked them where their home towns in China were. They knew their geography and their Chinese accent was all right so I let them in. The casualty has only a flesh wound and will keep till morning. I gave him plasma. We can't have lights anyway."

Those Chinese litter bearers deserve a lot of credit. They worked under fire just like American medical corpsmen. With our four thousand Chinese casualties at Myitkyina we averaged only 3.8 per cent mortality in the cases that reached us alive, though some were gasping their last breath. Very few died in the plane on their way to base and two large base hospitals assured me, months later, that only ½ per cent died after reaching them. This was a record to be proud of in view of the ghastly wounds the casualties at Myitkyina had sustained. The wounds were no more horrible than those of other battles, but in other battles they didn't reach us alive. That they did so in Myitkyina was due not only to the fact that we were never more than two miles from the fighting but also to the efficient service of the Chinese litter bearers. Every American casualty knows that it was more comforting to be carried on Chinese litters by Chinese than on American litters by Americans.

During the first two months of the Battle of Myitkyina we had confined our air support to the use of fighter bombers to pinpoint targets, then strafe, hoping we might save part of the town for our own use later. Soon fighters were based on our field. On days when work was light the nurses would climb to the top of the east revetment wall and watch them take off to bomb, screaming with delight as one plane after another peeled off into a power dive, dropped its load, and shot up into the sky again, then circled and strafed with his machine guns blazing. Any decent missionary would have reprimanded the girls for their actions or reminded them that perhaps the bombs and bullets were hitting their own relatives and friends in the city. But all I could remember was the unspeakable misery these girls had suffered as refugees in India waiting for the chance to help drive the hated invaders from their country. And as to the bombs and the bullets hurting their relatives and friends—I wanted them to forget it.

But still the Japanese defense didn't collapse—so B-25's were sent for. They came in squadrons, dropping so many sticks of bombs that their explosions sounded like the rattle of a super machine gun.

One day a prematurely aged man and an eight-year-old boy walked in. It was Esther's Uncle Boganaw and his youngest son. Boganaw had been headmaster of the mission school in Myitkyina and had elected to live out the Japanese occupation. At the time of Sein Myaing's and Dr. Mildred's escape from town he also might easily have escaped to the safety of the American and Chinese lines. Why he didn't do so I still don't know. Possibly he was skeptical of our ability to tear the Japs—and the town—apart. Perhaps it was only the apathy and fatalism of the Orient. Perhaps it was the oriental's determination to stick by his home. And, of course, it is very possible that, being the senior mission official of the district, he felt it his duty to stick it out and prevent as much as one man could the looting of mission property by the Japanese or the Allies. One day, when he and his youngest son were away from home, our B-25's came over and one

165

bomb dropped squarely in the trench occupied by his wife and five other children. When Boganaw returned home there was no sign of his children or wife except a small piece of flesh hanging on a nearby telephone wire. That was the end. He slipped out of town—a much more difficult feat as the battle drew to a close than at the beginning. The Civil Affairs officer set him to work recruiting Kachins. He finished this assignment in October, sick with malaria and half crazed by the loss of his family, and begged to join us as coolie, orderly, or errand boy, just to get away from the hateful memories of the last days of Myitkyina.

I've talked to a great many people who suffered the loss of family, friends, home, and property at the hands of our air force or big guns. As far as I know there was only one instance where any blame was laid on us. A Burmese woman, crazed by the loss of everything she had in the world, ran to the first American sergeant she saw after her escape, pounded his chest with her little fists, screaming, "You killed all my family. I hate you!"

The contrary, however, was the rule. Everyone, as did Boganaw and Ma Yi, admitted the right of the British and Americans to drive the Japs out of Burma and the necessity of using bombs, shells, and machine guns to do so. They blamed themselves for not having the common sense to clear out of the battle area when the war drew close. Long experience had convinced them that the allied planes and guns were aimed at legitimate Japanese targets, even if they didn't always hit the target on the nose. Civilians were hurt only when they helped the Japanese or when they remained too close to them.

General Merrill was in the hospital. General Boatner flew in to take command with Colonel Willey as chief of staff.

About a month before the town fell, Boatner got malaria and Brigadier General Wessels took his place. Wessels was rare in that he was one general officer who kept his medical units informed of the tactical plans. It was a relief to know what was actually going on and not have to lay one's medical plans on underground rumors. Either Wessels or Willey dropped in once a day to make sure everything was going well. It was during the beginning of the end that our unit reached its all-time high on total number of operations in one day—one hundred and ninety—and still we had six hours of sleep. Forty of the cases were skin-deep minor wounds. Our high-ranking technicians had had so much experience helping with major operations that removing the tiny shell fragments from these numerous "nuisance" cases was a treat for them. Bill Brough had a man whose flank had been struck by a .45-caliber bullet which, proceeding just under the skin, had come out near the navel. Under my direction Bill connected the two wounds with a long incision so as to be able to debride the muscles underneath and sew them together cleanly to prevent hernia. When he was done he called all his pals to show them the "abdominal" operation he had performed. "I took out his liver and both kidneys," he declared.

It was during this greatest inflow of casualties that a plane came in bringing with it the largest collection of American brass Burma ever saw. I was just finishing an operation when two major generals appeared so I went out to chat for awhile just as I was, in nothing but a pair of G.I. slacks and shoes and my rubber gloves. The generals refused to let me find a shirt.

They were astonished at the pigsty character of our operating room and the informality of our operating without gowns except for abdominal cases. I explained that in jungle fighting, medical officers have to sort out rapidly those things in surgery that are a sine qua non of success and those that are nonessential refinements. Many a capable American surgeon knows that 80 percent of modern techniques are refinements not absolutely essential to success. The first thing American medical units had to do in the jungle was to shelve these nonessential "Park Avenue" methods, as the army calls them, and learn to do good surgery without them. Our unit could make this change more easily than those fresh from the States, for Gurney and I had been learning through years of poverty in mission hospitals that many things are nonessential. We never masked the nose, for instance, even for abdominal operations—only the mouth. In surgery on casualties other than abdominals we didn't bother to mask the mouth. Sterile gowns are hard to get in the jungle so we used them only for abdominal cases. For others the body naked above the waist, or with only an undershirt, was sufficient. In the effort to keep his own body clean the surgeon keeps the patient's clean as well. A litter makes a good operating table. If night insects become so fascinated watching the operation that they drop into the intestine during an anastomosis, the surgeon wipes them away with gauze and doesn't turn a hair; for the patient will get well—also without turning a hair. Even the maggot, which should justly be-

167

come the golden symbol of war, rarely causes irreparable damage and sometimes helps the patient get well.

A combat surgeon had to learn to shrug off maggots if he wanted to keep from going mad. From May to August the real owners of Myitkyina were not Japanese, Chinese, British, or Americans—but the maggots. Chinese and American G.I.'s were in the lines for days at a time, their clothes constantly wet with sweat from the awful heat of the sun and from the frequent rains. Omnipresent flies laid myriads of eggs, and the uniforms of the casualties that came in, American boys as well as Chinese, were such a mass of maggots, tiny, medium, and full grown, that if you took the shirt off it would crawl away under its own power.

The generals saw another load of casualties arriving by litter and took their leave while I went back to work.

A few days later an important major on the general's staff came to "shoot the bull" one afternoon. He was a devoted friend of the unit, though he had definitely not started out that way. It had taken months at Ramgarh and a severe bout of illness to make him like us at all.

"Colonel, why don't you recommend two or three of your outstanding Burmese personnel for civilian decorations?" the major said. "Your recommendations would most certainly be approved. You're not being fair to them."

"They told me that at the end of the first campaign—both the Burmese Government and the U.S. Army," I replied. "I took my life in my hands and classified the group according to special effort in the face of danger or unusual technical skill. Not a word was heard from the Americans on the subject and the British gave each civilian a pat on the back in the form of a certificate saying they'd done something or other constructive. To the best of my knowledge the girls threw the things away. The fact is that except for Naomi, who makes a superb chief nurse—and that isn't a purely military trait—our work hasn't succeeded because of the work of any single Burmese girl or boy who stands out above the others. It has succeeded because we're a group of teams that form a larger team that's a powerhouse. It's not the Burmese girls or the Burmese boys or the American enlisted men or Gurney, Antonellis, Johnson, Dushkin, Ba Saw, or Hsang Yee, and it certainly isn't me that gets us by. It's the teamwork of them all. What they and I would appreciate most of all would be to have Stilwell line them up and give them each a handshake and a couple of words. But Uncle

Joe is so shy around these girls that I know he'll never do it."

"There are such things as presidential unit citations and unit citations from the theater commander," the major said.

"Those would be too good to be true," I replied. "There are many medical units that deserve such citations more than we, for to them the jungle is a real hardship, whereas to us it's home. If Stilwell is too shy to give us a formal nod and a couple of kind words, maybe General Wessels would do it."

Shortly thereafter a letter came in from rear-echelon headquarters saying that bronze stars were to be given to Dushkin, Gurney, and Antonellis, the officers who had led the detachment over the hills in the attack on Myitkyina airfield; that I was to make out a story at once of their labors on that trip. I complied. Then I wrote the following letter:

1. It has come to the attention of the undersigned that decorations are to be awarded to three officers of this unit for their meritorious services on the move which resulted in the capture of Myitkyina airfield.

2. The undersigned wishes to call attention to the fact that the following enlisted men accompanied these officers, sharing their dangers and difficulties.

3. On the occasion when the regiment served by this detachment resumed the march without notification and the detachment was abandoned in enemy-infested territory, these men, although not trained for that type of work, made litters and carried American and Chinese patients, who had also been abandoned, over mountain trails many miles to the nearest liaison strip whence they could be safely evacuated to base.

4. This action on the part of the enlisted men reflects great credit on the Army of the United States.

Months later Lieutenant General Sultan paid a visit to our hospital on the Irrawaddi bank.

"It seems almost every member of your unit is about to receive a decoration. I can't understand it," the general said with a twinkle in his eye.

"I can't understand it either," I said soberly.

That week orders came out awarding the Bronze Star Medal to all the officers and men of that detachment and the Oak Leaf Cluster, in lieu of second bronze stars, to Sergeants "Susie" Opas and "Bill" Brough. And on top of that came the notification that by presidential order, bronze stars were being granted to all our nurses who served in the first battle of Burma.

General Wessels' first two attempts to take Myitkyina were foiled by the general of the 30th Chinese Division refusing to obey orders. He either attacked a day early or a day late, refusing to support other divisions and consequently not being supported on his own unco-ordinated moves. His men were accordingly massacred, though by this time the Japs were out of 70-mm. shells.

Stilwell ordered the recuperating Boatner to fly back, get the general and ship him to Chungking for investigation. The day after the Chinese general left, Myitkyina was ours. Mogaung had fallen to the 38th Division and Kamaing to the 22nd. Stilwell had proved not only that the Chinese, when well trained and equipped, can fight, but that a war can be fought in Burma during the rainy season. The English, not to be outdone, had sent in their 36th Division, experienced English and West African troops who had fought in Ethiopia and elsewhere, and were carrying the fight down the railway south of Mogaung, while Chinese and Americans took a much needed rest.

PART FOUR: RETURN TO NAMKHAM

After the loss of Myitkyina, Japanese resistance in northern Burma crumbled. New Chinese, British, and American units were coming into the battle. Changes were made in the overall command, but the original Stilwell plan remained unaltered. On October 28, 1944, Lieutenant General Daniel I. Sultan assumed command of the American forces in the Burma-India theater. China became a separate American command under Lieutenant General Albert C. Wedemeyer.

From Myitkyina on, the allied advance was rapid. Bhamo fell to Chinese troops on December 14, 1944. The Ledo Road was now pushed forward to a point where it joined the old Burma Road. Chinese forces entered Namkham on January 15, 1945, and a few days later cleared the last Japanese roadblocks on the Burma Road at Wanting and Mongyu. On February 4, 1945, a convoy of American trucks, led by Brigadier General Lewis A. Pick who built the Ledo Road, rolled into Kunming, China.

16 THE TASTE OF PEACE

IT TOOK us two days to finish off the last of Myitkyina's casualties. General Wessels offered me a trip over town in a liaison plane and first priority in choice of a site for the field hospital we were to run for the rest of the rains.

We flew back and forth over where Myitkyina had been. Nowhere was a house intact. The shelling and bombing had been extraordinarily well done. Everywhere were pockmarks, especially around the railway station and other military targets. Near the riverbank on the northeast corner of town were two buildings that looked as though they could be repaired. The Baptist Mission area appeared hopeless. I flew back and pointed out my choice on the map. Two days later General Willey and I rode around there in a jeep. One of the buildings had an almost intact shingle roof, but the plastered mat walls had been blown out and the floors were ordinary wood. The tile roof of the other was completely

171

off, but the upstairs floors were teak and downstairs teak tile over cement.

S.O.S. and combat commands all needed sites, and General Stilwell had ordered a house on the bank of the Irrawaddi saved for himself, so Willey could give us only the tile house, the floors of which would be better for an operating room. For the hospital we were given a hundred yards of the riverbank south to a tall steel tower whence the telegraph wires to Tengchung, China, jumped across the river.

The task ahead of us was formidable, for we had to move the hospital as a going concern. We had stopped air evacuation with the close of the battle and had some two hundred patients in the wards at the airfield. For making the move we had only one broken-down jeep and trailer that we could call our own. Our enlisted men, having worked continuously all those months at the field, had not yet recovered from their forced march over the mountains. We had ten Burmese and ten Kachin coolies working for us under an Indo-Burmese boss and four Indian sweepers. With these men, our Burmese and Chinese boys and Dr. Hsang Yee to help me, we drove over to our new location to start cleaning up, while Captains Gurney and Antonellis and Dr. Ba Saw finished up the medical and surgical work and saw that our jeep was loaded with priority goods for each shuttle trip.

Upstairs in one bathroom I had noticed a flushing toilet completely modern and in perfect condition. The amoebae I had been incubating since the first days at the strip began to die at the sight of it! The other bathroom was a wreck except for one porcelain bathtub that had survived a 75-mm. shell as it passed through the bathroom wall. While the rest of us worked on the largest downstairs room, which I had set aside for surgery, the Burmese boys climbed to the roof to throw down the broken tile and gather the intact pieces together. I assigned one of our new men to tour the town and look for loot.

Leaving a few boys to scrub out the operating room with soap and disinfectant, the Americans climbed up on the roof to re-lay the good tile. I had seen marvels before but nothing like the speed with which that roof began to look like a roof. I set the Chinese to hauling water from the well and took the sweepers upstairs to sweep and scrub the teak floor. Then I took a peek into the good bathroom, just to gain strength from another look at that beautiful flushing toilet, and such a wave of anger swept over me that I couldn't even swear. My Burmese boys had carelessly filled the

172

toilet bowl full of broken clay tile and smashed it to a pulp.

It took three days to make a start at cleaning out a house that a Japanese general had used as his quarters. By the third morning so much of the roof had been covered with tile that one forty by forty tarpaulin could cover over the untiled area, and all but four of the nurses came over.

By this time some twelve scrubbings with disinfectant had removed all but a faint, mysterious aroma from the surgery and downstairs rooms. While the girls with dahs and sickles mowed down the yard-high grass from what had been beautiful lawns in the days of the English, our men and coolies filled in the numerous shellholes on our land, began erecting pyramidal tents for our male personnel, and put up the first ward tent.

The enlisted men whom I had detailed to bring in loot had located many broken and bullet-pierced tables, sets of shelves, almirahs and bureaus, four operating tables, and the framework of a settee just like those we had furnished the nurses in Namkham. I settled for a nice big downstairs room with a bathless bathroom on the end opposite the operating room. Gurney and Antonellis shared a smaller room in the middle. Gilbertson and Bullock appropriated the former dining room and pantry for supply and office. We fitted up the central entryway as a recreation room and library, and the girls took over the entire upstairs floor. In order to give them enough room we disconnected the porcelain bathtub and put it on the back verandah of the operating room to store water.

One of our sweepers was a tall, white-bearded Punjabi Sikh. He took one look at my cubbyhole of a "bathroom" and disappeared. Hours later he reappeared covered with smiles. In one hand was a framework of a commode and in the other a gorgeous chamber pot which he had looted from somewhere in town. After that I didn't dare use the officers' latrine for fear of breaking his heart.

Our fourth day was bedlam. Patients came over by the truckload and occupied the one ward tent, while the one they'd just vacated at the field was hurriedly put up in readiness for the next truckload. New nurses and coolies alternated mowing down grass for new ward sites. Older nurses received patients, sorted them and their charts, and gave the day's treatments.

In all of those frantic, work-glutted days, we never had to urge the Burmese on. Outline what had to be done and they did it even though it meant working on for an hour or two after quitting time. On four occasions, when our work became lighter, I had to order them to stop working at five o'clock. They laughed, sang, joked. And when we were alerted for our next combat assignment and I hoped possibly the Kachin coolies might be persuaded to follow us, the Burmese came in a body and demanded to be taken along.

"Why do they want to stay with us?" I asked their spokesman, Dr. San Yee.

"They say this is the first time in their lives they have been treated white," he replied.

We kept a few civilians in our wards, only those who would certainly die or need an amputation if we sent them out. I arbitrarily set the maximum number at fifteen so as not to interfere with the work for a total of five hundred beds for Chinese soldiers, which I knew would soon be filled and for whom I was requisitioning tarpaulins, cots, and blankets. But someone told General Willey that in order to care for those fifteen civilians, Seagrave was refusing to admit sick Chinese soldiers. That, if true, would have been a court-martial offense. General Willey very properly ordered me to get rid of all civilians at once.

We were deluged with natives needing treatment, many of whom had been treated without improvement at the civilian hospital. Portable surgical hospitals in the Mogaung, Kamaing, and Hopin areas continued to evacuate badly wounded civilians to us by train and plane for definitive treatment. How the civilians griped when we sent them away to the civilian hospital! Especially resentful were the Kachins. Most of their able men were in our army units helping us as Rangers and guerrillas as well as regular soldiers. Did that not entitle the sick and wounded of their race to our medical attention? It was especially embarrassing to me to have American soldiers pick up sick or hurt civilians in the street, many of them working as coolies for American units, and bring them to us, confident we would care for them, and then have to send them to the civilian hospital.

Furthermore, I couldn't rid myself of the idea that Stilwell had had some special reason for tolerating the existence of our "unorthodox, nameless, bastard" unit all those years—the desire to have someone to do unorthodox jobs in an unorthodox way to satisfy his sense of the fitness of things. His first assignment to us after our activation as the Seagrave Hospital Unit had been to care for civilian refugees in Assam in 1942. Then at Ramgarh we had wards for civilians. Then in the Naga Hills we had been ordered by

174

General Boatner, as our third duty, to obtain the friendship of the natives through medicine.

When General Willey returned from his furlough I pointed out these things to him and General Cannon, and assured them we had never refused admittance to Chinese, even to Chinese goldbricks, on account of civilians. Permission was immediately granted for us to continue helping needy civilians on this basis.

My interest in civilian medical care in Burma is a matter of long standing. When I express an opinion on the way certain medical matters were handled there, I stand on my record in Burma.

I doubt if any other foreign family has given Burma as many centuries of service as mine has. That service can in no sense be connected with exploitation—unless you can call education, medical and surgical care, and a bit of Christian preaching "exploitation." My family has not taken a cent of money out of Burma. On the contrary we brought into Burma many hundreds of thousands (lacs) of rupees of American money in the form of our salaries and appropriations for mission work, money that has improved the financial condition of a good many thousands of the people of Burma.

In Burma it was the practice to rotate doctors from one area to another every three years. But in any country a doctor has to root himself into the soil and struggle until the people nearby know him, especially if he is a surgeon. People the world over will go to quacks for medicine but not for surgery—not if they can help it. They want someone whose skill is known to themselves and their friends. And if that is true of the Occident how much truer it is of the Orient where the people still have to have the excellence of western medicine and surgery shown to them.

When an outstanding surgeon makes a name for himself in a district he should be left there or promoted in the same division. This will decrease rather than increase graft. His fame will bring in so many honest shekels that he won't need to resort to extortion. To avoid the smearing of his own reputation he will be much more rigid in supervising the professional work and morals of his subordinates.

You can't help loving the people of Burma if you honestly work for their good. The real surgeon would love his district and use his utmost ingenuity in laying out programs for its medical welfare. He wouldn't be satisfied to keep up the placebo (make-believe) hospitals he might have inherited.

175

For the sake of his own reputation he would make his district shine in medical matters instead of using the sins of his predecessors as an excuse for inefficiency. And surgeons who fail at their initial assignment should be given one in an entirely different area; for one part of Burma can psychologically and medically be so different from another as to seem part of another country.

We were really getting little tastes of peace as we worked away at our five-hundred-bed hospital. After supper it was everyone's delight to go to the riverbank and sit, watching first the majestic, swiftly moving stream and then gazing off at the mountains that marked the border of China.

When the sun sets in Myitkyina you do not face west: that's too common. You face east and watch the suggestive, reflected tints on the China mountains and the broad river. Right across from us were native houses, untouched by war, pasture ground, and beautiful trees. From the highest point of that sunset-hued ridge you can see Tengchung to the east and, to the south, the tip of the ridge on which stands Sinlumkaba, summer resort for Bhamo District and for peace lovers from all over Burma. And, from Sinlumkaba, the hills around Namkham! Just two hops and a skip yet to go.

Even in the Hukawng we heard G.I.'s sing about the moon over Burma. Poor fellows, they didn't know it was just an imitation there. In Myitkyina we not only had the moon over real Burma, we had the *Thadingyut* moon over Burma. In the rainy season the Buddhists have a Lent just as Christians do in the spring. During Lent they strive to be especially good Buddhists and that means going to monastery schools on their Sabbaths and listening to the reading of the Pitakas, the Buddhist scriptures. On Sabbath nights the merit-seeking Shans sleep at the monastery. Their Lent, too, has an Easter—at the full of the *Thadingyut* moon which usually comes in October. To the Burmese and Shans, *Thadingyut* is the greatest feast of the year. At night hundreds of paper fire balloons are released, carrying light high up into the sky. Every good family lights all the candles they can afford around their own houses, carrying others to the pagodas and monasteries, for is not this the Feast of the Lights?

How I berated myself for not remembering that this moon was *Thadingyut!* I could have begged, borrowed, or stolen—or even bought, if necessary—tissue paper to make balloons (as I had made them for John and Sterling in Namkham) and made the first *Thadingyut* back in Burma memorable for our poor, hungry-hearted Buddhist nurses. But our three blue-

176

blooded princesses, Louise, Pearl, and Chit Sein, did not forget. Louise came to me at sunset.

"Daddy, tonight is *Thadingyut*." She had to stop for five minutes while I cursed my memory. "Will you please let us go to the pagoda to place our candles? Captain Antonellis says he will drive us there in the jeep."

"Of course you can go," I said. Darn Antonellis anyway, I thought. He's always doing the right thing while I just go blundering along.

Much later that evening I turned out my light in my loneliness and went out to the verandah. There was the moon, high above the China hills, making a broad golden path across the Irrawaddi, and there, sitting on the bank of the river, their bodies sharply silhouetted against the perfect Burma landscape, were little groups of our personnel. Here an American boy and four nurses, there three girls and a couple of officers. Not a sound anywhere but you could feel them drinking in the beauty. Peace, peace again in Burma! The youngsters were out there enjoying it together. And I was all alone as usual. I went in, turned on all the lights, and set furiously to work. Myitkyina was no longer a combat zone.

For me now there were deep drafts of peace. By the time the hospital on the riverbank was a going concern, we had taken on some twenty-five new girls and boys as probationers. If they were to be worth much to us in Myitkyina, or beyond, they had to know what it was all about—more than Naomi could teach them in the operating room or Wasay and the head nurses could teach them in the wards. So I began to give them classroom work from ten to twelve every morning. The boys weeded themselves out in a week, but that didn't matter since they were a small minority, and in combat there is much an educated Burmese boy can do that coolies cannot—or nurses, either. At the end of another week I threw half a dozen girls out of the class, girls too stupid to learn, letting them act as orderlies on the ward, where they could ease the work of the graduate refugee nurses. The remainder were good or excellent.

If I had begun a regular course of training it would have been a year and a half before they would be worth much. I gave them instead a two months' bird's-eye view. First, three weeks of bandaging, bacteriology, and the parasitology so essential to surgery and to medical work among the Chinese, who are tanks for parasites. Then the twelve most common

177

diseases of C.-B.-I., teaching only a bit of anatomy and physiology here and there so they could grasp the inklings of pathology. A day or two on the benefits of fever—a thought that never occurs to an oriental. Another day or two on the importance of charting. It was fun.

Big Bawk had spent a postgraduate year with Captain Chesley in the laboratory at Ramgarh and, except with cultures, had become an extremely able laboratory technician. While my own knowledge of laboratory work was broader than hers, in the phases she had studied her knowledge was so much deeper that I never argued with her. In fact, I soon regarded her as infallible. We had the only microscope at the airfield during the entire battle for Myitkyina, and the decision as to whether an American soldier should be evacuated to base for malaria depended on the little Kachin girl's diagnosis as to whether the malaria was malignant or benign.

At the riverbank the laboratory work for a five-hundred-bed hospital was extremely heavy so I set Little Bawk, who hadn't been well for months, to work in the laboratory with Big Bawk, where she could sit at her work. I put new girls on in rotation to help as bottle, tube, and slide washers and specimen collectors. One day Naomi appointed Hkawn Tawng's pint-sized twelve-year-old sister Roi Ji as bottle washer in her lab. Roi Ji ate it up. In five days she was using the microscope herself. In seven she was identifying malaria parasites in the blood, amoebae and ova in the stools, and then passing the microscope over to Big Bawk for final diagnosis.

Two weeks later Little Bawk called me to the lab.

"What's that red splotch in the center of the field?" she asked.

I looked. "They're not tubercle bacilli, if that's what you mean," I said, recognizing the Ziehl-Neelsen stain for sputum.

I went on with my work. Two hours later, while I was at rounds in my Chinese officers' wards, the laboratory bottle washer came to me.

"Daddy," she said, "Little Bawk wants you in the laboratory at once."

"Confound it, these girls order me around and I haven't any more sense than to obey," I grumbled, walking back to the lab.

"Take a look at that specimen," commanded Little Bawk.

I obeyed. "Beautiful! Beautiful! That's a lovely stain! Those are real tubercle bacilli. Loads and loads of them, aren't there? You're getting good, Little Monkey!"

Silence.

"That's her own sputum," said Big Bawk in an undertone that meant, "You unspeakable idiot!"

"Good Lord!" I looked around. Little Bawk had disappeared. I went around the corner to my room and found her crying. I put an arm around her.

"Little girl, forgive me. I never suspected it was your own sputum. I can't understand it. I've examined you very carefully three times since you coughed up that blood at the field and have never heard a râle. Please don't quit on me. I'll take you to the 44th Field Hospital and we'll get an X-ray picture of your chest."

I stayed awake hours that night cursing the spirit that made me drive people until they broke down and caught tuberculosis. Yet I could never control my disgust at people who wanted to win a war from an armchair. I always insisted on my officers, enlisted men, and Burmese personnel going to bed with malaria and dysentery but hadn't put myself in bed for two years with either one. But my body could take that kind of thing and these poor little bodies couldn't. And what chance had Little Bawk? Unlike Julia, from whom she had caught the disease, sleeping in the same bed at Ningam because there weren't enough blankets to go around, Bawk couldn't stay still. Intense by nature, she had an overwhelming dose of thyroid secretion. With a much quicker brain than mine—although she hadn't learned a fraction of what I'd been taught—she would never be able to stay still.

And the X-ray didn't help. There was a large band of active tuberculosis in her left lung, with much acute inflammation.

I went to Big Bawk.

"Little Bawk has got to stay in bed. I'm sorry. Choose the nurse who will be most useful to you in the laboratory and I'll give her to you; I don't care who she is," I said, expecting her to ask for Kyang Tswi or one of the other graduates who had worked with Captain Chesley.

"Give me Roi Ji," Big Bawk said without hesitation.

"You're kidding, aren't you?" I asked, stunned.

"No, indeed. I want Roi Ji."

So pint-sized twelve-year-old Roi Ji was installed as assistant technician in the laboratory, and, as bottle washer under her, I appointed half-pint Emmie.

179

Two days later a new patient was brought in, in a state of collapse; his eyes were deeply sunken, his forehead moist but body dry and cold and the skin of his palms wrinkled. His pulse was rapid and very small.

I sent off a stool specimen for culture to the big laboratory at Chabua, and began treating the patient for what his symptoms indicated he had—cholera.

By the third day of treatment with glucose and plasma, our man was coming back to life. His body was reacting and warm and his eyes were coming back out of the walls of his brain.

On the day we discharged him as cured, our lab report came crackling over the radio: "Organism identified as *malleomyces pseudomallei*. Request complete report of postmortem examination."

We replied immediately: "Sorry, autopsy report unavailable; patient has gone home."

Later we learned that malleomyces pseudomallei caused a fatal disease with symptoms of cholera. Only two patients had ever been known to recover from it. Ours made three.

Our stay at the riverside was not all peace. To start our troubles Major Dushkin was given a well-deserved lieutenant colonelcy and that, in our unit, is tantamount to transfer. Then the American officers and men and the Burmese doctors and men were long overdue for furlough. While we were in the midst of increasing our ward space to the final high of five hundred and forty beds filled, a third of our male staff went off to Calcutta for two weeks. I had asked for a month in the States, not having been home for seven years, during which time my daughter Leslie had grown from a sixteen-year-old to a woman married to a naval ensign on duty on one of our big flattops. My son Weston had grown from a boy whose head reached my shoulder to a man whose shoulder my head would not reach and who was in the navy trying to qualify as a fighter pilot.

Don't let anyone talk to you about huge sacrifices made by foreign missionaries. They have the time of their lives. The only real sacrifice is that they can't watch their children grow up. I hadn't seen Tiny and the two little boys for two and a half years. I wasn't fed up with Burma. Far from it. But I could have enjoyed a few hours with the family, trying to remind them that I existed other than on paper, and censored paper at that. But I had reminded General Boatner

180

that if the leave were granted at the wrong time I would be unable to leave.

"It's up to you whether you take your leave or not," he said.

For the six weeks after Myitkyina fell I could have been away and no one would have missed me. Then the first third of our male personnel returned and the second third was leaving when catastrophe hit us. We lost nine men and Captain Johnson on the rotation plan. Gurney, the only officer other than myself from whom the nurses would take orders, needed a vacation much more than I did. He had not only gone more months without one but had been on several flank moves through the mountains and had been ill several times. Just before he was due to leave, my orders came through.

Gurney would gladly have given up his furlough in my favor but I would have none of it. He needed that vacation; and besides, not knowing Burmese, he couldn't teach the new girls. With only the rank of captain he couldn't manage the unruly Chinese officers' wards that he had to turn over to me. Having lost half our American personnel, the staff running the five-hundred-bed hospital was almost completely Burmese.

I radioed back turning down my leave. You can't work for a man like Stilwell without realizing the job comes before the man.

Colonel R. P. Williams, theater surgeon, whose special property we had always regarded ourselves, dropped in one day to chat. Our delight in his visit was dimmed by his information that Washington had ordered that we be anonymous no longer. We were to be activated as the 896th Clearing Company. It was too much trouble for Washington to remember, if we had no number, that equipment for an extra clearing company was always being needed in C.-B.-I.

"You will remain a lieutenant colonel," he told me, "and continue as before, with your civilian personnel. You will be assigned your full Table of Organization strength of thirteen officers and one hundred enlisted men but you won't actually get any more officers or men than you have now. Your additional officers and men will be put on detached service with other units who are short of personnel."

Strange are the ways of the army. Apparently, in spite of everything, we were to be the same "unorthodox, bastard" unit—but now with an illegitimate name as well. We would not only be assigned the old unorthodox jobs as whatever brand of hospital the tactical situation might demand, but now would have a new unorthodox job as a replacement pool for all the other units in the theater! The more I thought about it the more intriguing the thought became. Not by the widest stretch of the imagination could the "original" Seagrave Hospital Unit, as I always regarded the Burmese nurses and men, Captain Gurney and myself, be considered part of the 896th Clearing Company except for Gurney and myself. The Table of Organization of a clearing company calls for no nurses (certainly not for Burmese nurses) and for no civilians. No, we would be two units, the 896th Clearing Company with its dispersed American officers and men and the old Seagrave Unit. I would be the C.O. and Gurney the executive officer of both units, belonging to both.

There was nothing to do but wait and watch developments.

There were evidences that the war might begin again. A liaison strip had been built between our house and the movie show. The little planes roared over us hundreds of times a day on various missions, missing our roof by inches. I was anxious to get started on the new campaign before the pilots decided to fly in the nurses' windows. For the third consecutive time, and this time seriously, I invited all my American and Chinese friends to Christmas dinner in our bungalow in Namkham.

Our second group of vacationing personnel was just returning to duty when Colonel Petersen flew in from base.

"The 38th Chinese Division will begin to drive south on October 16," he said. "You will furnish a surgical team with the first regiment. The 43rd Portable Surgical Hospital will follow the second regiment, and you will move as a clearing company with divisional headquarters. There is no heavy Japanese concentration reported north of the Taiping River at Myothit, although an occasional patrol has been reported as far north as Nalong. Your first semipermanent setup will probably be at Dumbaiyang, a day's journey north of Nalong. You will march, and Major Davison, chief medical liaison officer with the 38th Division, will furnish you with animal transport. Evacuate all patients that will take more than three weeks to get well to the 73rd Evacuation Hospital, those that will take two weeks to the 25th Field Hospital at Tingkawk, and try to get rid of the rest to the 38th Divisional Hospital, leaving a maximum of a hundred beds filled here.

The 42nd Portable Surgical Hospital will move in and take over the hundred beds with your equipment."

Try as we would, we couldn't force the number of patients below four hundred. We could congratulate each other in the

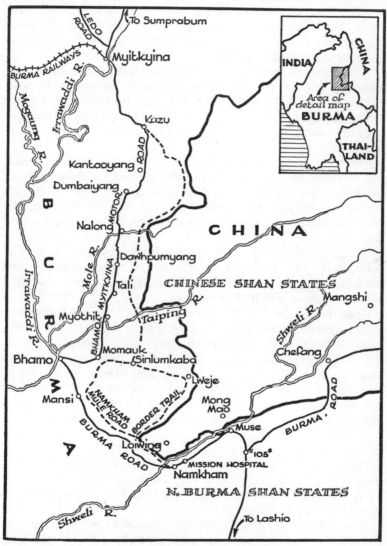

MYITKYINA TO NAMKHAM

morning as we put fifty or a hundred patients aboard planes for Tingkawk and Shingbwiyang, but in the evening the rail-head would send us in an equivalent number. The hospitals in Mogaung and Kamaing were also alerted for action and were unloading their patients onto us. Getting a little more stern, we forced the number down to three hundred, just as Colonel Petersen drove in with real trouble.

"The 48th Evacuation Hospital isn't ready yet," he said, "and the 38th Division has decided to send the divisional hospital south ahead of you. They have a hundred and twenty patients to evacuate tomorrow."

"Send them over," I said, as Major Stowe, the new commanding officer of the 42nd Portable Surgical Hospital, walked up. "We'll put up the ward tents that we pulled down today and admit them. Then we'll try to get the number of beds down to the two hundred Major Stowe says he can handle."

We took in the patients from the 38th Divisional Hospital but in spite of all effort during the remaining three days of work we still had three hundred beds to turn over to Stowe.

Colonel Hirschfield called up to say our vehicles must be ready at the main ferry at seven o'clock sharp the next morning.

Three of the girls with spots of tuberculosis, Saw Yin, Julia, and Little Bawk, were left behind. They pouted when we left, although I promised to have them flown to our first semipermanent installation.

"Let it not be longer than five days," ordered Bawk.

The ferry was an amazing thing. Four large pontoon boats, each with its own outboard motor, were bridged together. All of our personnel except the enlisted men and the coolies were packed on board with a jeep and trailer and a lot of baggage. Then the outboard motors started with a roar and we were off to the east bank of the Irrawaddi for the first time in two and a half years. We had to go downstream to round Plum Island first and then beat our way up against the current on the other side. At the far landing was a Shan village. I sent the jeep on to Kazu full of officers and Burmese boys, the trailer piled with baggage, while we walked to the headman's house. This was the first normal-life village we'd seen in Burma.

The nurses scattered through the village, meeting old friends and making new ones. Two of the girls stumbled on a native restaurant and brought me back a large dish of *hkow swai* (Shan noodles) and another of *wan toe poon* (pea jelly). Starved for good-tasting food, I gobbled them down with a prayer of thankfulness, enjoying even the hiccups that the hot chillies caused. Then Kyang Tswi whispered that I was invited to dinner at a nearby house. Real Burmese rice! I filled up again on their very good curry and hot salad. The first large meal I had eaten in months made me sleepy, and I was just dozing off on a wooden bench when I heard someone asking for the colonel. This was no time for visitors. I shut my eyes tight and they went away. When the arrival of the last of our equipment awoke me fifteen minutes later, one of the nurses informed me that I had missed a chicken curry dinner in another home because they hadn't wanted to wake me.

That afternoon we shuttled down to Kazu, the "end of the road," in the two jeeps and the weapons carrier. Captain Gurney had been assigned an old Japanese-Chinese camp on the bank of a deep swift river. There were a lot of flies and it was hot in the sun but it was interesting to sit and watch the Chinese being ferried across the river on single pontoons with outboard motors.

Early the next morning, while a battalion of artillery was forcing its horses to swim the river, the local engineers began bridging two pontoons together for our jeeps. By two in the afternoon our equipment and the artillery had completed the crossing. Then the pontoon boys took the nurses on a motorboat excursion up the river.

I sent Gurney ahead to find a camp site, while I remained to see that all the nurses were herded onto the shuttling jeeps.

Since our fifty-five horses could move less than half our stuff, we left the rest with Sergeant Brough in camp in a glade and marched on to Kantaoyang, only to find that Antonellis and his detachment had pushed on to Dumbaiyang that very morning. Antonellis now had only three horses instead of sixteen so his equipment was left at Kantaoyang in the care of Lieutenant Breger and a Burmese boy. For bivouac we had been assigned the bald brow of a hill beside two new Chinese graves, and the merciless sun beat down on us. Cross at the heat and rather stiff from the first day's march, I found a tiny stream some distance away and sat in the shade of some bushes, determined to do nothing until the cool of the evening. When I walked back to camp Breger and the nurses had put up a lot of parachute tepees and were busily engaged sorting out mountain rations. Hkam Gaw rescued us from a supper of "health biscuits" by discovering a sack of Burmese rice abandoned in some nearby underbrush.

Major Davison was still in camp and pulled out a map to

185

show me what was cooking. Advance Chinese units were halfway from Nalong to Myothit on the great Taiping River which empties into the Irrawaddi at Bhamo. They hadn't seen a Jap.

"No one can understand why the Japanese have let us have all this gigantic area without a fight," Davison said. "Kachins say the Japanese grand strategy is to suck us all into the Bhamo area and then wipe us out from the rear, but General Lee is guarding against this very thing by deploying the 112th Regiment on the right flank."

After we had all had a gorgeous bath in the cold stream, Colonel Burns, chief liaison officer, and Major Davison returned for a visit in the delightful parachute tent Antonellis and his boys had built for me.

The next day's march was a mess. We had no sooner started when the battalion of artillery insisted on passing us. As soon as they got in front of us they stopped for a rest. It was positively nasty. I called the noon halt hours before noon and let the artillery get out of the way.

The Nalong plain was not nearly so hot and being a Shan plain (the name means "Great Rice Paddies") there were vegetable gardens and fruit trees growing everywhere.

"Why don't they let us choose our own site and then we could camp here and get a full stomach for once," grumbled one of the girls.

The site picked for us was an old monastery with a shrineful of Buddhas. Japanese had camped there and it was filthy and lousy with sandflies. There weren't enough shade trees for the men to hang up their jungle hammocks. Although we were next to the field where the liaison planes would be landing the next day, we were two miles from the dropping field and farther than that from divisional headquarters. Colonel Burns and Dr. Taubenfliegl rode off on horses to find us a better bivouac area.

From then on Taubenfliegl became a charter member of the 896th Clearing Company Reconnaissance Patrol. The site he chose was perfection—another monastery in a temporarily deserted Shan village with unlimited shade and surrounded by weedy vegetable gardens and fruit trees. The girls fitted into the monastery and one room of the nunnery, which we covered with a tarp, and I took another room in the same building. While the girls collected fruit and vegetables and chatted with the natives, who came out from the hiding places in the jungle when they saw Burmese nurses, the boys

186

went to the dropping field and came back with—delightful surprise—sacks of Louisiana rice.

The 38th Division pulled out and left us at Nalong. If we had to linger somewhere, that was the spot for me. Our horses went back for another load near Kazu. Our coolies caught up, staggering along under the weight of our power unit. Then orders came in by phone for us to push forward to Dawhpumyang with horses from the artillery battalion. The artillery promised us seventy horses and turned up with fifty. There was a flurry as we abandoned cases of rations right and left—much to the delight of the natives—and scattered bottles of medicine and pyrethrum (mosquito) bombs around for the nurses and myself to add to our own packs.

We crossed a little ridge, rounded a corner, and there were the Dawhpumyang rice paddies spread out below us. I stopped, rubbed the cobwebs and sweat out of my eyes, and looked again. It couldn't be. But there it was. The Dawhpumyang fields were the beginning of the forest-floored Bhamo plain, and there, in the distance, was the same blue ridge of mountains west of the Irrawaddi at Bhamo upon which I had gazed so many hundreds of times in the past twenty-two years. I pointed out the Bhamo area to the nurses and they quickened their pace as if they intended to sleep that night in Bhamo. The refugees were getting home to their own mountains.

Major Davison was beside the road near some dilapidated Kachin houses he had selected for our bivouac. "The 113th Chinese Regiment has occupied Myothit and rubber boats are being dropped to them tomorrow," he said. "The 114th has taken the suspension bridge over the Taiping River on the border trail and is pushing on to Sinlumkaba. Their last battalion leaves the road ten miles south of here at Tali tomorrow morning to join them there. Have a detachment with three officers ready to do a double march tomorrow to catch up with them. They will have twenty horses. You will go tomorrow to a tiny village called Numfang half a mile this side of Tali. You will have thirty-five horses. No one can understand why the Japs don't try to stop us. General Lee says he will be in Bhamo in a week."

I selected Captain Gurney, Dr. Taubenfligl, and Dr. San Yee. Since we had only five enlisted men available I included all my good Burmese technicians and enough new Burmese boys to do the dirty work. Boganaw went along as interpreter, for this was Kachin country. Wong Jack went as cook.

187

"I hate to send you off on this flank, Doctor," I said to San Yee who always begged to stay with me, "but you may strike directly across the hills to Namkham and get there before us. Give your wife and child my love, if you do."

San Yee chuckled.

The rest of us sat back to await developments. Interesting things occurred sufficiently frequently to keep us from too complete boredom. The 30th Chinese Division marched in and began to supply us with patients. There was a swarm of scrub typhus cases—the Shitsugamushi fever of Japan. This was unknown in Burma before the war but is one of the legacies to remain with Burma long after the Japanese themselves were driven out. Scrub typhus had caused more havoc among the Marauders before Myitkyina than had malaria.

There was the sound of a gasoline engine one afternoon and a jeep drove in. Two Americans had floated it across the rivers at Dumbaiyang and Nalong, wrapped up in a tarpaulin. It was an omen that before long our own jeeps and other vehicles might catch up with us. Then Captain Whedbee and his clearing company marched in and we knew it was time for us to leave and catch up with the 38th Division. Orders arrived the next morning.

South of the Taiping the road was at first heavily graveled and then asphalted. On a good many of the world's worst trails the nurses had frequently beat me into camp. But this asphalt road was too much for them to take. Unused to walking on hard roads, their arches gave way and I had rapidly to increase the rest periods to twenty minutes, then thirty minutes per hour. Finally some of them toddled away for ten minutes at a time, and some removed their G.I. shoes and went barefoot. At camp at the fifteenth-mile post they flopped on the floor of the house Major Davison had selected for their quarters. For the first time in three years of army marching they couldn't be enticed out for a bath.

Gurney and his men had completed their flank move to this same camp and were operating as we came in; but Momauk, the first large town near Bhamo, had just been captured and they moved on the next morning while we set up a clearing station and liaison planes flew into our back yard to evacuate patients.

Esther was preparing to give an anesthetic the next afternoon when she looked up and there was her brother standing in the gateway. It was perhaps just as well for me that I didn't see the actual meeting. By the time I came along Esther

188

had calmed down a bit and told me, starry-eyed, that her father and mother, her elder doctor-brother Albert, and her adorable younger sister Pansy were alive and well and living only four miles away from us in a jungle village.

As one girl after another found her people, the other girls from farther south began to smile and laugh from sheer good spirits, accepting the omens as portending happy days in store for them also.

The Chinese had now debouched on the entire Bhamo plain, had wiped out company after company of Japanese, had cut the Namkham and Sikaw motor roads, and had backed a thousand Japanese into Bhamo town where they were completely encircled. Gurney's detachment was five miles outside Bhamo. We in the main unit made one last march down the asphalt road to Momauk town, arriving to the music of rifle fire as a company of Japanese was slowly being wiped out a quarter of a mile away.

For our new location Major Davison had picked out the best part of Momauk. A huge, well-built Buddhist monastery and its outlying nunnery and resthouses gave us a perfect hospital setup, while across the asphalt main road, two two-story wooden houses gave us quarters for nurses. Our Chinese detachment and coolies and sweepers appropriated two thatch houses. About ten days later Colonel Burns, chief liaison officer, suddenly woke up and complained to Major Davison that Seagrave had taken over the best part of the town.

"Doesn't he always?" chuckled Davison, who had at last obtained his dream: the perfect medical setup for a Chinese division. The 43rd Portable Surgical Hospital in two detachments, one with each of the two regiments on the Namkham Road, and Gurney's surgical detachment with the third regiment on the Momauk Road were less than two miles from the fighting front. Most of their casualties reached them by litter in less than an hour after being wounded. From the portables the casualties were being jeeped back on an asphalt road to our hospital. Just beyond our hospital the Chinese field hospital was taking all the medical work and much of the minor surgery. A quarter of a mile away hospital planes were taking on our evacuation patients for the short run to big institutions at Myitkyina. More than 50 per cent of the casualties never needed to be evacuated, and long before the fall of Bhamo two hundred casualties had been returned by us to the front—a whole company of troops. Davison had a right to be a bit smug.

A few nights later the Japanese, fed up with the barrages

of 155-, 105-, and 75-mm. howitzers that had been pounding them for two days from positions on three sides of Gurney, pulled up their remaining big guns to the very Chinese lines and threw fifty shells at point-blank range into Gurney's hospital area, hoping to destroy the ammunition dump beside them. When Gurney and his men emerged above ground in the morning, their operating-room roof and their jungle hammocks and blankets were full of shellholes. I brought them back to our monastery, since patients could reach us within ten minutes of the time they had been reaching Gurney.

Our monastery was now really three hospitals. The upstairs floor was a field hospital, caring for patients who would take three weeks or more to get well. The larger area downstairs was a clearing station for patients who would be well in less than two weeks and for those who needed to be evacuated to the rear. The remainder of the downstairs was a portable surgical hospital operating on casualties direct from the front. The nunnery was a civilian hospital, filled with badly shattered natives, and the rest-house was an American hospital. Life was interesting.

After Thanksgiving the American infantry began to march past. As the boys caught glimpses of the nurses, choruses of whistles and catcalls rent the air. One group was given a breakfast halt right in front of us and dropped to the ground and started making coffee in their canteen cups over their canned heat. Pin-up girl Big Bawk stepped daintily across the road toward the hospital.

"Ann Atomy! *Hao-bu-hao!*" called an infantryman.

"That must be the Seagrave Unit," said another.

"Sure it is," said a third.

"What are they doing down here so close to the front?"

"They're always at the front. They operated on me in Myitkyina."

They thought I was out of hearing, as I sat wishing that our unit could be allowed to serve the American infantry. Just then Colonel Esterbrook stepped into the room.

"Doctor," he said, "I have a problem on my hands. We're ordered to march double stages around Bhamo and south and west toward Shwegu. We have no time to build liaison strips and no way to evacuate our road casualties. Is there any way you can help us?"

"The five-mile bridge and the eight-mile bridge on the Namkham Road have both been bombed by our air force," I replied. "I think I can ford the first stream and float a jeep across the second wrapped up in a tarp. If so, I can shuttle your casualties back here and fly them back to Myitkyina after a night's rest."

I set off with our coolies, intending to bridge the narrow deep channel across the first stream and look into the possibilities of the second. To my amazement Chinese engineers had already bridged the first with a part pontoon, part pier bridge constructed of captured Japanese pontoon boats and salvaged timbers from the outskirts of Bhamo, and were already halfway across the second. My only real opportunity to serve the Americans turned out to be too easy. Still it was fun and I made one ambulance trip myself, hoping the boys would get a kick out of having a lieutenant colonel for an ambulance driver.

After the infantry was out of the way the heavy guns began to roll by. It was the first time we'd seen our own 105's and 155's. Colonel Levell stopped in to pay his respects.

"Are you going to shell Bhamo?" I asked.

"Yes."

"Can we come down and watch you?"

"Sure. Come tomorrow at ten o'clock."

"Colonel," I went on, "I understand that in Namkham the air force has ruined only my operating room, but all native reports agree that the mission hill there is the center of the Japanese activities, not the town. In Namkham the Japs can't build their usual deep dugouts for they will strike water about six feet down. All their real defenses will be around the hospital."

"That is indicated by our intelligence reports," the colonel agreed.

"Sir," I said, "I feel the same way about that hospital of mine that a father feels about a dying son. He stands the son's death better if he can be present and helping. I am sure you will have to shell that hospital, but I wish you would promise me that when you do you will let me pull the first lanyard!"

"It's a promise."

The nurses and enlisted men who went with me to watch the barrage on Bhamo were properly impressed. The 114th Chinese Regiment under Colonels Chen and Peng had learned at last how to move in behind an advancing barrage and it was exciting to watch the officers in contact with headquarters and air observers giving orders and having the orders expertly obeyed. By afternoon the 114th Regiment had obtained their objective and captured their north end of the town. Now it was up to the 113th Regiment to take the rest of the town.

And then the tanks rolled by, lights and mediums. Colonel Brown, freshly discharged from the hospital, flew down and spent one night with me. Brown planned to attack Bhamo and show everyone how to fight.

Everyone felt Bhamo was in the bag, so Captains Antonellis and Fair and Dr. Ba Saw started off in the morning to begin a flanking move with the 112th Chinese Regiment on Namkham. Their vehicles had no sooner left when word came that the Japs had evacuated Bhamo.

It was reported that two hundred Japs had escaped south along the riverbank, and Antonellis and his companions expected to run into an ambush at any moment during their first day. Colonel Brown was disgusted that his tanks hadn't had a chance to fight and sent several of the light tanks south in a futile effort to catch the enemy. The last effort on the part of the Japs before leaving had been to throw all their remaining 70-mm. shells at the 43rd Portable Surgical Hospital area.

The following day Major Davison informed me that he was going to visit the 43rd and congratulate them on their narrow escape, so I drove him down, hoping we could sneak into Bhamo by the back door and take a look at the wreckage of the large stone church I had built there. Two of the officers of the 43rd joined us. Stepping warily to avoid mines, we had only reached the south edge of the town when we saw my friend Colonel Peng also viewing the remains. Peng stopped his tour and insisted on escorting us all over, by paths that had been cleared of mines. There was nothing but destruction. The only building I saw in town that could be used for living purposes was the old Burmese Anglo-Vernacular School. I didn't see the north end. Shops where I had bought stores for years and the entire bazaar area, including the famous clock tower, the "Circuit House," Deputy Commissioner's and Civil Surgeon's houses, the Government Hospital—especially the hospital—were a complete loss.

Diagonally opposite from the hospital was my church. From the front no damage could be seen, save that the corrugated asbestos roof had been blown off. We entered and there was a huge oval hole in the rear wall where a 75-mm. gun had scored a direct hit. But my belief in cobblestone architecture was well justified: over the shellhole, the overhanging stone structure had not fallen and only part of one

192

corner of the building nearby had been cracked. The pews had all been stolen but the complicated electric wiring remained, still usable after a bit of untangling. The mission could repair the building and make it as good as new with an expenditure of about a thousand dollars. Under my heavily reinforced concrete porte-cochere was written the reason for the shelling of the church: an arc cut an inch deep in the cement floor, on which the base of a Japanese 70 had rested. I went back to Momauk happy—and crazy to start for Namkham.

17 HOME

FOR THREE long years I had been inviting everyone to Christmas dinner in Namkham, first in 1942, then in 1943, and now again in 1944. We were now only forty miles from our objective but still couldn't fulfill our Christmas obligations. It was irritating that not only were we not in Namkham for Christmas but had to be separated from each other. Our personnel liked to be together.

We could remedy the first defect somewhat. On the day before Christmas I called the nurses whose homes were in the Namkham area and we drove up to a point beyond Kaitik from which we could see, fifteen air miles away, the central portion of the Namkham Valley spread out before us. Namkham and the hospital area were hidden by the mountain from which Chinese mortars were still driving the last of the Japanese. While we were exploring for a better view a lone Japanese sniper, hidden in the brush a hundred yards away, tried ineffectively to pick us off.

At the thirty-second mile we found that the Kachins of the villages nearby had braved stray Japanese and the Chinese outposts to come down, welcome us back, and share Christmas with us. They had brought pigs, chickens, and eggs, and were already cooking the feast. Our stomachs full of fresh food, we had a short Christmas service together and then they went off home, their old-fashioned rifles and muzzle-loading shotguns ready for the Japanese.

We couldn't remedy the second defect completely, for Captain Antonellis' detachment was miles away over jungle paths. But it wasn't difficult to reach an agreement with the 13th Medical Battalion. They were anxious to let their men have Christmas Eve off duty so they could get tight, if they wanted to, and try to forget that they weren't having Christmas at home in the States. We wanted dinner with our main unit at Madanyang on Christmas Day. We therefore took all the medical responsibility for Christmas Eve, while the 13th assumed responsibility for Christmas Day.

While the 13th had their Christmas Eve party we built a huge bonfire and sat around it till midnight, singing carols and chatting. Many of the 13th's guests slipped out to join in our carol singing for half an hour or so. We were unhappy because we were still forty miles from Namkham at Christmas but there was a feeling of peace as we sang.

We couldn't drive through Madanyang Christmas morning, for engineers of the tank battalion were blasting the granite-hard limestone cliffs at the sharp curves to make them passable for the tanks. But, by shuttling, we arrived in time for dinner. There was no fresh turkey but our boys had done their best with a bit of canned turkey and fresh venison, and a very good best it was.

There had been few casualties and we weren't busy. We had learned patience in our years of army service and we spent our time watching the engineers bulldoze and blast the road to twice the width of the original English road. Everyone was restlessly stamping around waiting for the 30th Division to take Namkham so they could get on with the war. The first through convoy for Kunming, China, was forming at Myitkyina.

But the 30th Division was bogged down. Impatiently the 112th Regiment of the 38th Division took matters into its own hands and walked into Loiwing, capturing the airplane factory site and landing field. Then it plunged on to the Mansawn ferry and back up the motor road toward the 30th. Still more impatiently, Colonel Levell of the heavy artillery begged Colonel Brown of the tanks to set his bulldozers to cutting a direct road down to Panghkam, near the Loiwing airplane factory, in order that the artillery and tanks could reach the plain ahead of the 30th Division and smooth things out so they could capture Namkham. Colonel Brown snapped at the suggestion and came to me with Colonel Sliney for help on a reconnaissance to locate the best short cut to the old mule road to Panghkam.

The nurses yelled *S'taing ga* after me as I set off with great dignity in a train of jeeps with a brigadier general in front and countless full colonels behind. We drove through to the fifty-second mile, where the Chinese told us we could go no farther as Japs were entrenched two hundred yards beyond. But that was far enough. We were at the entrance to the short cut and in sight of the hospital buildings at Namkham. Something had certainly happened. Even with binoculars, the outline of the buildings was indistinct, whereas the last time I had looked back from this spot, the naked eye could clearly see the red-roofed, pearly gray stone buildings, set like a jewel in the green of the foothills above Namkham, with the great twin seventy-five-hundred-foot mountains behind. Now the blur was so indistinct you could hardly be sure you were looking at the right spot.

While I gazed at the physical evidence of what was left of my lifelong dream, the tank officers explored and found a steep but steady descent by which they could reach the old mule trail, after a mile of bulldozing through the jungle. Colonel Brown decided this would be the route for his tanks and the artillery.

New Year's Day passed rather quietly. I sent the nurses down the hill to celebrate with the bigger group while I remained on duty. All returned after midnight except Big Bawk, who had come down with a severe chill and fever and had to be left behind.

The 30th Division Headquarters finally moved on from Kaitik and the 38th Division settled there immediately. Major Davison asked me how long it would take our entire unit, patients and all, to move from our two locations to Kaitik. Predicating my reply on the use of the level ground at the pass, I replied that we could complete the move in twenty-four hours.

To my vexation the level area at Kaitik was still pre-empted by 30th Division Artillery who had no intention of moving. There was nothing left but a Chinese cavalry camp on a hillside and some rice paddies. It was a steep climb for the nurses to carry their barracks bags, and men were scarce for they were driving vehicles, loading and unloading, erecting ward tents and a kitchen. The nurses, children, and I did our best to drag bedding to the top of the hill but broke down and had to beg our coolies to help us. Girls put up their own parachute tents. The ward tents were placed in the rice paddies and patients were left on their litters on the ground.

But our troubles were still not over. Though it was raining the 38th Division Chinese Field Hospital, deciding they needed a nice long rest, unloaded swarms of patients on us while we were frantically trying to get our own patients out of the mud. If it hadn't been for the extraordinary efficiency of our enlisted men, acquired through long experience with difficult moves, our professional work would have broken down. Our three staff sergeants, Probst, Stolec, and Mortimeyer, especially distinguished themselves.

On the ninth of January, Lieutenant Rathje, our finance officer, had but one day to complete payment of the enlisted men with Antonellis, so we obtained permission to contact them. With Little Bawk, whose home was in the valley, and two of our former Marauders, we hopped into a jeep and set out to see how far Colonel Brown's dozers had succeeded in pushing their new short cut. They were already well down the mule trail and there were tracks of a jeep beyond the dozers. So we pushed on and, after almost running over a decayed Jap in a small stream, burst out onto the plain at Panghkam. We drove into the battalion command post and discovered one of the finest, most courteous young Chinese officers I'd ever had the good fortune to meet, a Major Shu. He furnished two guides to lead Lieutenant Rathje and the two Marauders up the jungle trail to Antonellis' hospital, while he led Bawk and me around the area, showing us the wrecks of the airplane factory and letting us use his binoculars.

This time it was possible to see quite clearly that the operating-room end of my stone hospital was in ruins. But the house Tiny and I had built seemed untouched. If only one of the buildings I had built remained unscathed it could become the nucleus for rebuilding the whole plant. But I crushed my hopes as they sprang again to life. The latest Chinese G-2 information reported six thousand Japanese still in Namkham. The 10th Air Force was not done with me yet—dive-bombing was going on at that very moment—and the heavy artillery had not yet begun to shell.

Major Davison was excited when he learned on our return that we had actually driven to Loiwing and asked me to reconnoiter the location with him the next day.

"Major," I said, as we drove around the Panghkam area, "this is the place for a field hospital. There are no Japs between here and the river. The 30th Division has at last captured Manwing, where the motor road debouches on the plain south of us, and the 112th Chinese Regiment holds the flank on our north. You can see that there's no danger from the nonchalance of the Chinese soldiers, wandering without guns all over the plain in search of food. The only imaginable danger would be from shelling by 150-mm. guns."

"Yes, and they would be trained primarily on the Loiwing airfield to the north and the English fort to the south," the

196

major replied. "Furthermore, you could hide a huge hospital in the area where Major Shu has his command post, if he moved out, and you could take shelter behind the high embankment of the irrigation ditch if the Japs started to shell you."

"The map doesn't show them all as motorable," I added, "but there are five motorable roads that come together at Panghkam over which casualties could be jeeped to us. If Namkham turns into a big battle like Myitkyina this would be the ideal spot."

We were invited to have dinner with Major Shu and found his command post full of distinguished guests, Generals Sun, Lee, Tang and their staffs and a couple of photographers.

During dinner we learned that the motor road was clear at last so we completed the round trip through Manwing and back by the Burma Road to Kaitik. Knowing Colonel Bob Thompson would approve anything he recommended, Davison gave me the "all clear" to begin moving to Panghkam the next day.

"It's almost twice as far as our last move and we have many more patients," I warned. "We may need three days to complete the move."

"Take as much time as you need," Davison said.

We made it in two days. Not only our old-timers but all our new personnel were crazy to see the valley the old man had thought worth spending his life in, and they worked with a will. They even failed to complain at having to tear up the Kaitik hospital before the finishing touches had been put on it and build a new one. And because we thought the conquest of Namkham would take at least a month, we made this the best tent hospital ever. Knowing it was around somewhere, I searched and found the cement floor of the shack where Al Anderson had set up his motor department when the airplane factory had been bombed out almost five years before. On this the Burmese boys put up an excellent operating room, while the coolies put up seven ward tents.

Ever since the day the chaplain of the 20th General had told me at the Pangsau Pass how glad he was to get out of Burma, I had heard Americans complain about Burma, its climate, its customs—everything but its people, whom Americans seemed to like instinctively. They had complained in the Hukawng, at Myitkyina, and at Bhamo. They didn't like the mountains between Bhamo and Namkham. Why good Americans should be forced to fight for a country like this was beyond their comprehension. But now all was changed.

197

Everyone who took one look at the Nankham Valley gasped and took a deep breath of fresh air.

"Gee, Doc, this valley—it's beautiful! Beautiful! No wonder you want to get back!"

"And it's rich," I would reply. "Look at those thousands of stacks of rice waiting to be threshed. Yet the people haven't planted all their fields. The best rice in the world grows in this valley."

An hour later I saw San Yee on duty. His face was deeply lined and he looked years older.

"My wife, sir. She died five months ago of malaria because no one had any medicine for her. My son is still alive."

And five months ago we had been impatiently but comfortably settled in Myitkyina curing Chinese of malaria by the hundreds, while San Yee's wife sickened and died of neglect.

On the afternoon of the fifteenth Colonel Van Natta walked in.

"How would you like to move?" he asked.

"Any time, any place," I replied, trying to look pleased but expecting him to give us another flank move. "Where are we going and when do we start?"

"How about moving to Nankham?" the colonel said, a twinkle in his eye. "The 30th Division walked in this morning!"

I was positively delirious and screamed out the news to the nurses.

That night General Sliney and Colonel Brown drove in to congratulate me.

"General Sun and Colonel Van Natta are going to escort you personally into Namkham tomorrow," Sliney said. "You are to be at Manwing headquarters at ten o'clock."

I couldn't sleep that night. We were at headquarters soon after nine-thirty but General Sun had already left. Colonel Van Natta told us that the time had been changed to nine-thirty and we would have to hurry to the suspension bridge area. In front of the Manwing bazaar Colonel Van Natta found some engineers who reported that there was no bridge across the Mawswihka and that there were huge bomb craters in the center of the road. Furthermore, their own dozers hadn't arrived. Van Natta told me to walk on beyond the Mawswihka to meet General Sun and he turned back to beg the use of Colonel Brown's dozers.

I found General Sun near what was left of the great

suspension bridge. He had the two cameramen with him and they photographed our meeting.

"Where are the pontoon boats operating, sir?" I asked.

"There are no boats."

"We could cross by the Mansawn ferry."

"There might be snipers beyond."

So there had been no intention of walking into Nankham at all. Just picture taking! The conqueror of Namkham welcoming the Burma Surgeon home! I detest having my picture taken but it had long since been impressed on me that if the army thought they wanted pictures of you, you submitted. I would have gone anywhere to oblige General Sun and the photographers, without having a pretended trip to Namkham thrown at me.

On our way back we met General Sliney who hadn't been informed of the change in time and had sincerely desired to escort me into Nankham, since he was the only old-timer left besides myself who had walked out with Stilwell. He was out of humor at not being informed of the change, and when he discovered no actual crossing had been planned he became purple in the face and went on to the suspension bridge to cool off.

Staff Sergeants Probst and Stolec and Dr. San Yee were also in need of calming, so I suggested we explore the jeep road just to see if we could reach the ferry at Mansawn. As it turned out, on the way we passed within a hundred yards of a wandering Jap but we proved that jeeps could reach the river. Then we worked off the rest of our impatience with a game of baseball.

On the morning of January 17, 1945, I spent some time with air force engineers exploring the possibilities of a C-47 airstrip nearby. Just as I was returning to camp a jeep hurried up and an officer informed me that this time they were really intending to escort me to Nankham but that since they had to ride horses, they couldn't allow my personnel to follow me. I must be at the location of our 155-mm. guns in fifteen minutes. I decided to take Stolec, Probst, San Yee, and Ba Saw with me anyway and let them trail along on foot after the horses.

At the trysting place I found General Sun and his staff poring over maps and I noticed his finger tracing a path from the spot where we then were to the Mansawn ferry.

"You can drive a jeep to that ferry, sir," I said. "I drove there myself yesterday."

For a full fifteen minutes Sun lectured his staff because

they hadn't known the road was jeepable. Then he ordered me to lead the train of jeeps.

We drove straight to the site of the big ferry and then noticed no one was following us. Probst went back to make inquiries and learned that some Chinese soldiers had led the general and his party off to a different, smaller ferry crossing. We hurried along but they were out of sight and it took us half an hour to find where they had crossed to a large island in the middle of the stream. We reached the other branch, however, before they finished crossing and the Chinese gave me priority. Newsreels cranked and the cameras clicked, as General Sun welcomed me to the valley all over again. Then, without waiting for the rest of my party, we walked out of the village and started across some paddies.

"This is the road to Namkham over here," I pointed.

"The general is going to Nawngkong first, to see General Tang," an aide explained.

"I'll wait by that big banian tree," I said.

"Don't move till I come back," the general said.

"Okay, sir."

We waited for an hour, then started toward Nawngkong to find out what had happened. On the edge of the village a cavalryman met us and pointed to where the general's party had taken to horses and was heading across the paddies direct for Namkham. That released me from my promise to sit, and we marched down the road on the double-quick in an effort to catch up. San Yee and the rest of my party had taken an even more direct route to Namkham. Since his wife was dead San Yee was even more determined to see his son and he was letting no generals or lieutenant colonels force him to go slowly. All we saw of him was a small patch of dust. I was just as anxious as he to see what was left of my baby, the hospital I had built up in Namkham, but with all the brass hats, photographers, and correspondents around I had to bite my nails and do it in style and like it.

Namkham! There was nothing left of the poorer Chinese quarter of the town, although the wealthier Chinese traders' houses were still intact. Occasional houses had been destroyed by bombs but for the most part the dilapidated condition of the Namkham houses, as of those in all the villages of the valley, was due to the Shans themselves. Without being taught, they had learned dispersion. They knew that if they remained in the towns they would be bombed, so they pulled down the essential parts of their houses and moved out bag and baggage to the rice fields, where each built himself a tiny grass shack as far from his neighbor as he could get.

After we crossed the Namkhamhpong River the destruction caused by bombs began to appear. And then I noticed a peculiar thing. When the British first took over the Shan States sixty years before, Shans had ambushed and killed an English captain. As a reminder to the Shans that they must not do these things, the government buried the captain in the exact center of town beneath a huge banian tree and built a stone tomb over him, surrounding the grave with a wire fence fastened to concrete posts. A thousand-pound bomb had fallen right into the captain's tomb. Only the two concrete posts at the foot of the grave remained. Had the air force also destroyed Gordon Junior's grave? I was more anxious than ever to push on and see.

On the other side of the open area had been the great monastery of Namkham, the center of the town's Buddhism, a monastery so sacred that I had entered it only once in twenty years, and then with my shoes off out of respect for the religion of other people. It was in complete ruins, but out of the ruins still stood the great image of Gautama, the Buddha, almost untouched, the mosaic on the back of his throne still gorgeous in its beauty. Christians will read many meanings into the freak destructions of their churches in this war. Perhaps we will concede the Shans also the privilege of making something out of their great Buddha, sitting serene and unmoved amid the havoc of war.

Generals Sun, Tang, and Lee were inspecting the wreckage of the monastery. General Sliney and the staff were resting outside the abandoned shop where the nurses used to buy their silks and satins with money saved up from the pitiful stipends of sixty cents a month which was all I could afford to give them while they were in training. Probst, Stolec, and I, sat too. An hour passed and the generals reappeared. I had been sitting within a mile of the hospital for an hour, unable to go farther. Now, surely, the wait was over. I stood up expectantly. But then General Sun sat down. Orderlies ran hither and yon, bringing tea, biscuits, and candy. I managed to choke one biscuit down. General Sliney watched me sympathetically. He was as eager as I to see what was left of my hospital.

At the end of the second hour General Sun decided he would push on. We passed by the all but ruined bazaar buildings; the Namkham bazaar had been the biggest and most colorful in the Federated Shan States. I had hoped the air force had had sense enough to destroy the awful post-office building but it was untouched, an ugly living monument to the unimaginative architectural ability of the Public Works Department. A battalion of Chinese were passing us now and they had impressed some natives into portering for them. I stopped. "Well, well, folks," I said in Shan, "how are you making it?"

They glanced at me, looked again, threw down their loads and grasped my hands. "Our doctor, our doctor, our doctor!" The newsreel camera began to grind.

General Sun turned to look, covered with smiles. "They recognize you, do they?"

"Shucks, they'd better! I've taken care of them since they were pups!"

As soon as I could tear myself away we marched on, way-laid frequently by other small groups. And then we were climbing the mission hill at last. At the foot of the hill was a sign in Japanese: "HEADQUARTERS, NAMKHAM GARRISON, IMPERIAL JAPANESE ARMY." In three years the Japs had not cut a weed. Branches of trees shattered by bombs were strewn across the road. We had to climb warily lest the Japs had laid booby traps. The center of the hospital gateway was occupied by the crater of a thousand-pound bomb. Other craters were everywhere. But the southwest corner of the hospital was intact. Again I was officially welcomed back to Namkham for the sake of the newsreel man, who posed me several times in the way to demonstrate best the feelings he thought I had at the time. All I wanted was for them all to go away and leave me alone. At last the photographers were tired and the generals, exhausted, went away to rest. General Sliney, God bless him, deliberately chose a different route for his exploration and left me alone with Stolec.

A small feeling of satisfaction came strangely over me as I walked around. A thousand-pound bomb had struck within five feet of the wall of the men's wing, but all it had accomplished was the destruction of a three-foot pillar between two windows on the ground floor; the second story wasn't hurt. But the most extraordinary thing was that either God or the air force seemed to have decided that I was to practice no more gynecology or obstetrics, for the men's wards were all up except for the bathrooms and the women's wards were all down—except for the bathrooms. The ma-

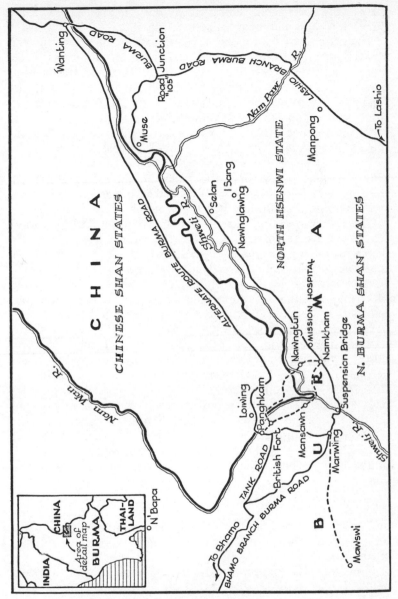

NAMKHAM AREA

ternity wards were completely destroyed but the children's ward and the ward for newborn infants were still there. My office and one private room were untouched except for bullet holes. The operating-room section and the women's wing were destroyed completely, but it had taken three direct hits and ten near misses to do it.

The iron roof had been torn almost completely off and what sheets of iron remained were full of countless holes from machine-gun strafing. Even the undamaged wards were deep in litter. Unwilling to sleep on teakwood floors, the Japs had built bamboo platforms a foot off the floor. In three years the place hadn't once been swept.

Out in the patio one of Tiny's red roses was bravely blooming as if to show the war was over at last.

I went over to the nurses' home. One of the front-door pillars had been smashed, the ballroom floor had collapsed, the roof was full of holes, and everywhere was Japanese filth; but otherwise the building was unharmed.

Then I started my search for Gordon Junior's grave. I feared the worst when I saw that the enemy had completely disposed of the banian tree beside him. It was incredible that the weeds could grow so high even in three years. Finally I found the grave, completely untouched. Roses were blooming in spite of the neglect, and beside the grave our poinsettias were in full flower. I felt much better.

Only one of the cottages which we used for private patients had been wrecked. The other cottages and the old dirty hospital building to which I had first come twenty-two years before and which I had often threatened to burn down was still there and immediately usable. The machine-gunners hadn't missed these roofs either; there wasn't a single roof on the entire mission hill that hadn't been riddled.

My other buildings were also usable. The damage to the stone church was slight, but the wallboards and the partitions of the house where Tiny and I had lived for eighteen years, and those of every other house in both compounds, had been torn off by the Japanese to build sheds and lean-to's.

On the Kachin compound was complete devastation. Only one small cottage and the schoolgirls' dormitory could ever be repaired. What our air force had not destroyed the enemy had.

Now that I'd inspected all the buildings of our working plant, I was free to visit the little cottage of stone Tiny and I had built for ourselves and used for two short years. The Japs had torn off all my copper screening from the doors, windows, front and back porches. They had torn off the paneled doors of our built-in closets. There was a hole in the dining-room floor. Not a stick of furniture anywhere. Then I opened the bathroom door. The Japanese had broken the toilet bowl loose from its moorings. The bathtub was gone. The washbowl had been torn out and was set into Tiny's neat closet on the back porch.

General Sliney obtained permission for me and my party to separate from the rest and go back to Panghkam alone. At the foot of the hill, in the ruins of the recently burned Christian Kachin homes, were the twisted ruins of five of our iron beds and our bathtub, the enamel completely destroyed. I was told later that the Japanese had used them for the comfort of the Korean and Japanese prostitutes. The first Chinse shell thrown into the area, a phosphorus shell, had lit squarely in the area and burned both houses to the ground.

San Yee had been lost all this time. Ba Saw undertook to go find him in the rice fields to the southwest of Namkham where he had located his brother, cousins, and the son he had never seen. It took half an hour to pry San Yee loose from his son but when he came his eyes were shining and his face wreathed in smiles. "Such a nice big boy with bright red cheeks and so fat!" he chuckled. Ba Saw and the American boys were just as enthusiastic. San Yee had something to live for again.

The bamboo raft was just landing as we reached the river. We crossed the ferry and it was darkening as we entered Mansawn.

On our return the girls crowded around to hear the news.

"When are we going to move to Namkham?" they demanded, excitedly.

"Not until Major Davison says okay," I replied. "He knows how anxious you all are to go. It won't be long. But Dr. San Yee and ten coolies can certainly go over tomorrow and stay and clean up the nurses' home for you."

Dr. San Yee had just set out by the ferry route when Major Davison appeared.

"Let's go over and reconnoiter," he said.

"By the ferry?"

"No, the engineers have already thrown a pontoon bridge across. We can drive over."

We hurried. Davison hunted for booby traps and made inquiries about the disposition of troops. "I don't see why you can't come over right away," he said. "Your only danger will be from the Japanese 150-mm. rifle and you've been shelled before. Your whole hill is dotted with dugouts and trenches for you to jump into."

It was after twelve when we got back to camp.

"All the original unit nurses and Burmese boys will leave immediately for Namkham," I shouted. "Trucks back up to nurses' quarters immediately for baggage. Probst and Stolec and all Burmese coolies on board! Everyone else will follow tomorrow with the patients."

I was too excited to eat. The girls, convinced that Major Davison wouldn't hold them back, were already packed up and ready. Within half an hour we were away on the last lap. Then, for the first time in many weary months, the girls began to sing at the tops of their voices as we rode along.

I had thought I was excited but I was calmness itself compared to the nurses as they jumped out of the jeeps and ran into their home, tripping over the heaps and piles of junk the coolies had been clearing away. Each of them ran to the particular corner where her bed had been three years before and dumped her musette bag there, as one who would stake out a claim to a gold mine. Then they began to explore. They were delighted that the destruction wasn't more extensive. One girl found, in a bathroom, the first sheet of typewritten notes on anatomy I had been teaching her when we left Namkham for the Shan States front. Suddenly there was a burst of laughter from several of the nurses and they began to tease a companion who, running to a corner of the attic, had found there just what she hoped to find: a bundle of love letters from her sweetheart of three years before.

Then they ran out to the jeeps and brought the worn-out brooms we had looted months before in Momauk and set to work with a will. Soon they raised such clouds of dust that it was impossible to breathe. They tied handkerchiefs over their noses and continued to sweep but I ran out, to find that the coolies had stopped work to enjoy the delight of the nurses at their homecoming.

"Come on, let's go!" I shouted. "I promised we'd be ready for new admissions at noon tomorrow and we have three hundred old patients to bed down before then. Burmese boys, clean out the cottages! Half the coolies to the old wooden hospital! The rest, clean out what's left of the stone hospital wards! The nurses will cook our supper!"

Everyone became infected with my mad frenzy, and tons of Japanese dirt and trash began to fly out from the windows and doors. It wasn't safe to walk anywhere for fear of having a load land on one's head and shoulders.

Early Friday morning we set to work again keeping half a step ahead of the patients as they came over by the truck-

206

load. Heroically, the nurses bedded down patients on the wooden floors, saving the cots for wards with cement floors. Then they tagged the patients' foreheads with adhesive tape to correspond with their new positions, renumbered their temperature charts, and began dosing them with medicine and putting on fresh dressings. I must have walked ten miles that day without leaving our compounds, for the Shans had heard we were back and had turned out three hundred strong with dahs, shovels, and bamboo baskets.

"These people are from Manhong, Nawngsang, and Man-hkam villages," said their respective headmen.

"Good! We need you!" I replied. "I will pay grownups one rupee per day and children proportionately."

"You won't pay us anything. You've been away three years and we had given up hope of your ever coming back. The Japs forced us to labor every day for nothing. Now for once we are going to do something just because we want to do it and not for money. Every village around Namkham is going to give you three days of free labor. There will be another group of villagers in tomorrow."

I felt like a candidate for president of the United States. All the Christians grasped my hands, while the Buddhists insisted on the complete *wai*. Then a group of girls ran up and I saw Hseng Hun, the Shan girl Tiny and I had put through the English high school. Excitedly I threw my arms around her and gave her a big squeeze while bystanders applauded and her mother stood by smiling delightedly.

"Are you married yet?" I asked.

"No," Hseng Hun replied demurely.

"What the Sam Hill do you think I put you through school for?" I demanded.

Paw Hpying Awn, the coolie I had trained to be a master mason and who had been the chief of those who built the hospitals, nurses' home, our cottage, and the church in Bhamo, pushed his way through the crowd, his eyes streaming with tears, his mouth set in a broad grin. I almost kissed him.

"I want you to work for me again. We must rebuild this hospital. Will you help me?"

"*Aw hka.* Yes, sir," was all the reply he could produce that day.

"I wish someone would tell Sein Hla Tha, the old headmaster, and Chief Nurse E Hla and the rest of my old staff that I'm home again," I said to everyone at large.

Koi's old father and mother came up and I drew them aside and asked Big Bill to give them two hundred rupees on account. Even a group of Shans who hadn't cared tuppence for me in the old days came to shake hands as if I were their long lost brother. I walked on, watching the villagers at work.

"That's he! That's our old doctor!" said a twelve-year-old to her younger sister.

"How he has aged!" exclaimed one after another of the old friends.

In the middle of the morning the new patients began to arrive to add to the melee, although I had set noon as the earliest permissible time. Dr. San Yee's brother Hsang Hsam, who had been prime minister of Hsenwi State, his cousin Hkun Hsam Myat, the lord mayor's son, and their cousin Hkun Myat Hsa, a barrister-at-law, also called to pay their respects. They looked starved and haggard. The Japanese had been offended at their non-co-operation and had deposed them, forcing them to relinquish the title of *hkun* or prince and compelling them to start truck gardening. With them were San Yee's sister-in-law and son. No wonder everyone was delighted with the boy. The nurses began to strive for his affections. Looking at the beautiful girl who was his aunt, I began at last to place San Yee's charming wife whose name I had not previously recognized. He had really suffered a great loss.

I tried to organize the work of clearing away the rubble, saving up piles of stone and gravel for future use so that when bulldozers came to fill in the bomb craters they wouldn't bury stone that we could use again. It was a nerve-racking ordeal. In the middle of giving instructions in Shan to the coolies, American officers would stroll up to congratulate me on my return. As I chatted hurriedly with them a nurse would break into the middle of a sentence with a demand in Burmese for instructions. Before long I couldn't be certain what language would pour out when I opened my mouth. I began to talk in Shan to nurses and in Burmese to Americans. Then the presents began to arrive. By Shan custom a present must be made in your home, the fruit, vegetable, or rice being laid on a table. But I had no table. Hour after hour I had to drop my work and walk to the kitchen, formally accept the gifts, and try to find some container to hold them.

Saturday morning the engineers drove in a dozer which I might use straight through the twenty-four hours. I didn't dare trust the bossing of the bulldozer crew to anyone else.

Every minute of the day before, I had been planning just how the dozer could fill craters without pushing the remnants of the hospital down or burying precious materials that could be used in rebuilding. The dozer boys and I spent the day together. By the time they left, all the important craters around the big buildings had been filled and our roads cleared, widened, and in use again. The dozer was still filling craters farther away when I fell asleep.

Sunday morning Sein Hla Tha walked up.

"How did you learn I was back?" I asked.

"That mason, Paw Hpying Awn, ran all the way up the hill to tell me," he said. "We have been living in the woods behind Oilaw ever since the Japs came."

"How are Rosie and the children?"

"Rosie is well. She had a little son nine months ago but during the rainy season he suddenly died without anything seeming to be wrong with him."

There went another dream. After all my operations she had finally had a son, only to have him die before I could come back and take care of him.

"Is Little Bawk's father all right?"

"He was, the last I knew."

"Can you send a messenger to tell him she's back and wants to see him?"

"I'll send one in the morning."

"When are you coming back to stay?"

"Will they let us come back?"

"Certainly. You don't live on the main road. The villagers who live on the Burma Road can't come back yet, for some of their villages are being used by the army. But all of the Christians can come back and if anything is said I will tell them that I need you to work for me, and I do! I can't rebuild without all the workers who worked for me before and I need you teachers, Kachin as well as Shan, to act as foremen for me. I can't do all this myself; there's a war on!"

"What about the preachers and the schools?"

"As soon as the army gives me permission to bring back Dr. Ba Saw's wife and family from India, we're going to start a little school on our own. It will be done without government assistance. The nurses and I will pay the teachers' salaries out of our own pockets. Perhaps some of my officers and those of other American units will help. As for preachers, that will have to wait. That doesn't mean we're not going to have church services. Already officers of four different American units have come to me begging me to repair the church before I repair the hospital so they can have a nice place to worship. The army has repaired the church I built in Bhamo and is using it as a church for all denominations. That's what I'm going to do here. When the church is repaired chaplains of every denomination, including Catholics and Hebrews, will be invited to conduct services here."

That night we had our sing in the stone cottage. Though the piano had been stolen, the nurses sat cross-legged on the floor as in the days of old and it was nice to have Sein Hla Tha's baritone voice with us.

The next day Ai Pan, the Shan pastor, his new daughter-in-law Nurse Htawnt, and Hkam Gaw, who had taken care of John and Sterling, suddenly appeared. I threw an arm about each girl and squeezed, and I mean hard. Htawnt laughed and laughed and Hkam Gaw cried and cried. It was fifteen minutes before I could get loose and even then I couldn't stop Hkam Gaw's crying.

"We thought you were dead," she sobbed. "Three times the Japanese announced they had captured you. Once they said they had captured you and thirty Burmese nurses in the Hukawng Valley. Then they said they had captured you and five nurses and were taking you to Rangoon. The last time they just mentioned they had caught you and put you at forced coolie labor at Sagaing and I knew you couldn't stand that. It was only a few weeks ago that the airplanes dropped leaflets prepared by the O.W.I. saying that you and the nurses were all safe and already in the Bhamo area with the Chinese and American armies and we knew the Japanese had been lying."

"Come over to the house and I'll show you the family pictures," I said hurriedly, hoping to stop the sobs.

I drew out the pictures of Tiny, of Leslie and Weston, of John and Sterling. Hkam Gaw sat on the floor and spread the pictures out on my cot. When she came to Sterling's picture she pressed her face down on it and began sobbing again as if her heart would break. This was no good. I turned to Htawnt, a lovely Shan girl who, to my regret, had not gone out with us.

"Who told you you could go and get married?" I scolded fiercely.

Htawnt and her husband smiled. Nobody was scared of me any more.

"And how many offspring have you produced?" I demanded.

"One already and I am producing another at the moment."

"I'll say you are! I left you a young girl and here you are an old woman already!"

We continued to rail at each other until Hkam Gaw began to return to normal.

Things were happening every day and all day long. Ma Hkun, the first girl trained by me to become head nurse at Namkham, came down from the mountains, children and all, and with her was Ma Nu. Seven months' pregnant, she had walked twenty-five miles on mountain paths in one day just to welcome me home. Ma Nu, of Htawnt's class, was distinctly unhappy.

"You didn't come, and you didn't come," she complained. "My folks insisted on marrying me to a man I didn't want but I held off until I gave up hope of your ever returning. And now that you're back I'm pregnant and I can't start nursing with you again!" and Ma Nu also dissolved in tears.

My return was causing more tears than laughter.

"Listen, woman. We're going forward soon. Go on home and stay till the baby is born and then, when you hear we're back in Namkham, get a servant girl and come down and start nursing again."

"Will you take me?" she asked, astonished, her tears stopping and her eyes beginning to shine.

"Of course I will, you little fool! You're one of the best nurses we ever had."

Colonel Petersen flew down all the way from Myitkyina to congratulate me on my return. We were sitting on the front steps of the cottage chatting when around the corner appeared Ai Lun, my medical student, and now hospital superintendent at Namkham, and—yes, there was E Hla! I ran past Ai Lun and threw my arms around her.

Colonel Petersen delicately withdrew and we all went in and jabbered for an hour.

"How many children do you have?" I demanded.

"Two of my own and the little orphan girl we adopted," E Hla replied.

"Are you coming back to work?"

"We came down to inquire if you wanted me."

"Silly girl, why didn't you bring the children and all your possessions down at once? You knew I'd want you."

"It will take a truck to bring us all down."

"You can have it. Where are my two Irish terriers with the pedigree from Ireland two pages long?"

"They took sick and died," she replied, looking away.

211

The next day at dinner Little Bawk was seething, as if she had something on her chest, so I took my messkit over to a corner to eat with her.

"E Hla says she lied to you yesterday about the two dogs because she thought you couldn't stand the truth. What actually happened was this. The Japanese were extremely provoked when they failed to capture you here. When they learned that Buddy and Podgy were your dogs they hung them up by the neck to a tree and split their bodies open while they were still alive."

I stopped eating.

In the evening E Hla brought her whole family to sit by the fire and talk. With her was Hkam Yee, one of the former teachers in our middle school who had served with our unit at the Shan States front and was in Selan when the Japanese came in.

"They caught Pastor Paw Hkam and his son and executed them in front of us all," he said. "The executioner's bullet broke Paw Hkam's hip and he fell to the ground. Then the executioner stepped up and slowly hacked off his head with a dull sword. When Paw Hkam was dead I heard the Japanese commander say they were going to execute all the people who had worked in your unit. They didn't know I was one of them. So I took off into the woods and warned all the others and we hid for months until there was a new commander."

On Tuesday, the twenty-third, General Cannon came in to congratulate me.

"Well, Doc," he said, "what do you want to do now? Remain here in Namkham permanently?"

"Sir," I said, "we're in the army now. I have no choice as to what I will or will not do. But if I do have a choice I want to stay with combat until combat's mission in Burma has been completed."

"But if you remain with combat you will have to move forward," the general warned.

"I realize that, sir. But none of us expected to remain in Namkham permanently after our first arrival. We all expected to push on."

"Of course some of your personnel will have to remain here to guard the place and supervise the rebuilding. You must start rebuilding at once!"

"Sir, I accept that as an order. We have already begun to rebuild." I couldn't keep my delight from showing. I had thought I might have to beg for permission to rebuild. "But in order to rebuild in wartime we will need a lot of engineer supplies," I added.

"What engineer supplies will you need?" the general inquired, cagily.

"Cement and iron and stuff like that," I replied boldly.

"Certainly you will need cement. The engineers won't be able to give you much, of course, but they undoubtedly will give you some."

Was I getting the breaks again? An hour later I was sure I was. Lieutenant General Wheeler, formerly commanding S.O.S. in India and now on S.E.A.C. staff, also flew in to congratulate me. With him was Colonel Hirschfield of S.O.S.

"You're going to rebuild, aren't you?" the general asked.

I explained about General Cannon's remarks and my statement about cement.

"I told Colonel Hirschfield on the flight down that he must supply you with everything you need."

"That's an order, Colonel!" I said, turning to Hirschfield.

I sent out invitations to everybody from General Sultan down to come to a feast and entertainment on Thursday afternoon to celebrate our homecoming. Then I scouted around for Chinese, Shan, and Burmese cooks so everyone would find some dish to his taste. The American boys cooked steaks and creamed potatoes and made delicious pies.

I had expected some three hundred Shan guests, a hundred and fifty Kachins and, if lucky, about three hundred Americans. As it turned out we fed sixteen hundred people— or tried to. Many went away empty or half-filled. The Shans had for days been welcoming us with open arms, and according to Shan custom this was my special dinner to them. The Kachins, once a year, put on a great dance called a *manau* which combines sex, religion, and war. The Japanese were so afraid of them, however, that they forbade the Kachins to hold a *manau* and it had been three years since the last one. The Kachins were uncertain what the Chinese and Americans would do to them if they had the big dance and were intending to postpone it further when they heard I had come home. That gave them an idea. If they had the *manau* under my auspices, they were sure nobody would interfere. I regarded it as a great compliment to their knowledge of my tolerance that they were so certain I would permit this heathen ceremony on Christian ground; but I was appalled

213

when I saw some three hundred and sixty Kachins come in from the mountains to the west and another hundred and fifty from the mountains to the east where the Japanese patrols were still operating.

The greatest compliment of the day, however, was the arrival of whole villages of Palongs, timid Buddhist mountaineers. To have the Palongs pass through the Chinese lines in order to welcome us home was a compliment indeed.

But the guests of honor—the American officers, Chinese officers of field rank, and the sixty correspondents who were following the first convoy through to China—were late. General Sun at the last moment had invited them all to a party celebrating the arrival of the convoy. To make matters worse, there were, as the news broadcasters admitted, still two Japanese snipers with rifles on the road. What the broadcasters neglected to state was that the snipers' rifles were 150-mm. rifles! So the generals were fighting a war and Sun's party also was late. I gave up hopes of their coming at all, and since I already had two brigadier generals, Sliney of the artillery and Pick who built the Ledo Road, I decided to start dinner with the twenty guests who had arrived. We had no sooner sat down when the others poured in, General Cannon with them. Still we were minus the three chief Chinese generals, Sun, Lee, and Tang.

I suggested the usual toasts: to the Chinese First Army, conquerors of Namkham; to the artillery, the best part of the Chinese Army; to the liaison officers; to the tanks; to the engineers who built the Road; to the pipeline; to S.O.S.; to the convoy; to Generals Sultan and Stilwell. But I brought the house down with my last toast: "To the 10th Air Force and their precision bombing of the Namkham hospital!" Everyone shouted "*Kambei!* Bottoms up!"

Having welcomed the U.S. Army to that first Christmas in Burma at Ningam, I now welcomed the army to Namkham and told the guests I hoped that I was the only American soldier to return home and find everything he owned destroyed by his own air force! We had prepared some authentic items. The Karen singing—all the girls in adorable Karen costumes—was the real thing and very beautiful with its close harmony. Nurses put on a parody of a Chinese dance, dressed in modern Chinese clothes which they had made from torn silk parachutes. Princess Louise and M.T. Lu did solo Burmese dances and M.T. Lu a duo dance with a Burmese boy. This dancing, too, was authentic. Two pretty Kachin nurses sang a duet. They were suffering from

214

stage fright but their gorgeous Kachin clothes, heavy with silver plaques, and their beautiful faces made them an immense success. The prime minister had secured expert Shan male dancers who put on a series of skillful sword dances with two swords, which made the front-line spectators wish they'd taken standing room in the back after all. The rest of the program was just for fun. But the crowd had to go outside for the last number, the most authentic of all: the great Kachin *manau* dance with two hundred dancers.

The Kachins had fenced off a large area of the football ground. In the center were two *nat* poles, reminiscent of the totem poles of the American Indians. All the men were armed with drawn swords and with rifles or muzzle-loading shotguns on their backs. All, men and women, were a bit tight. Two chiefs, who outranked all others, had on high feathered headdresses and led the dance. Between the *nat* poles were the musicians playing on native pipes, gongs, cymbals, and drums. The music was weirdly exciting, with a powerful rhythm. In long rows they danced back and forth, sometimes like a snake dance. To an unsophisticated observer the steps were all the same, but I had seen *manaus* done for fun before and had heard stories of the unfettered *manaus* in the animist areas. Whether these Kachins would go to the usual extremes or tone the dance down because they were on Christian land I could not know.

Flashlight bulbs were exploding and radio-recording men were at work in the midst of the dancers, who tolerated them unconcernedly, grateful for the protection the U.S. Army gave them. But five or six correspondents, who had been tight and noisy all evening, decided they would show the Kachins how their *manau* looked to a foreigner and, jumping into the enclosure, began to interfere with the dance. I lost no time in gruffly ordering them out of the ring and insisting that the sober correspondents keep them out! It would seem that correspondents aren't accustomed to reading any but their own writings, for these men should have known that a Kachin in a trance is nothing to be played with; these two hundred Kachins were in a religious, sexual, alcoholic war trance, the first they had indulged in after three years of abstinence.

But I had to leave early. A Chungking Radio broadcaster who was too much of a rugged individualist to record while others were recording, had insisted on a midnight séance and I had to order the tired girls and boys out again. By the time he was done with me I was stammering like a Sunday-school child reciting his first poem.

The next day Colonel Brown's tanks cleared the road junction at the 105th-mile post of the two large-barreled "snipers." The great convoy was forming, ready to start for Kunming. I decided to do the thing in style. Ever since the fall of Burma in 1942 we had been serving the troops who were fighting to get convoys into China and now the first one was going through. General Sliney, the only other officer besides myself still left of those who had walked out with Stilwell, was just starting back for the States. Stilwell himself was gone. I had welcomed the army into Burma. Who was better entitled to bid them Godspeed on their way to China? I turned the jeep off the road, backed it to right angles, stood up on the hood, and took the salute. Generals, colonels, majors, sergeants, and even buck privates entered into the spirit of the occasion and gave me "Eyes Right!" and stiff, precise salutes, though they had broad grins on their faces at the presumption of that queer bird, the Burma Surgeon.

Last night I lay awake hours remembering my old ruined dreams. Perhaps they were gone forever. But I could still dream of rebuilding so that my successor would start his work with a beautiful, modern hospital and not with a mass of rubble. And perhaps something still more wonderful might prove possible—a hospital of a thousand beds instead of three hundred; a hospital where young medical students could come for internship and surgical training, where the men of Burma would catch the spirit that seemed so beautiful to me in the girls of our unit; not a Baptist hospital alone but a Christian hospital; a hospital that would appeal to Americans whether church members or not; a hospital above denomination where Buddhists and animists could come and receive loving care when sick and learn that peace comes only to men of good will.

It was a beautiful dream—and outside the stars were shining.

EPILOGUE

IT IS exactly fifteen years since the Japanese were driven out of Namkham and we were permitted to return to find all our hospital buildings bombed out by the United States Air Force. These fifteen years have seen extraordinary changes not only in Namkham but all over Burma, politically, sociologically, economically, medically.

After V-J Day I spent my six months' terminal leave as Chief Medical Officer for the Shan State under the British Military Administration and during this period we used the same practical measures I had used during the building of the Burma Road to reactivate all the hospitals in the Shan State. By the time the British Military Administration turned the country over to the civilian government all of our war nurses had been scattered through the Shan and Karenni (now Kayah) States assisting doctors, where there were doctors, and running other hospitals under my direction when no doctors were available. In March 1946 I returned to Namkham to reopen our nurses' training school on a large scale, to train in surgery such doctors as were available and to supervise by monthly tours the state hospitals of the Shan State. People never had believed in surgery until we brought surgery into their own home towns. We never kept spectators out, so everyone began to realize surgery was a science. This last duty I continued until the end of 1948—the year of Burma's independence from Great Britain. The pro-Socialist Government of Burma then took over all hospitals except private hospitals such as ours at Namkham and its nearby branch dispensaries.

When, in 1946, we had the hospital and the nurses' training school well organized, I left for a six months' lecture tour in America. In Boston I contacted the president of the American Baptist Foreign Mission Society, who held the lease on our property at Namkham, and explained to him my desire to have a separate non-sectarian, non-political, non-profit making organization in the States to support our work and requested that the property be made over to me without retaining any connection with the American Baptist Mission

217

in Burma. As soon as the president learned that I had no intention whatsoever of fighting the American Baptist Mission in Burma but would continue to help them medically in their other stations to the best of my ability, he agreed to my plans. We have been a non-sectarian mission organization since that time.

With the help of friends in America, including such men as Gen. Frank D. Merrill, Gen. Wild Bill Donovan, and Dr. (Gen.) I. S. Ravdin of the University of Pennsylvania as well as Johns Hopkins classmates of mine, we organized the American Medical Center for Burma, incorporated it in New York State with headquarters, now, at Three Penn Center Plaza, Philadelphia, Pennsylvania. There my friend John F. Rich is still Executive Vice-President. On my return to Burma I organized a Namkham Hospital Committee of Burmese citizens to parallel our American Committee. This Burmese Committee was ineffective during the time that I was under arrest in Rangoon, but on my advice Dr. Ai Lun reorganized the committee as soon as he took over and the committee has been of tremendous assistance since that time.

By the end of 1958 our hospital buildings had been rebuilt out of funds and materials which I secured to a state in which they could be satisfactorily used. To this day there is still bomb damage apparent everywhere, which we have not had sufficient funds to repair. The Shan State, however, had given us financial assistance towards building a new two-story medical block and a twin extension of the pre-war nurses' home. Our training school had grown to 250 pupil nurses and was the largest in Burma. There were some seven doctors, the senior of whom was Dr. Ba Saw of war days assisted by Dr. Tu of pre-war days, besides my sister Grace and myself on the staff.

From 1949 on, Burma suffered more different simultaneous insurrections than any of the "new" post-war countries has ever endured. It is a great credit to the stability of Burma that the country was not completely destroyed and that the insurgents, in spite of trying to join each other, have now passed from organized insurrection into a phase of armed banditry. This is especially remarkable because General Aung San, the chosen leader of the country, was massacred together with half his cabinet of influential men before Independence Day. Because I fought for the integrity of the hospital and training school when Namkham was overrun by insurgents, suspicion was directed against me in 1949 and

218

I was arrested a year later on charges of treason. In America only a citizen can be arrested for treason, but the Burmese Treason Law includes foreigners as well, who, in America, would be accused merely of subversion or spying. When I was taken to prison in Rangoon my sister Grace promised to see that the hospital continued its service until I was permitted to return to Namkham — even if she died doing it. She kept her promise literally, becoming unconscious a year to the hour from the day I was arrested and dying a year to the hour from the time I was put in prison.

The Burmese treated me well while I was in jail, and when the trial court gave me six years of hard labor I became the only first-class convict Burma ever had, with a separate house to live in. They even gave me a bat-boy and an electric fan. My "hard labor" consisted of finding a way to spend my time!

Even after the Supreme Court cleared me of all charges I was not permitted to return to Namkham, in spite of American and English public opinion. But when Burmese public opinion demanded it, the Government permitted me to return immediately. This puts Burmese democracy way ahead of the type of democracy in the Union of South Africa, where the opinion of the majority and the decision of the Supreme Court mean nothing to the Government.

On my return, there were only about thirty patients in the hospital. But as soon as the people of North Burma discovered that I was really back in Namkham, the number of patients increased until we were completely filled. The Namkham Hospital Committee had to assist us in securing funds for putting up a large two-story building to take care of the large number of well-to-do patients who demanded private rooms. By that time we had a 250-bed hospital in which this last year we had at one time 50 patients on the floor besides those on beds. There were about 25 nurses still in training on my return. With the help of scholarships from the Fulbright Board, we now have approximately 100 nurses in training. My term in jail was the best publicity the Namkham hospital was ever given in Burma.

Dr. Ba Saw, for some reason which I shall never understand, disappeared with the insurgents when they were driven out at the time the Burma Army recaptured Namkham in 1949. To escape the Burma Army, the insurgent leader led his group, including Dr. Ba Saw, across the border into what was then Nationalist China. When the Communists took over, Dr. Ba

Saw was unable to return and make his peace with the Burma Government, and we have no knowledge whatsoever of his whereabouts or even whether he is still alive. A month after Ba Saw's disappearance, Dr. Tu contracted the variety of influenza-pneumonia which was so prevalent around the world during 1918, and died in two days. The other doctors all disappeared and Dr. Ai Lun alone was in charge when I returned from Rangoon. A Goanese-Indian doctor, Olwen Silgardo, who had been my executive officer while I was with the British Military Administration, had been sent by me for two years' training in America. A few months after I returned to Namkham from Rangoon he rejoined us and now, even if we have 300 patients in the wards, there are just Dr. Silgardo and myself to carry on, with the assistance of our excellent nursing staff, who now total 17, and of the nurses in the training school. We have four of our United States Army nurses on the staff.

"Grandma" Naomi, Emily and Saw Yin left me temporarily in 1946 to help our English Doctor Gurney reopen his medical missionary work in the Southern Shan States. "Grandma" and Emily returned here when Dr. Gurney went to England on furlough and are respectively matron and assistant matron. "Grandma's" skill in surgery and anesthesia still stands out preeminently. Emily has become one of the finest obstetric nurses in the world and is, in addition, the chief of all "sister tutors" who teach nursing in the training school. Esther, who had always stayed in Namkham, ranks next to "Grandma." In late 1947 I sent her and her younger sister to America for a year's training in laboratory technology. Saw Yin, on leaving Dr. Gurney, ran a small hospital in the Southern Shan States until she and E Kyaing, the nurse with the club-foot, were swept away by the insurgents. After about three years of wandering in the jungles, Saw Yin managed to get free and return to Government-controlled Burma and is now house-mother in charge of the nurses' home. Koi, who was chief nurse during the first battle of Burma and served in the OSS during the last months of the war, was sent to the Mayo Clinic by the State Department for a year and a half of post-graduate training. On her return she rejoined us and stayed until the insurrection almost destroyed the nurses' training school, when she went to Taunggyi and organized the training school in the Government hospital. She was married a year later and is now living in Namkham, where she does private practice and is raising a family. While she is not on our staff, she is

220

honorary lecturer in the nurses' training school and is always appointed as senior nurse examiner in the Government Examinations for nurses. "Big-Bawk" married a relative of the Shan Sawbwa of the State where she was running a hospital and still does some private nursing. "Little Bawk" eloped with a Burmese doctor on our staff and is living in Taunggyi. Hla Sein or "Lassie" is supervisor in a big hospital in Jersey City. Ruby is in Philadelphia, married to an American, and has twins. The others are scattered all over Burma and are all, I believe, married and raising families of their own.

The best class of nurses we have trained here since the war was the group of new girls who joined us in the middle of the battle for Myitkyina in 1944. The best was Daisy, who was first in all Burma when she took her Union Government examinations. Since my return from jail we have had in the training school three second-generation nurses whose mothers had been trained here before the war. Two of the girls we have trained during this time have been girls who were born after I operated on their mothers for primary sterility. One of the girls now on our staff was an orphan whom my mother adopted long before the war. Another on our staff was an orphan whom we raised in our hospital until we could have her adopted by a very fine childless couple. The father of one of our staff nurses was executed by the Japanese for being an American spy just before the end of the war. Another now in training lost both father and mother from illness and exposure when they were caught up in the wave of insurrection. Several others have suffered extremely as a result of these same stupid rebellions.

The picture in the hospital itself has changed. As a result of all the publicity given me in the Burmese newspapers in 1950-51, we get patients from much greater distances than ever before, and the number is so large that there are now three bus lines operating into Namkham from Lashio and many jeeps operating both regularly and irregularly bringing patients from Bhamo. Tuberculosis, which was no major problem in North Burma before the war, is much more important in this hospital now than malaria used to be. All varieties of cancer which were rare before the war are now very common. The anemias are terrible. Dr. Silgardo had a patient with a uterine tumor who had only 10 percent hemoglobin. A nurse gave her a half pint of blood, Silgardo gave the patient another pint of his own blood, operated next day and she is almost ready to go home. Patients sometimes still come to us from as far away as Rangoon or the Irrawaddy Delta, or even from Arakan on the Bay of Bengal, and from as far north as the snow mountains and the disputed border arear near China. In obstetrics I might say that we are paying the penalty of having urged women for so many years to come to the hospital to have their babies, especially their first baby. Maternity cases and pediatrics cases have long since overflowed from the maternity building and are found in every ward for women in the hospital. With increasing age I have turned all the wards, excepting the maternity and pediatrics wards, over to Dr. Silgardo and I act as teacher and consultant. Dr. Silgardo also does all the surgery except obstetrical surgery and surgery on nurses.

As a result, first, of the insurrections and, second, of the taking over of China by the Communists, relatives of patients who follow them to the hospital do not dare stay elsewhere and we have to give them sleeping space on the floors of every ward except in the Private Building, where they are furnished with beds.

We still receive patients from Communist China, but whenever we admit any our chief clerk checks their credentials. If there is anything suspicious about them they are reported either to the Civilian Government or to the army, and in this way quite a number have been taken over and tried by the Government. We no longer permit our nurses even to approach the Chinese border which passes down through the center of the valley. Abnormal labor cases from the other side of the border must be carried across the border to the main road where our nurses pick them up and bring them into the hospital. Recently Communists from China leave us alone. One group, two or three years ago, came as out patients and was actually so ill-advised as to try to indoctrinate me. As soon as I discovered they were Communists I escorted them to the door and saw them off the premises.

The army has been exceedingly helpful to us, especially when the Chinese Nationalists were fighting the Government in Burma; and to this day are a protection against Communist Chinese as well as Burmese insurgents. During the year that General Ne Win took over as Prime Minister the army enforced discipline all over Burma. When independence reaches a new country in Asia or Africa the people tend to think of independence as a lack of discipline. The idea of freedom under law is now beginning to be understood in Burma at least although there are always the die-hards.

We still have with us two jeeps, a weapons carrier and

two trucks which belonged to my unit during the war and which are occasionally operable. The only reason they can still run is because of the skill of our chief mechanic, who was one of the first babies I delivered in Namkham. The people of the United States through CARE have given us a wonderful four-wheel-drive jeep ambulance as a special gift through us to the people of Burma and it has proved extremely valuable.

With Communist China one air-mile away across the valley, with groups of bandits who call themselves insurgents trying to undermine the Government and even attacking and robbing nurses on their way back from vacation, with a budget for a 300-bed hospital about sufficient for one with a hundred beds, with a huge new Russian-built hospital in Taunggyi being run by my wartime protégé Dr. San Yee, with a personal salary of ninety dollars a month — with all these there is no security for an American doctor with a hospital at Namkham. But there is adventure. There is a real happiness to be obtained in loving the people of Burma and in curing them of their ills even without sufficient funds to do anything in the way we would like to do it.

On January 1 of this year Tun Shein, who made possible all of our work for the United States Army during 1942, returned to us as Administrator of the hospital. He has relieved Dr. Silgardo and myself of all responsibility for the administration of the hospital as such and all the skills he has developed in his lifetime are making it possible for Dr. Silgardo and myself to confine ourselves to purely professional and educational work. A visa has been issued for Dr. and Mrs. Myron Donald Olmanson and their three children of St. Peter, Minnesota, to come to Namkham. They are scheduled to sail from New York tomorrow. With all his skill in the practice of medicine and surgery — which will be much more up to date than our own practice — we should at last be able to give to the people of North Burma the sort of medical and surgical care which they deserve and which the great drug companies of the United States as well as our many friends in America have made possible through their person-to-person gifts.

Often, during the past fifteen years, correspondents have asked me whether I would say, "This is a one-man hospital." If women are to be excluded from the human race then perhaps, during my first ten years, this was a one-man hospital. But even during the first five years we could not have done hospital work without Burmese nurses. The larger the hospital grew, the more important the Burmese personnel became. I

223

take pride in regarding our work as an example of Burmese-American cooperation for the welfare of Burma. The continuity of that Burmese-American cooperation on a person-to-person basis is the most important thing in the world to me.

GORDON S. SEAGRAVE, M.D.
NAMKHAM, AUGUST 3, 1961

This is not the end of the Burma Surgeon's story. Dr. Gordon Seagrave carries on his dedicated work in the Namkham Hospital with the same determination that marked his earlier years. Today the hospital cares for almost 15,000 patients a year. And today Dr. Seagrave and his associates are still overworked, understaffed and in great need of supplies and funds. A group of private Americans has sought to aid Dr. Seagrave in his merciful work through the American Medical Center for Burma. Under the leadership of former ambassador to Burma, David McKendree Key, this organization's support has enabled the hospital to continue and to grow despite recurring crises, not the least of which has been financial.

The publishers of this book believe that many of you, after learning of the extraordinary life and accomplishments of the Burma Surgeon, will want to help him to continue providing medical care and training to the Burmese people. Your tax-deductible contribution will be most appreciatively accepted by the American Medical Center for Burma, Inc., Six Penn Center Plaza, Philadelphia 3, Pennsylvania. All of us can take pride in Dr. Seagrave's remarkable example of humanity and perseverance. By giving generously to his lifework we will assure its continuity.

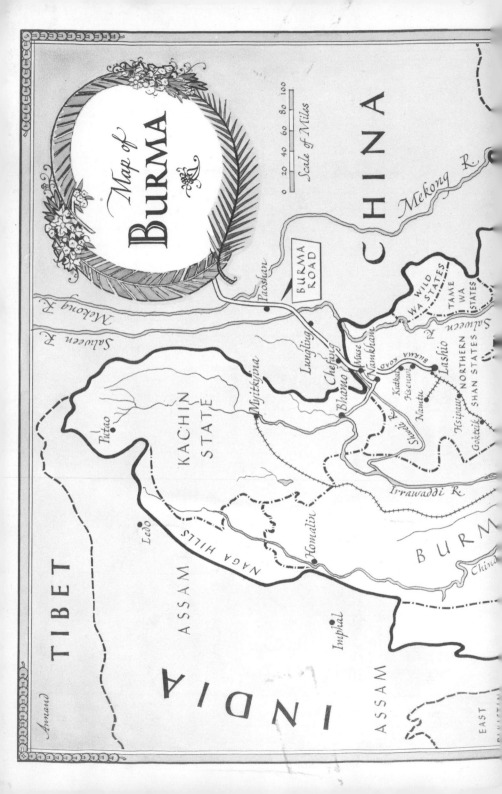